Psychologists in Word and Image

Psychologists in Word and Image

Nicholas Wade

A Bradford Book
The MIT Press
Cambridge, Massachusetts
London, England

This book was set in Palatino by The MIT Press and was printed and bound in the United States of America.

Library of Congress Cataloging-in-Publication Data

Wade, Nicholas.
Psychologists in word and image / Nicholas Wade.
p. cm.
"A Bradford book."
Includes bibliographical references and index.
ISBN 0-262-23180-8.—ISBN 0-262-73112-6 (pbk.)
1. Psychology—History. I. Title.
BF81.W33 1995
150'.9—dc20 94-31482
CIP

Dedicated to the psychologists who do not appear here in word or image.

Contents

Preface

This book grew out of an exhibition at the International Congress of Psychology, held in Brussels during July 1992. The aim of the exhibition was to encapsulate the history of psychology graphically, by presenting portraits of eminent students of mind and behavior in an unconventional way: portraits were combined with motifs which reflected their contribution to psychology. Fifty portraits were exhibited, and it was during the exhibition that I met Harry and Betty Stanton of The MIT Press. The seeds of the present book were sown during our conversations, and I am very grateful to them for their subsequent enthusiastic support.

I refer to these illustrations as "perceptual portraits" and over one hundred are presented here, some of which were among the original fifty exhibited in Brussels. The aim of the perceptual portraits is both artistic and historical. The illustrations generally consist of two elements—the portrait and some appropriate motif. The nature of the latter depends upon the endeavors for which the portrayed person was known. In some cases the motif is drawn specifically to display a phenomenon associated with that person; in others it is derived from a figure or text in one of his or her books, or on apparatus which the person invented. The portraits and motifs have themselves been manipulated in a variety of ways, using graphic and photographic procedures involving high-contrast film (as described in my book *Visual Allusions: Pictures of Perception*). The illustrations often require some effort on the part of the reader to discern the faces embedded in them. I have found that such perceptual portraits both attract attention and engage the spectator's interest to a greater degree than do conventional prints or photographs. It is hoped that this visual intrigue will enhance the reader's desire to discover why particular motifs have been adopted, and in turn to learn more about the persons portrayed: it is intended to be an instance of art serving science.

The historical starting point is taken at the onset of the scientific Renaissance as it applied to the study of mind—with Francis Bacon, Thomas Hobbes, and René Descartes. All the men and women were chosen because of their importance in shaping the present state of psychology. Reducing the history of psychology to about a hundred prominent contributors has necessarily involved some arbitrary decisions, but they have been informed by several criteria. The first was that those selected should be deceased. There are so many living psychologists who have made and are continuing to make valuable additions to our knowledge that it would have been invidious to select some but not others; moreover, the filter of time has not had a chance to sift through contemporary ideas to determine those which will last. The second criterion was that the subjects should reflect the wide range of ideas affecting psychology. That is, they were not selected for their individual merits alone but also for the areas they examined and the issues they exposed. Even though this approach might seem to bypass current theories or techniques, it is seldom the case: the precursors of the ideas are likely to be included and so the current ideas can still be introduced. Third, the emphasis is on those who have made psychology an empirical discipline. Despite these criteria there are still personal choices. Indeed, it is difficult to see how it could be otherwise.

The history of psychology is typically described in terms either of the great contributors or in the context of the Zeitgeist—the spirit of the time. In reality, these two approaches are so intertwined that they cannot be separated in any simple way. The spirit that is reflected at any time is not impersonal—it is distilled from the wisdom of those individuals addressing fundamental questions about the nature of human endeavor. Here, the passage of time is reflected in the chronological sequence of portraits: they are arranged in order of birth date. By so doing, the differing viewpoints become enmeshed, as they were historically—the British empiricists did not present their ideas en masse nor were the early behaviorists a group isolated from their opponents. The convenience of recapitulation has encouraged many historians to adopt an approach in terms of topic rather than time.

It is of interest to note that conventional portraits are used increasingly in histories of psychology, and in textbooks generally. Why are we so interested in the portraits of people long dead who are known for their thoughts rather than their appearance? When we do recognize a portrait it is only by association with others we have seen of that person. There is rarely evidence concerning the accuracy of resemblance of a particular portrait, and in some cases there may be very few portraits from which to select. (This sidesteps the issue of whether a static two-dimensional representation can adequately resemble a dynamic three-dimensional face—the perennial problem of the portrait artist, whether painter or photographer.) The subjects of portraits are usually portrayed when they are old and established, whereas their important work was mostly carried out when they are young. This book is intended to engage the widespread interest in the characteristics, both intellectual and physiognomic, of the pioneers of psychology.

The format adopted is of one page of text facing a full-page perceptual portrait. The text presents details about the persons portrayed and their ideas, and also includes a title of the picture. The titles are often intentionally cryptic. The source of the portrait and of the motif is appended; when no details of the motifs are given they have been drawn specifically for the portrait. Interrelations between the people portrayed are stressed, so that common threads running through the work of particular groups will be apparent; this provides the deeper level at which the many facets are integrated. I have avoided citing references in the text, but a list of references consulted is given in the Bibliography. In all cases the quotations are taken from works of the person under discussion. The sources of the quotations are listed in an appendix in the order in which they appear.

The history of any discipline involves social as well as intellectual dimensions, and the same applies to the writing of histories. Many friends and colleagues have encouraged me in this enterprise and are due my gratitude, most particularly Mike Cowles, Ross Day, Malcolm Macmillan, Mike Swanston, and Alan Wilkes, all of whom have offered their sober perspectives on this history of psychology. Despite their best efforts the responsibility for the errors that remain rests with me alone. My greatest debt is to my wife, Christine, who has provided constant encouragement and inspiration.

Introduction

The eye of psychology does not have a single lens to focus the problems it addresses; it does not form a single image. Rather, it reflects many viewpoints concerning the nature of mind and behavior, more like the facets of an insect eye: these operate independently of one another at first and then are integrated at a deeper level. The multifaceted nature of psychology is evident both in its origins and in the disciplines it has embraced since its inception. These many viewpoints are here presented in terms of its subject matter and the subjects that mattered. That is, the theories and procedures that are now grist to psychology's mill are described in text relating to perceptual portraits of those who have generated them. Art is rarely considered to be one of the facets of psychology, but here it is applied in the service of science. The significant figures in the history of psychology are portrayed in an indirect manner—allusions to their contributions are made visually. The perceptual portraits themselves pose puzzles for the perceiver; the portrayed person might be difficult to discern, and the source of the visual distraction is itself significant because the motif molded with a portrait speaks to the endeavors of the person portrayed. In addition, brief descriptions of the subjects and their ideas are presented. It is my hope that a visual introduction to the origins of ideas in psychology will engage the reader's interest in the history of psychology generally.

Psychology has a fascinating history because it conflates ideas from diverse disciplines. Many of the major figures presented in this book would not now be classified as psychologists even though their work has had a profound impact on what we call psychology. It is these multiple influences that are celebrated here. Psychologists often pursue their profession with scant regard for the past: all that is worth knowing is seen as in the present or lies ahead. The preoccupation with the present can blind us to insights from the past. Our current ideas were not conceived immaculately; they have evolved over decades, centuries, or millenia of thought and debate. The language surrounding particular ideas has often changed, but the kernel remains constant. There are many excellent texts on the history of psychology, and this is itself an area of research that is undergoing both transformation and expansion. It is not my intention here to present an alternative history of psychology, but rather an alternative way of presenting that history.

From the seventeenth century, the scientific methods that had proved so successful in the physical and chemical sciences were seen as relevant to life processes. The anatomy of the senses and the brain were gradually elucidated, and these anatomical structures were related to function; the behavior of the insane was observed and classified, and the lessons of science were absorbed into philosophy. Descartes did distinguish between the mechanical body and the immaterial mind, but his application of scientific rigor to understanding the senses set psychology on a course from which it has seldom wavered. Interaction with the world through the senses provides the basis for much in philosophy and physiology, the twin precursors of modern psychology. Disturbances of sensory function are features that distinguished the majority from those who were called mad. In the nineteenth century psychology emerged as the interface between philosophy and the natural sciences. It addressed the eternal questions of philosophy by deed rather than by word: it embraced scientific methods to frame the questions empirically. The methods adopted initially were adapted from other sciences, most notably from physics and physiology. From the mid-nineteenth century new methods were developed for studying perception and performance that distinguished psychology from both philosophy and physiology, and the arbitrary birth of the independent discipline is often taken as the founding by Wundt of the Institute of Experimental Psychology at Leipzig in 1879. Among the founding fathers of psychology were Weber, Fechner, and Helmholtz—who all influenced Wundt. They were students of perception, and their more general contributions were based firmly on their perceptual research. In the words of Thomas Reid "All that we know of nature, or of existence, may be compared to a tree, which hath its root, trunk, and branches. In this tree of knowledge, perception is the root, common understanding is the trunk, and the sciences are the branches." Thus, in addition to presenting perceptual portraits of the principal figures in psychology's past, I emphasize the perceptual dimension in the development of ideas in psychology.

When Ebbinghaus said, a century ago, that psychology has a long past but a short history, he was reflecting upon the age-old questions of human existence that were being addressed by novel procedures. The same statement could be made today. The armory of methods amassed by psychology in the last century is impressive, but the questions remain much the same. How do we derive knowledge about the world? How is the mind related to the body? What are the causes of mental illness? Why do individuals differ? While psychology's past reaches back to the first records of human endeavor, the subject as it is now constructed is much more modern. Psychology is neither philosophy nor medicine, but it has drawn on both disciplines in its long past. Philosophy can be thought of as providing a buttress between religion and science—asking questions that the former answers with authority but without evidence and to which the latter provides evidence suggesting there are no answers. Medicine can be considered as building a bridge between magic and science—reducing the ritual associated with the treatment of disease while often retaining mystical concepts concerning their genesis.

For two thousand years, prior to the scientific Enlightenment, the interpretation of mental processes in the western world was dominated by the wisdom of Greek philosophers. They brought some degree of order to the study of mind, although the ideas they expressed were widely divergent. Of the plethora of opinions associated with Greek thinkers only two strands will be mentioned—those associated with Plato and with Aristotle—because they have continued to impinge on psychology. Plato (427–347), distrusted the senses and sought truth through abstract reasoning whereas Aristotle viewed the senses as an important source of knowledge about the external world. Plato believed that the world of appearances was one of illusion, as opposed to the world of thought in which ideal forms existed. The forms reflected the universal qualities of objects rather than the features which can be sensed. The abstract forms could be investigated by reasoning rather than observation, and this resulted in a preference for rational rather than empirical inquiry. Plato's position demonstrates the influence that language has had on philosophical thought: particular members of a category that are given a single name (e.g., horse) do not reflect their universal characteristics. The senses are concerned with particulars rather than universals and so were not considered to furnish useful knowledge. Plato distinguished between the body and the soul: the body was part of the material world, whereas the soul was immaterial. He likened the rational soul to a charioteer steering the competing horses of emotion and appetite; the rational soul was considered to be morally superior to the others and should guide their actions. These distinctions were to have considerable significance because they later permeated both philosophy and Christian theology. A simlar mind-body dualism was at the heart of Descartes's philosophy as well as a constant current in Christian theology. The latter also placed great emphasis on the moral superiority of reason over irrational feelings and passions.

Plato was a philosopher and a poet, whereas Aristotle was a scientist and a systematic teacher. Aristotle (384–322 B.C.), who was one of Plato's students, displayed detachment from his mentor in developing his own philosophy. Aristotle adopted more naturalistic explanations of phenomena which did not denigrate the senses. He was interested in universals but believed that they could best be understood by the study of particulars. Therefore he preferred an empirical approach to a rational one. He is often considered to be the first psychologist because of his emphasis on observation and because he tried to order phenomena in a systematic manner. Many of his classifications of natural phenomena are still used, and he studied a broad range, from botany to behavior. He placed humans at one end of a continuum of living things that extended to plants. The distinguishing feature was the possession of mind—the ability to reason. Aristotle's conception of the soul was quite different from that espoused by Plato. He considered that soul imbued the body with life and it was neither mystical nor a metaphor for mind. There were three types of soul. The vegetative soul was shared by plants, animals, and humans; the animal soul was restricted to animals and humans; and the rational soul was confined to humans. The soul was not a thing but a process that could control the movements of the organism. Movement and change in the material world were cardinal problems Aristotle addressed as he wanted to determine their cause. He proposed that nature could be described in terms of four causes. Material cause relates to the substance of which objects are composed (e.g., marble); efficient cause transforms the substance (as with a sculptor chiseling the marble); formal cause reflects the transformation (a statue); and the final cause refers to the aim or purpose of the object (reverence to some deity). All material was considered to have a purpose and all change was determined by a prime mover. However, it was in the area of logic that Aristotle's influence was greatest and longest lasting. He devised rules of deductive logic based on syllogistic reasoning that would permit proofs of propositions. A syllogism consists of two statements (a major and a minor premise) and a conclusion. A familiar example is: All men are mortal, Aristotle is a man, therefore, Aristotle is mortal.

Aristotle's studies of the senses were extensive and he suggested that sensations were brought together to form a "sensus commune," which he located in the heart. He added to the phenomena of vision by describing afterimages, aftereffects, and binocular double vision. He argued that light was received by the eyes rather than emitted from them; the latter view was held by most of his contemporaries. He discussed many other psychological phenomena including remembering, thinking, dreaming, and development. Both Plato and Aristotle elaborated theories of memory. For Plato memory was like making an impression in a wax tablet—the impression would be retained and recollection from it could later be made. Individual differences could be related to the different consistencies of the wax and the ease with which impressions could be made in it. Aristotle wrote much more extensively on memory and elaborated the wax tablet metaphor. He also made a clear reference to the association of ideas by similarity and contiguity. Thus, for the first time a range of psychological issues were examined by observations of behavior and their interpretations were in terms of natural processes.

Despite this progress in general psychology, explanations of abnormal behavior were influenced by the prevailing views of magic, medicine, and religion; some of those displaying the behavior were described as being possessed by spirits. The spirits were mostly considered as demonic, in which case the treatments were cruel and barbaric; occasionally they were thought of as benign, in which case the utterances of those afflicted were taken as sage and prophetic. Plato distinguished between natural and divine madness. The mentally ill did not have any obvious injury or disease to which the medicine of the day could be applied, and the history of their treatment until recent times is mostly a record of cruelty, oppression, and inhumanity. Molding abnormal behavior back toward the normal was seldom undertaken. While Greek medicine did much to assist in the treatment of organic diseases, relatively little was written about mental disorders. Concepts of the soul developed by philosophers like Aristotle were incorporated into psychological medicine: the vegetative, animal, and rational all had their own properties, disturbances of which could lead to abnormal behavior. Indeed, philosophical speculations were the driving force of Greek medical practices, which were as diverse as their underlying philosophies. Both philosophy and medicine were based on what were taken to be self-evident truths, from which conclusions could be reached by deduction.

Aristotle lived during the declining years of the golden age of Greece and of the Greek city states. Both Platonic and Aristotelian ideas were elaborated in the next centuries and Greek science and medicine were retained throughout most of the classical Roman period. While there were great technological and legal advances in the Roman Empire, there was relatively little innovation in philosophy and science. Philosophy and monotheistic Christian theology became enmeshed in the fourth century A.D., prior to the sacking of Rome and the descent into what are called the Dark Ages. Greek writings were preserved and advanced in the eastern Mediterranean and in North Africa, where Islamic scholars translated them; many were housed in the vast library at Alexandria. Certain areas, notably mathematics and optics, were developed considerably, but much of the ancient Greek thought was no longer available to medieval Christian philosophers. It returned to southern Europe gradually from the thirteenth century onward when the works were translated from Arabic into Latin, and it was one of the principal factors leading to the Renaissance. There were many other factors that fashioned the Renaissance during the fifteenth and sixteenth centuries. These included the decline in the power of the Roman Catholic Church, as evidenced by the Reformation and the establishment of Protestantism; the invention of printing machines; and the Copernican revolution that placed Earth as a peripheral part of a larger universe.

During the Renaissance nature was examined again, with a human rather than a divine eye. Art was one of the first areas in which this rediscovery of human potential was expressed. The invention of linear perspective in the early fifteenth century was influenced by translations into Latin of medieval *Perspectivas,* which described both physical and physiological optics. Theories of image formation on a surface in front of the eye resulted in paintings that mirrored more precisely the optics of the real world, and actual as well as allegorical scenes were portrayed. It took two more centuries before the link between linear perspective and image formation in the eye was appreciated. Much of the delay was occasioned by the absence of an accurate anatomy of the eye. Medieval medicine was practiced according to the tenets of Greco-Roman authorities. Even anatomical dissections rigidly followed the structures described by Claudius Galen (ca 138–201). It remained to Andreas Vesalius (1514–1564) to observe human anatomy through his own eyes. With the newly found knowledge of ocular anatomy Johannes Kepler (1571–1630) elucidated the workings of the eye as an optical instrument, describing the formation of an inverted and reversed image on the retina. Descartes built upon Kepler's discoveries and extended the anatomical understanding of the eye and its relation to vision: he suggested that the eye can focus on objects at different distances by changing the curvature of the lens, and that the nerves from corresponding points on each retina project to a single site in the brain. William Harvey (1578–1657) applied the same empirical principles to function, describing the heart as a pump which circulated blood through the body via the arteries and veins. Anatomical structure was related to physiological function, and both were applied initially to the study of the senses and later to the intellect.

Aristotle's system of logical reasoning was referred to as the *organon* or instrument for philosophical investigation. It achieved ascendency from the thirteenth century when Aristotle's works were reintroduced to the West. However, it became dogma that stifled scientific inquiry. Conclusions were reached by deductive reasoning, starting from self-evident universals and culminating in particulars. Bacon reacted against this dogma of syllogistic logic and suggested in its stead a reliance on scientific experiment. That is, the interpretation of natural phenomena should be based on the accumulation of evidence from experiments rather than by recourse to the rules of logic. Bacon's method of inductive science was not widely adopted, but its significance lies in the shift from logical to empirical procedures. His emphasis on experiment was to influence the empirical philosophers of the seventeenth and eighteenth centuries. It is at this point that the present history commences.

Psychologists in Word and Image

Portrait after an engraving in: *The Gallery of Portraits: with Memoirs,* Vol. 7. Under the superintendence of the Society for the Diffusion of Useful Knowledge. London: Charles Knight, 1837.

Motif after text in: Bacon, F. 1620. *Novum Organum sive Indicia Vera de Interpretatione Naturae.* Londini: Billius.

Inductive Scientist

Francis Bacon (1561–1626) represents the dawning of the scientific era as it was applied to natural phenomena because of his emphasis on observation rather than a reliance on reason. He lived in an age of intellectual and social turmoil, when the old order of deference to received wisdom was being replaced by new views of religion, government, and nature. It was an age of geographical discovery and conquest. Bacon, later Lord Verulam, was trained in law and rose to high office in government, becoming Lord Chancellor in 1618. His descent from power was precipitate following conviction for bribery in 1621. Throughout his life he wrote extensively on law, history, and learning as well as on natural philosophy. His *Novum Organum* (1620) described the science of induction—"a form which may solve experience, may separate things, and, by means of due exclusions and rejections, conclude necessarily." He argued that data should be accumulated and compared so that the underlying causes could be induced, rather than deducing particular events from universal principles. His opposition to Aristotelian logic was virulent and was harbored from an early age. Bacon's philosophical position was initially outlined in *The Advancement of Learning* (1605) and his advocacy of the methods of empirical science instilled a spirit of experimental inquiry that was to culminate in the formation of the Royal Society in 1662. Despite instigating this new experimental philosophy, Bacon remained isolated from or opposed to many of the great scientific discoveries of his day, like Kepler's laws of planetary motion and Harvey's account of the circulation of blood (despite being a patient of Harvey's). The inductive method itself, involving exhaustive classification, was not widely adopted, but it was the emphasis on experiment rather than syllogism that was significant. In *New Atlantis* (published posthumously) he described a house of Salomon in which marvels of the natural world could be explored: "We have also perspective-houses, where we make demonstrations of all lights and radiations; and of all colours. . . . We have also houses of deceits of the senses; where we represent all manner of feats of juggling, false apparitions, impostures, and illusions." This has been taken as a model for many of the modern museums of exploration in which natural phenomena can be observed and manipulated.

Bacon is depicted in text from the *Instauratio Magna* of the *Novum Organum,* the new instrument that was to replace Aristotle's organon of logic. The text describes the essentials of inductive science, and it cautions against placing too great a reliance on the senses because of the two fallacies to which they are prone: they either fail or they deceive. Bacon states these fallacies are overcome either by providing substitutions where they fail and rectifications where they deceive, that is, by making experiments.

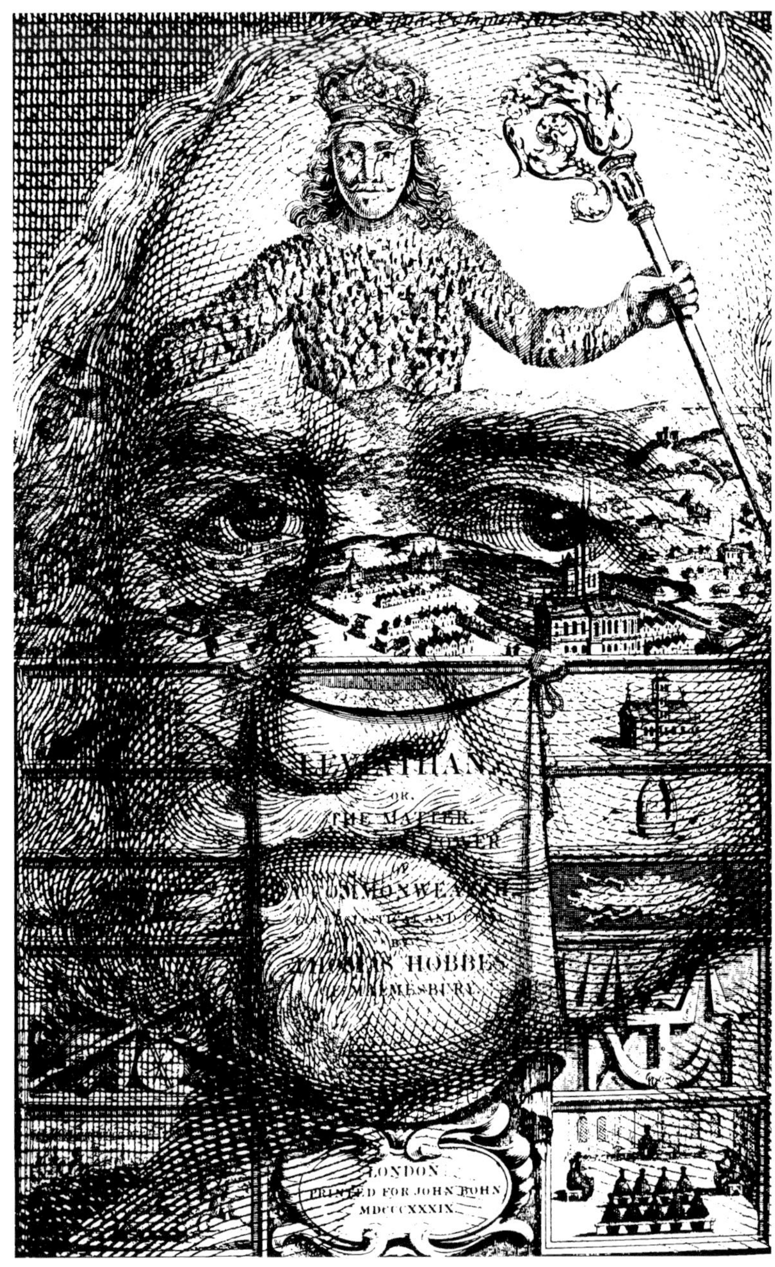

Portrait after a frontispiece engraving in: Molesworth, W., ed. 1839. *The English Works of Thomas Hobbes,* Vol. 1. London: Bohn.

Motif after a frontispiece engraving of the title page of *Leviathan* in: Molesworth, W., ed. 1839. *The English Works of Thomas Hobbes,* Vol. 3. London: Bohn.

Leviathan

Thomas Hobbes (1588–1679) was a political philosopher who saw an understanding of human nature as essential to an appreciation of government. Although he served briefly as Bacon's secretary, he did not adopt the method of inductive science but was more attracted to the deductive method that had been applied with such success in astronomy. Hobbes considered that all nature consisted of matter in motion and, as parts of nature, humans were machines, too. In his introduction to *Leviathan* (1651) he wrote, "For seeing Life is but a motion of limbs, the beginning whereof is in some principall part within; why may we not say, that all *Automata* (Engines that move themselves by springs and wheeles as doth a watch) have an artificiall life? For what is the *Heart,* but a *Spring;* and the *Nerves,* but so many *Strings;* and the *Joints,* but so many *Wheeles,* giving motion to the whole Body, such as was intended by the Artificer?"

Hobbes painted a pessimistic picture of human nature. Humans were said to be motivated by self-interest, seeking quarrels with one another because of the desire for power. These were taken to result in individuals striving for their own advantage and at war with one another, thereby living in "continuall feare, and danger of violent death; And the life of man, solitary, poore, nasty, brutish, and short. . . . The Passions that encline men to Peace, are Feare of Death; Desire of such things as are necessary to commodious living; and a Hope by their Industry to obtain them." Government is required to keep such forces in check and, for Hobbes, the most appropriate form of rule was by sovereign power.

Hobbes laid the foundations for empiricist philosophy. He placed the senses as the source of all knowledge: "there is no conception in a mans mind, which hath not at first, totally, or by parts, been begotten upon the organs of Sense." In this regard, his empiricist ideas were in direct conflict with Descartes's dualism. Hobbes also presented a fledgling theory of association. The "Trayne of Thoughts" were a consequence of their coherence (or simultaneous occurrence) and could be random or regulated; the latter were guided by desire and habit, and associations could be strengthened by frequent repetition.

Hobbes was educated at Oxford and served for much of his life as tutor to various Dukes of Devonshire. In this capacity he made three grand tours of Europe, meeting Galileo and Descartes, as well as other French philosophical luminaries. Hobbes's long life saw the founding of the Royal Society in London, from which he was excluded primarily on the basis of his unorthodox political and religious beliefs.

Hobbes is portrayed as part of the Leviathan, the macrocosm of the state that is inseparable from the microcosm of man: "The multitude so united in one person, is called a Commonwealth. . . . This is the generation of that great Leviathan."

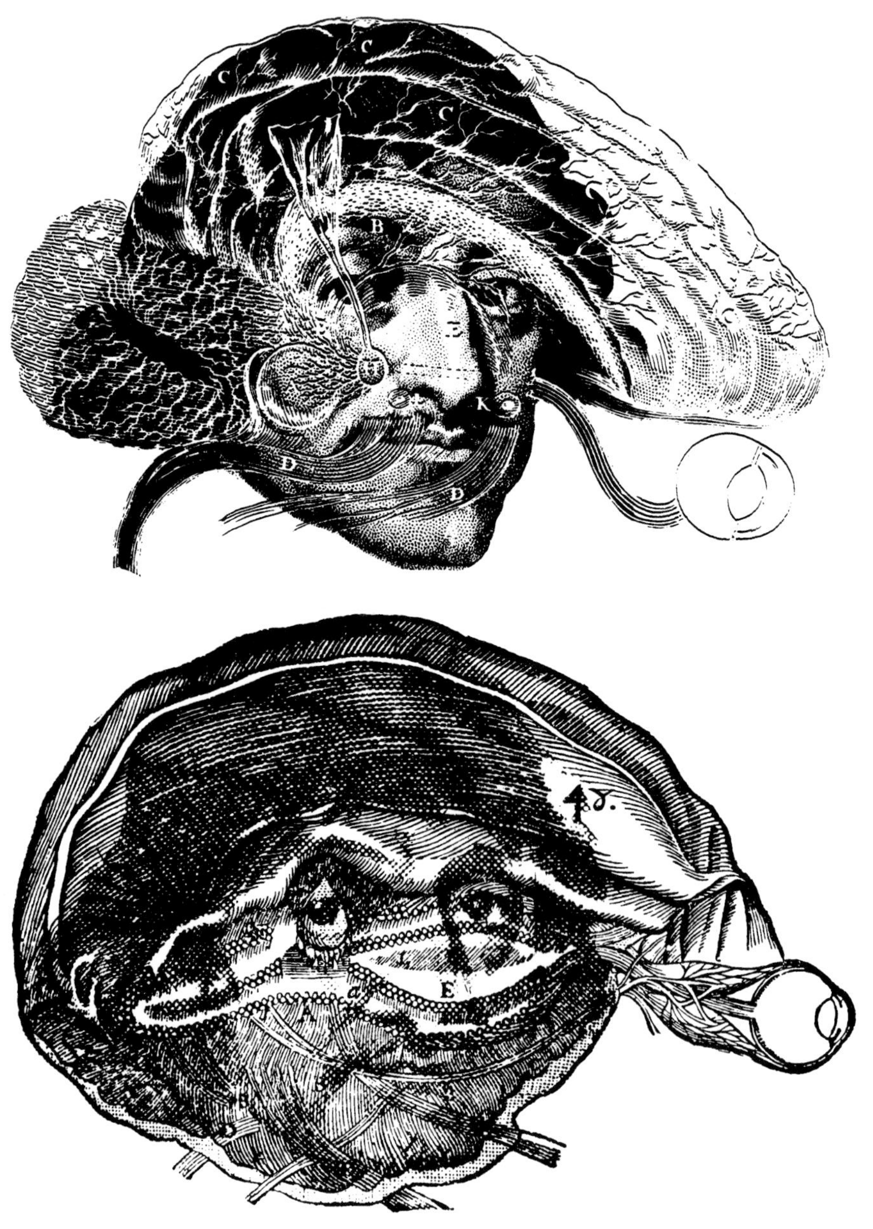

Portrait after an engraving in: *The Gallery of Portraits: with Memoirs*, Vol. 4. Under the superintendence of the Society for the Diffusion of Useful Knowledge. London: Charles Knight, 1835.

Upper motif after a diagram of the brain in: des Cartes, Renatus. 1662. *De homine figuris et latinitate.* F. Schuyl, trans. Lugduni Batavorum: Leffen & Moyardum.

Lower motif after a diagram of the brain in: Descartes, R. 1664/1909. *Traité de l'homme.* In *Oeuvres de Descartes*, Vol. 11. C. Adam and P. Tannery, eds. Paris: Cerf.

Cartesian Dualism

René Descartes (1596–1650) was the herald of modern science. He applied mechanistic interpretations to bodily processes while maintaining that the mind was immaterial, thus retaining the Platonic distinction between body and soul. Like Bacon, he studied law, but he also received a solid grounding in mathematics. As a young man in Paris he was fascinated by the hydraulically operated statues in the royal park at St. Germain; they made lifelike movements even though they were entirely driven by water power. In 1619, during military service in Germany, Descartes had a series of dreams that were to structure his subsequent thinking. They inspired him to search for new methods of inquiry rather than adopting those of past philosophers. After all, centuries of philosophical inquiry had not resulted in any generally accepted account of human nature. His method was to reject all ideas about which there could be any doubt. He was left with the irreducible fact of his own existence—I think, therefore I am. That is, Descartes's sceptical inquiries led him to the view that only thought and reason were beyond doubt, and were the bases upon which philosophy should stand, and these were the province of humans alone. The body, on the other hand, worked by mechanical principles that Descartes did much to advance. Of particular importance is his introduction of the reflex concept, which involved the nerves acting like pipes connecting the receptors to the brain which sent messages to the muscles. Communion between mind and body was achieved via structures in the brain, particularly the unpaired pineal body. These ideas were described and illustrated in his *Treatise of Man,* which was written in French but first published in Latin (*De homine*) in 1662, twelve years after his death. The translation into Latin was from a defective copy, but the engravings are far more detailed than the woodcuts that appeared in the first French edition (*Traité de l'homme,* 1664), and which are more frequently reproduced.

A portrait of Descartes, after the famous painting by Frans Hals, is presented twice: above in an engraving of the brain taken from *De homine,* and below in a woodcut illustrating the same text from *Traité de l'homme.* "Conceive surface *AA* facing cavities *EE* to be a rather dense and compact net or mesh, all of whose links are so many little conduits which the spirits can enter and which, always facing toward gland *H* [the pineal] whence the spirits emanate." Descartes considered that movements of the pineal gland (controlled by the mind) redirected the animal spirits (carried along the nerves) to move the muscles.

Portrait after an engraving in: *The Gallery of Portraits: with Memoirs,* Vol. 5. Under the superintendence of the Society for the Diffusion of Useful Knowledge. London: Charles Knight, 1835.

Tabula Rasa

John Locke (1632–1704) rejected one of Descartes's principal concepts, that of innate ideas, initiating the continuing debate between nativists and empiricists. Instead of accepting that some ideas, such as unity or God, are inborn, Locke proposed that all knowledge derives from experience. In *An Essay Concerning Humane Understanding* (1690) he wrote: "Let us then suppose the Mind to be, as we say, white Paper, void of all Characters, without any *Ideas;* How comes it to be furnished? Whence comes it by that vast store, which the busie and boundless Fancy of Man has painted on it, with an almost endless variety? Whence has it all the materials of Reason and Knowledge? To this I answer in one word, from *Experience:* In that all our Knowledge is founded, and from that it ultimately derives it self. . . . Our Observation employ'd either about *external, sensible Objects;* or about the *internal Operations of our Minds, perceived or reflected on by our selves, in that, which supplies our Understandings with all the materials of thinking.* These two are the Fountains of Knowledge, from whence all *Ideas* we have, or can naturally have, do spring." The senses provided the only route through which knowledge could be acquired, and what is perceived is always an idea rather than an object. Simple ideas, like whiteness, were produced passively via the senses, whereas complex ideas, like snow, resulted from active reflection by the mind. The transformation from simple to complex was effected by a process of mental chemistry. In this regard, Locke was influenced by the atomistic concepts of chemistry, and he was a close associate of one of the foremost chemists of the day, Robert Boyle (1627–1691). Thus, Locke rejected the Cartesian rationalism prevailing in continental Europe and established empiricism in Britain. He shared with Bacon a distrust of language as a basis for understanding nature, and he built upon Hobbes's materialism. In later editions of his *Essay* he proposed that ideas could be associated with one another, providing a basis for learning.

Locke was trained in classics and taught philosophy in Oxford. He lived through the heady political times of the English Civil War, and politics was his first love. He became a Fellow of the Royal Society and was acquainted with the leading scientists of his day, including Newton. It was not during his time at Oxford that he wrote on philosophy and politics; he left there to study medicine and subsequently found a more congenial atmosphere for his views in the diplomatic service. His *Essay* was published after almost twenty years of preparation, some of which was spent in exile in Holland.

The portrait of Locke has been rendered in line form by the photographic process of solarization. In order to represent the importance of the senses in Locke's philosophy, the eyes, ears, nose, and mouth have been covered by a blank, transparent sheet of paper (tabula rasa) and then the portrait was photographed once more.

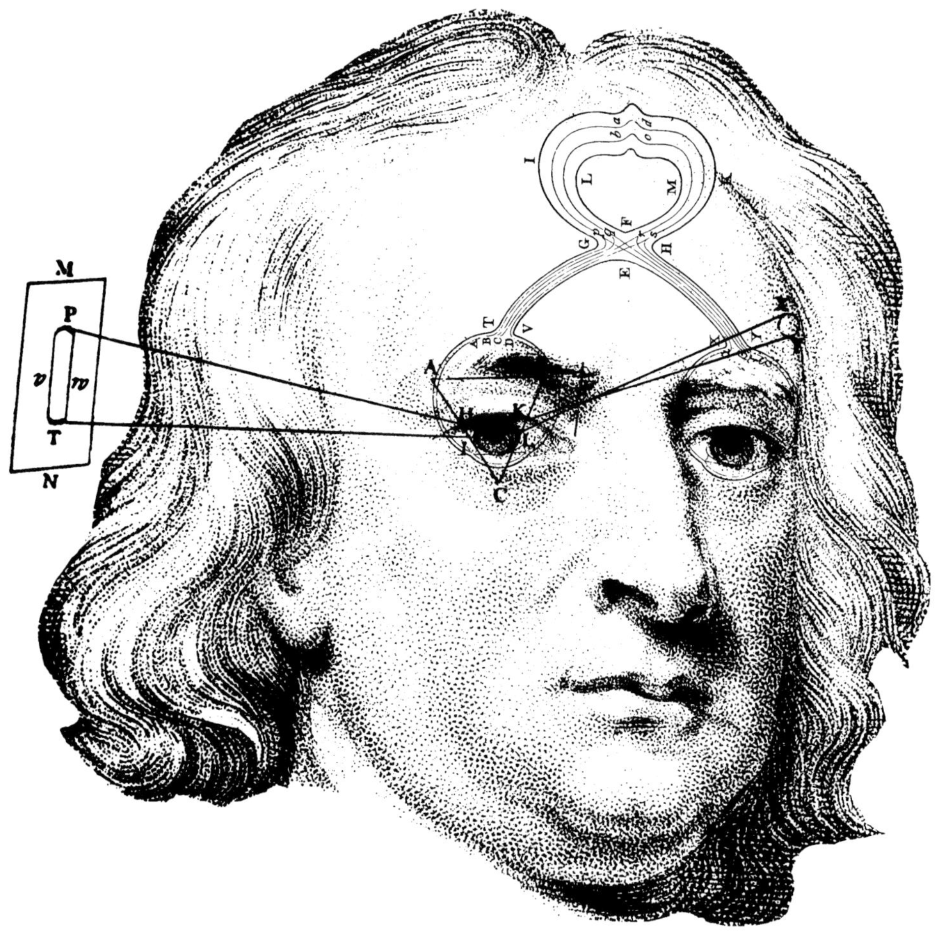

Portrait after an engraving in: *The Gallery of Portraits: with Memoirs*, Vol. 1. Under the superintendence of the Society for the Diffusion of Useful Knowledge. London: Charles Knight, 1833.

Motif of the spectrum after a figure in: Newton, I. 1704. *Opticks: or, a Treatise of the Reflections, Refractions, Inflections and Colours of Light.* London: Innys.

Motif of the visual pathways after a figure in: Brewster, D. 1855. *Memoirs of the Life, Writings, and Discoveries of Sir Isaac Newton.* Edinburgh: Constable.

Visionary

Isaac Newton (1642–1727) formulated the theory of universal gravitation and set science on a deterministic course from which it would not stray for centuries. By emphasizing that the motions of the planets could be described mathematically and that the same principles of gravitational attraction applied to all bodies, Newton removed the need for an Aristotelian prime mover. Natural phenomena should be accounted for in natural rather than supernatural terms, involving concepts of space, time, matter, and force. Newton's direct contributions to psychology were principally in the domain of vision—elucidating the nature of light, establishing rules of color mixing, estimating the duration of visual persistence, and expanding the knowledge of binocular combination. These are described in his *Opticks* (1704), although the initial experiments were conducted decades earlier. The germ of almost all his major insights were sown during a period of enforced absence from Cambridge during the years of the plague (1665–1666). At this time he purchased a prism at the annual Stourbridge Fair and used it in his experiments on returning to Cambridge. By making a small hole in the shutter of his darkened room in Trinity College, sunlight could fall on the prism to be refracted onto a sheet of white paper: "This Image or Spectrum PT was coloured, being red at its least refracted end T, and violet at its most refracted end P, and yellow green and blew in the intermediate spaces. Which agrees with the first Proposition, that Lights which differ in Colour do also differ in Refrangibility." Newton believed that there were seven colors in the spectrum, in accord with the seven tones in an octave, and they were arranged into a circle based on the musical intervals of the octave. Colors that were opposite one another were complementary, because when mixed they produced gray, and white was in the center. Newton's work displaced the study of color from objects to light.

When observing rapidly moving illuminated objects, Newton realized that the process of vision took a measurable time, which he tried to determine. He also carried out dissections of the visual pathways and in an unpublished manuscript described, for the first time, the partial decussation of the optic nerve at the optic chiasma.

Newton was born at Woolsthorpe, a small village in Lincolnshire. He studied at Cambridge University, and was appointed Lucasian professor of mathematics at the age of 26. He was appointed Master of the Mint in 1699, was elected president of the Royal Society in 1703, and was knighted in 1705. He is represented together with diagrams of the prismatic spectrum and of the visual pathways.

Portrait after an engraving in: *The Gallery of Portraits: with Memoirs,* Vol. 6. Under the superintendence of the Society for the Diffusion of Useful Knowledge. London: Charles Knight, 1836.

Monadologist

Gottfried Wilhelm von Leibniz (1646–1716) made a lasting achievement in mathematics with the formulation of infinitesimal calculus, independently of Newton. His mathematics fashioned his ideas on the philosophy of mind. Leibniz did not accept that extension and motion were the primary qualities of the universe, as both Descartes and Locke had argued, because length and motion could be successively divided into infinitesimally small parts. In their place he proposed that the universe is composed of an infinity of noninteracting forces called "monads," and their activity is expressed as perception. Monads are ordered hierarchically, according to the clarity of their perceptions of the world, being rational, sentient, or simple. Simple perceptions could accrete to yield awareness, but there was a limen, or threshold, below which awareness would not occur. Thus, the possibility of unconscious processes was also introduced. In his attack on materialistic models of mind Leibniz employed a powerful metaphor that has been much used since: imagine a mechanical brain that could think and feel and was so large that it would be possible to walk round it; all the moving parts would be visible, but what would correspond to perception?

Leibniz was born in Leipzig, where his father was a professor and he was a student. As a young man he traveled to Paris and London, meeting the leading thinkers of the day. Most of the rest of his life was spent in the service of the Houses of Mainz and of Hanover, being librarian in the latter. He was instrumental in founding the Academy of Sciences in Berlin and in St. Petersburg. The range of his interests was astounding, extending from mines to minds, though it was so widespread that he rarely completed one enterprise before being distracted by another. In his own lifetime he was often treated as a figure of fun, being satirized as Dr. Pangloss in Voltaire's *Candide*: in spite of all the ills that befell him, the optimistic fictional philosopher continued to believe that all is for the best in the best of all possible worlds! Although Leibniz wrote extensively and corresponded with a wide circle of intellectuals, the depth of his understanding was only appreciated after his death, with the publication of his private papers.

The illustration is composed of a multitude of tiny, independent units that can be actively organized into the portrait of Leibniz (with his characteristically flowing black wig); the individual dots lie below the threshold for their perception. Like the act of perception itself, it is easier to report on appearances than to appreciate the processes underlying them: Leibniz is here contained within the letters spelling the basic units of his system, though the letters themselves are not easy to discern. "And all this makes one indeed think that the *noticeable perceptions* also arise by degrees from those which are too minute to be observed."

Portrait after frontispiece engraving in: Fraser, A. C. 1871. *Life and Letters of George Berkeley, D.D. formerly Bishop of Cloyne; and an Account of his Philosophy.* Oxford: Clarendon Press.

The Perception of Distance

George Berkeley (1685–1753) published *An Essay Towards a New Theory of Vision,* (1709), upon which his reputation is principally based, when he was 24 years old. He refined the empiricist philosophy of Locke by arguing that appearances are all: existence is perception. That is, the matter from which materialism is constructed is itself open to question. If all we have are our perceptions, how can we prove the existence of an external world? A problem with this position is that if perceptions are transitory, so is existence. Does an object cease to exist when the eyes are closed? Berkeley sought to salvage this slide into solipsism (that nothing other than one's own ideas exist) by arguing that God alone perceived an external reality.

Despite this idealist stance, Berkeley made important steps toward understanding how we perceive space, and how the different spatial senses are integrated. He commenced his *Essay* by stating "My Design is to shew the manner, wherein we perceive by Sight the Distance, Magnitude, and Situation of Objects. Also to consider the Difference there is betwixt the *Ideas* of Sight and Touch, and whether there be any *Idea* common to both Senses. It is, I think, agreed by all that *Distance* of itself, and immediately cannot be seen. For *Distance* being a Line directed end-wise to the Eye, it projects only one Point in the Fund of the Eye, Which Point remains invariably the same, whether the Distance be longer or shorter." He proposed that we learn to see distance by associating sight with touch. Moreover, the degree of muscular contraction involved in converging the eyes are also correlated with distance, and provide a source of association with sight for perceiving distance. This interpretation of space perception was presented in preference to that based on geometrical optics: "Those *Lines* and *Angles* have no real Existence in Nature, being only an *Hypothesis* fram'd by *Mathematicians,* and by them into *Optics,* that they might treat of the *Science* in a *Geometrical* way."

Berkeley was born near Kilkenny, Ireland, and became a fellow at Trinity College, Dublin, in 1707. Following extensive travels throughout Europe he journeyed to America in order to set up a missionary college in Bermuda, returning in 1731. In 1734 Berkeley became Bishop of Cloyne, an office he held until his death.

Berkeley's portrait is embedded in a pattern of points, representing extended lines, only one of which is directed to the fund of his left eye; the others would be seen as lines. His argument about the projection of an extended line to the eye is restricted to monocular vision: with both eyes open the line would be a point for only one eye and extended for the other. Berkeley is deliberately represented close to the threshold of vision because he introduced the term "minimum visible."

Portrait after frontispiece engraving in: Reid, T. 1821. *An Inquiry into the Human Mind, On the Principles of Common Sense.* London: Bumpus, Sharpe, Samms, Warren, & Reilly.

Common Senses

Thomas Reid (1710–1796) reacted to Berkeley's idealism and Hume's skepticism by arguing that the evidence of external reality is provided by the common activities of the senses and is supported by commonsense intuition. "Let scholastic sophisters entangle themselves in their own cobwebs; I am resolved to take my own existence, and the existence of other things, upon trust; and to believe that snow is cold, and honey sweet, whatever they may say to the contrary. He must either be a fool, or want to make a fool of me, that would reason me out of my reason and senses." Thus, Reid founded the Scottish "commonsense" school of philosophy, of which Dugald Stewart (1753–1828), Thomas Brown (1778–1820), and William Hamilton (1788–1856) were the principal protagonists. Their ideas were to be influential in the development of psychology in America in the nineteenth century. The school was opposed to associationism, particularly when it was couched in physiological language. Reid also proposed a faculty psychology; faculties were innate properties of the mind which exerted control over habits, or behavior. His descriptive psychology could be studied by reflection on mental activity, by an analysis of the use of language, and by observations of behavior. He provided a bridge between the extreme rationalists and empiricists. His belief in the power of reason was tempered by a desire to accumulate evidence empirically. He conducted experiments on space perception to show how people with squints gradually overcome double vision: "One who squints, and originally saw objects double by reason of that squint, may acquire such habits, that when he looks at an object, he shall see it only with one eye: nay, we may acquire such habits, that when he looks at an object with his best eye, he shall have no distinct vision with the other at all." This was supported by evidence from examinations of the visual acuity in each eye of twenty such persons. He believed that the perception of objects was given directly by divine assistance but that sensation derives from physical objects themselves. Although they are described similarly in language, he considered that they were different—sensations referred to the immediate actions of the senses, whereas perceptions are always associated with objects that continue to exist whether or not they are perceived. Perceptions could be innate or acquired. The separation of sensation from perception has remained with psychology to the present day. Paradoxically, it was the modern standard-bearer of direct realism, Gibson, who dismissed this distinction.

Reid was born in Strachan, in the northeast of Scotland, and entered the ministry after studying at Marischal College, Aberdeen. In 1752 he became professor of philosophy at King's College, Aberdeen, and he was appointed successor to Adam Smith (1723–1790) as professor of moral philosophy at Glasgow University in 1764—the same year *An Inquiry into the Human Mind, On the Principles of Common Sense* was published. He is represented in the context of his common senses.

Portrait after an engraving in: *The Gallery of Portraits: with Memoirs*, Vol. 7. Under the superintendence of the Society for the Diffusion of Useful Knowledge. London: Charles Knight, 1837.

Motif after text in: Hume, D. 1772. *Essays and Treatises on Several Subjects*, Vol. 2. *Containing An Inquiry Concerning Human Understanding; A Dissertation on the Passions; An Inquiry Concerning the Principles of Morals; and The Natural History of Religion. A New Edition.* London: T. Cadell.

Humean Understanding

David Hume (1711–1776) stands in the empiricist line from Locke through Berkeley, and he rejected the rationalist notions of cause and effect in favor of skepticism. Hume proposed that while events occur in sequence, the perception of causality is a consequence of repeated mental associations between contiguous impressions, and the true nature of causality could never be known—hence he is often referred to as the skeptical philosopher. While he accepted that all experience derives from the senses, he did not make appeal to a higher perceiver, as Berkeley had; rather he considered that external reality is unknowable.

Hume was born and died in Edinburgh, though he spent much of his life in England and France. It was during his first visit to France that he wrote his celebrated *A Treatise of Human Nature* (published anonymously in 1739 and under his own name in 1740), laying the ground for a "science of man" based on observation and experiment; he followed this eight years later with a shorter version entitled *An Inquiry Concerning Human Understanding*. Hume's science was modeled more closely on Bacon's inductive than on Newton's deductive approach, and he did much to foster a realization that all areas of human endeavor require an understanding of human nature.

Hume placed great emphasis on the association of ideas and, despite its origins in Greek philosophy, he considered it to be his most important contribution to establishing a science of the mind; it has had a profound impact on psychology, particularly on behaviorism. Hume referred to it initially as the "connexion of ideas," but in the text presented opposite he used the term "association of ideas," as had Locke earlier. On the page following that reproduced he states that the three principles of association are resemblance, contiguity in time or place, and cause and effect. Contiguity refers to the likelihood of remembering experiences that occurred frequently together; the sight of a glass of beer can evoke its bitter taste. Association by cause and effect was considered to be the most important; events that occur in sequence, and may appear to be causally related, are recalled together. The stone thrown in the water is linked with the ripples it sets in train.

The example he gives of association by resemblance is that "A picture naturally leads our thoughts to the original." The original in the case of the portrait shown here was an engraving by William Holl which in its turn was after a painting by Allan Ramsay.

Portrait after an engraving in: *The Gallery of Portraits: with Memoirs,* Vol. 5. Under the superintendence of the Society for the Diffusion of Useful Knowledge. London: Charles Knight, 1835.

Motif after an engraving of Rousseau's tomb in the gardens of Ermenonville, near Paris, in: Urmson, J. O, ed. 1960. *The Concise Encyclopaedia of Western Philosophy and Philosophers.* London: Hutchinson.

Noble Savage

Jean-Jacques Rousseau (1712–1778) represented quite a different philosophical strand from the rationalists and empiricists. He urged that feelings and emotions played the prime role in human behavior, rather than reason and experience, and he ushered in the Romantic movement. Contrary to Hobbes's pessimistic outlook on humankind, Rousseau considered that humans are inherently good, but can develop otherwise due to the corrupting influence of social forces. "The fundamental principle of all morality . . . is that man is a being naturally good, loving justice and order, that there is no original perversity in the human heart and that the first movements of nature are always right." In *The Social Contract* (1762) Rousseau proposed that life in a community is possible because of a general will which operates to the advantage of the society, but it is not necessarily in harmony with the desires of the individuals composing it. Thus, the individual who escapes the constraints of social institutions, the noble savage, would be happy as well as free. "All is well, coming from the hands of Nature, the Author of all things; all degenerates in the hands of man."

The importance of education was stressed in *Émile* (1762), which charts the course of a developing child. Rousseau considered that education should capitalize on the inquisitive nature of children, being an active process of acquisition deriving from nature and nurtured through discourse between teacher and pupil. Children were not to be considered as imperfect adults, but as having positive characteristics that should be stimulated by education. Rousseau placed development firmly in the province of psychology.

Rousseau was born in Geneva where he endured several childhood misfortunes, losing his mother shortly after birth and being abandoned by his father at the age of ten. He left a remarkably candid record of his life in the four books of his *Confessions* (1781–1788). Although never married, he lived with an illiterate maidservant who bore him five children, none of whom they raised themselves.

Rousseau's moral philosophy was the source of much adverse comment in his day. Indeed, with the publication of both *The Social Contract* and *Émile* in 1762 a warrant for his arrest was issued and he had to flee Paris. David Hume offered to befriend him in England; their initial correspondence was effusive but, as with most of Rousseau's contacts, friendship turned to emnity: in Hume's words, the "honest savage" became "a black-hearted villain." Rousseau did eventually return to Paris, where he achieved some contentment before his death.

The illustration reflects the ultimate stage of development, and the grand scale in which Rousseau was honored by his adopted countrymen. He was accorded far greater eminence in death than throughout his life.

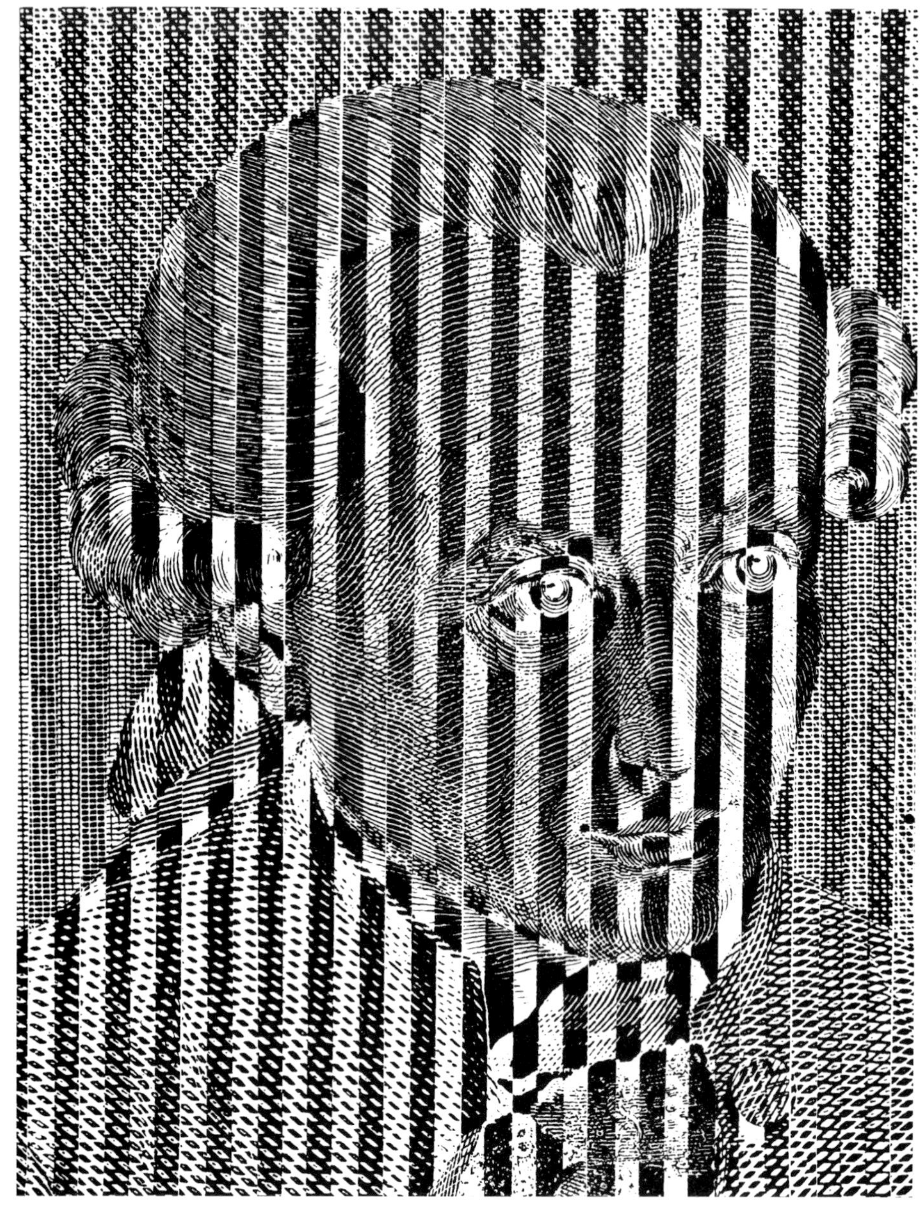

Portrait after frontispiece engraving in: Hartenstein, G., ed. 1853. *Immanuel Kant's Kritik der reinen Vernunft*. Leipzig: Leopold Voss.

Apperception

Immanuel Kant (1724–1804) was initially an orthodox Leibnizian philosopher who became aroused from "his dogmatic slumbers" on reading Hume's analysis of causality. Kant developed a transcendental theory of mind which drew upon both rationalism and empiricism without being allied to either. Rather than accounting for ideas in terms of experience, as Hume had done, Kant adopted the opposite strategy of accounting for experience in terms of concepts. That is, our conscious, phenomenal world is a cognitive construction. He accepted that all knowledge arises from the senses, but it is not treated in a passive way. "Though all our knowledge begins with experience, it by no means follows that all arises out of experience. For, on the contrary, it is quite possible that our empirical knowledge is a compound of that which we receive through impressions, and that which the faculty of cognition supplies from itself." Certain concepts, like intuitions of space and time, were considered to be independent of experience and are used to order perception. "Space does not represent any property of objects as things in themselves, nor does it represent them in their relations to each other." The case for nativism was championed in a more specific way than Descartes had proposed. Perception was taken to be an active process of organization rather than a passive accretion of sensations. He made a distinction between the world of things and that of appearances, and was pessimistic about whether the latter (and hence psychology) was open to scientific inquiry. That is, he did not consider that the inner world was open to precise measurement, and therefore could not be classified as a science. Nonetheless, Kant's ideas have had a long-lasting influence on psychology in general, and most notably on the emergence of Gestalt psychology. Kant wrote about human nature in his *Anthropology* (1798), but the *Kritik der reinen Vernunft* (Critique of Pure Reason) (1781) contains the main features of his philosophy as it relates to psychology.

Kant rarely strayed far from his native Königsberg, where he studied, lectured, and held the chair of logic and metaphysics from 1770 until his death. He was a meticulous man who shunned popularity; the regularity of his daily pursuits was such as to act as a timepiece for his fellow citizens and any departure from his routine was cause for concern. He was once late for his daily constitutional having become engrossed in Rousseau's *Émile*! In a display rare in the annals of academia, the Königsbergers showed their appreciation of him by staging a funeral on a grand scale.

Kant replaced Descartes's self or ego as the ultimate reality with "the transcendental unity of apperception." Apperception referred to the active ordering of our experience to achieve meaning, and it is applied in recognizing Kant's portrait: neighboring vertical bands are in opposite contrasts, but despite this the figure is seen as representing a face against a patterned background.

Portrait after an engraving in: Hilgard, E. R., and J. R. Hilgard. 1975. *Hypnosis in the Relief of Pain.* Los Altos, Calif.: Kaufmann.

Motif of a mesmeric séance after an engraving in: Darnton, R. 1968. *Mesmerism and the End of the Enlightenment in France.* Cambridge, Mass.: Harvard University Press.

Animal Magnetism

Franz Anton Mesmer (1734–1815) set in train a branch of medicine which proved to be one of the motive forces for later dynamic psychology. "I named the property of the animal body that renders it liable to the action of heavenly bodies and of the earth *animal magnetism.*" Physical magnetism, first elucidated by William Gilbert (1544–1603) in Bacon's day, was also considered to cast its subtle influence on the nervous system. Mesmer wrote of animal magnetism, "that all bodies were, like the magnet, capable of communicating this magnetic principle; that this fluid penetrated everything and could be stored up and concentrated, like the electric fluid; that it acted at a distance." Moreover, harnessing its forces could "cure nervous disorders directly and other disorders indirectly."

Mesmer, a Viennese physician, was attempting to provide a scientific explanation for some remarkable cures he had effected by requiring patients to grasp magnetized iron bars. He considered that this procedure resulted in restoring equilibrium between the patient's animal magnetism and that prevailing in the environment. Later, cures were achieved without the use of magnetic bars, by rhythmic movements, by fixating, and by stroking the body. Despite his desire for academic respectability, Mesmer was forced to leave Vienna, and moved to Paris in 1778. There the medical profession was as skeptical as it had been in Vienna, but in 1784 Mesmer's claims were put to the test by two commissions, one of scientists and the other of physicians. The verdict of the commissions was that animal magnetism did not exist. The cures that undoubtedly did sometimes result from the treatment were said to be a consequence of imagination and imitation. In the course of their inquiries the commissioners carried out some of the first genuinely social psychological experiments, manipulating expectancies and controlling stimulus conditions, to show that the same effects could be produced in the absence of any magnetizing fluid. Mesmer's reputation was tarnished by this conclusion and he faded into obscurity, unlike the process he had uncovered, which was renamed *mesmerism.* Mesmerism was transformed into hypnotism by James Braid (1795-1860), who realized the potential of altered states of consciousness for surgery.

Mesmer is represented in combination with a contemporary portrayal of a mesmeric séance. He recommended treatment in séances, which were conducted with much theatricality: patients, connected to one another by cords, would sit round a tub, or *baquet,* of "magnetized" fluid, grasping iron rods that protruded from it. Mesmer and his assistants, called magnetizers, would pass among the patients, occasionally stroking the body or the afflicted part. Patients often experienced convulsions during treatment, after which they were taken to a padded "crisis room" where they usually passed into a trance before returning to their normal state.

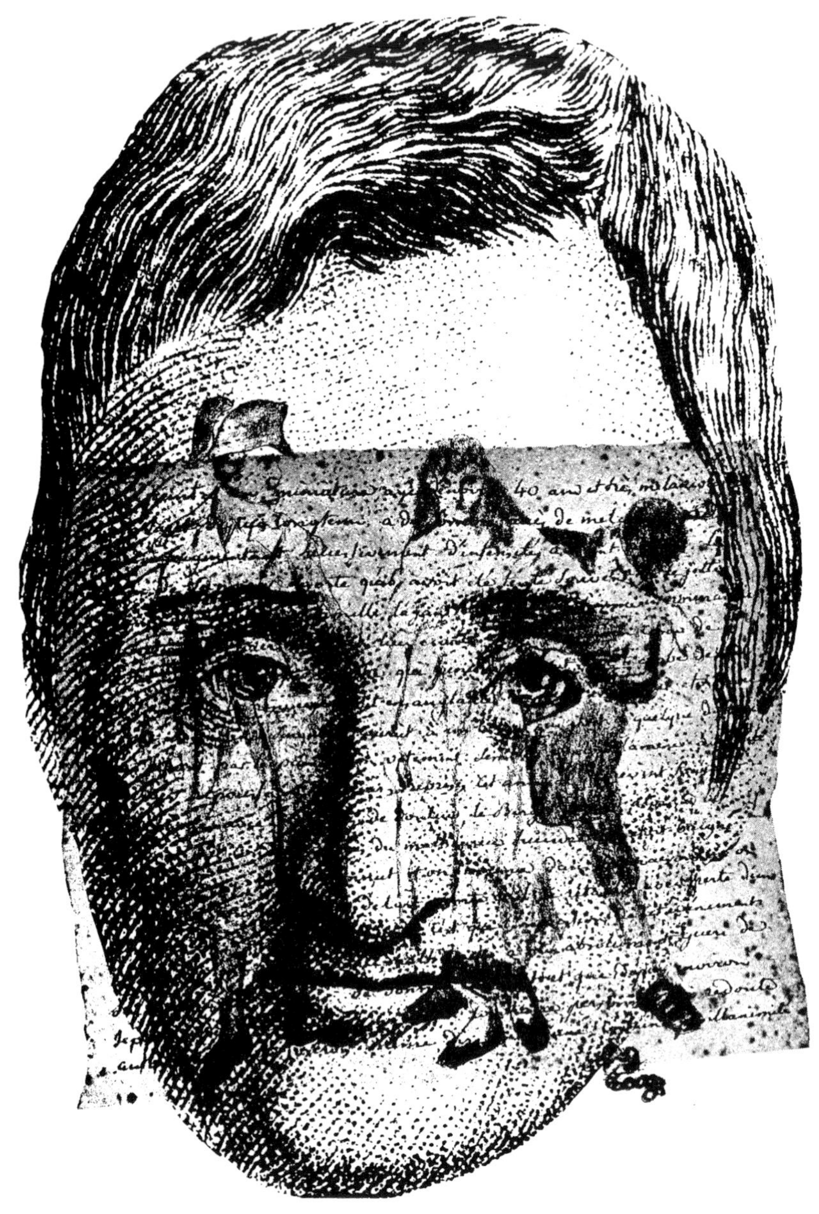

Portrait after a frontispiece engraving in: Pinel, P. 1818. *Nosographie philosophique, ou la méthode de l'analyse appliquée a la médecine.* ed. 6. Paris: Brosson.

Motif of text after a case history by Pinel in: Zilboorg, G., and G. W. Henry. 1941. *A History of Medical Psychology.* New York: Norton.

Embedded motif after a detail in the painting by Robert-Fleury of Pinel unchaining the inmates of the Bicêtre mental asylum in: Urmson, J. O., ed. 1960. *The Concise Encyclopaedia of Western Philosophy and Philosophers.* London: Hutchinson.

Emancipator

Philippe Pinel (1745–1826) moved to Paris to practice medicine in the same year as Mesmer, but his concerns were quite different. Rather than treating the well-to-do ladies of the city, he dealt with the destitute and disposessed inhabitants of the asylums for the insane. Conditions in the asylums were appalling; one report recorded that there were four times as many patients as there were beds, and many of the patients were fettered. On his appointment as chief physician at the Bicêtre in 1792 Pinel entered the hospital and ordered the patients' chains to be removed. Pinel's decision was questioned by the Revolutionary authorities, and he was required to defend it: freedom was not for all the French. Following the accusation that he himself was mad "to unchain these animals" Pinel replied, "it is my conviction that these mentally ill are intractable only because they are deprived of fresh air and of their liberty." Not all the inmates were subsequently unchained, and many that were had suffered such severe psychological scars from years in shackles that freedom of movement was impossible. Nevertheless, Pinel considered it a success: "The mentally sick, far from being guilty people deserving punishment are sick people whose miserable state deserves all the consideration that is due to suffering humanity. One should try with the most simple methods to restore their reason." Among these simple methods were frequent visits to patients, involving conversation and taking careful note of their behavior and replies. This emphasis on recording detailed case histories is another tribute to Pinel's humane approach to the mentally ill. "In medicine there are few topics as fruitful as insanity, because of its many points of contact and because of the necessary relation of this science to moral philosophy and to the history of human understanding. But there are even fewer topics against which there are as many prejudices to be rectified and errors to be destroyed."

In 1795 he was promoted to take charge of the Salpêtrière hospital, which he found in much the same state as he encountered on his arrival at the Bicêtre, but which was similarly transformed from a prison to a hospital. Pinel retained his administrative posts throughout the turbulent years of the Revolution and its aftermath. His example of treatment for mental patients and the organization of mental hospitals was followed initially in Britain and eventually throughout the world.

Pinel's act of unchaining the patients was of great symbolic significance. It has been celebrated in two paintings, details from one of which are incorporated in the portrait; the third element is a copy of a case history taken by Pinel.

Detail of a portrait after an engraving in: *The Gallery of Portraits: with Memoirs,* Vol. 4. Under the superintendence of the Society for the Diffusion of Useful Knowledge. London: Charles Knight, 1835.

Silhouette after a figure in: Lück, H. E., and R. Miller, eds. 1993. *Illustrierte Geschichte der Psychologie.* Munich: Quintessenz.

Romantic Eye

Johann Wolfgang von Goethe (1749-1832) was a poet, novelist, and playwright of enormous popularity who also wrote on science and philosophy. His major work, *Faust* (1808 and 1831), in which a wandering conjuror sells his soul to the devil in return for superhuman powers, was an early influence on Freud, and his belief that life was motivated by opposing forces like good and evil find their echo in Jung. Goethe, in line with many Romantic philosophers, rejected the experimental approach to the study of nature because it was too constrained. In its place he proposed the astute and intuitive observation of natural phenomena, setting in train the method of phenomenology. This is best seen in his *Zur Farbenlehre* (Theory of Colours) (1810), which contrasted his observational approach to color with what he considered to be the physicalism of Newton: "A great mathematician was possessed with an entirely false notion on the physical origin of colours; yet, owing to his great authority as a geometer, the mistakes which he committed as an experimentalist long became sanctioned in the eyes of a world ever fettered in prejudices." The purity of white light was taken to be fundamental and indivisible, rather than white being a mixture of different colored lights. Goethe chose to observe and describe instead of experiment on color vision. He distinguished between what he called physiological colors (the experience of color) and physical colors produced by optical refraction. He did borrow a prism to repeat Newton's experiment of separating the spectral components of white light, but failed to conduct it appropriately; when asked to return the prism he simply directed it to a light and concluded that it still looked white! Goethe's theory of color was never taken seriously by the scientific community, but his observations have rarely been challenged. He reported many novel phenomena, like positive and negative color afterimages, irradiation, color shadows, and color blindness, in addition to contrast effects—both in the chromatic and achromatic domains. For example, the color or brightness of a piece of paper can be changed by surrounding it by differently colored or bright papers, as can its apparent size. In the broader field of science he introduced concepts in comparative anatomy, like homologous parts, which were to play their part in the emergence of Darwin's theory of evolution.

Goethe was born in Frankfurt-am-Main and studied law, somewhat reluctantly, at Strasbourg. As a consequence of his literary work he was invited to serve in the Court of Weimar to which he remained attached for most of his life.

The pattern of contrasting black and white, diamond shapes shown are rather like those in a figure from his *Theory of Colours.* The sizes of the elements vary very slightly, as can be seen by a good observer, to reveal an acute left eye—that of Goethe—enclosed in his silhouette.

Portrait after an engraving in: Polyak, S. 1957. *The Vertebrate Visual System.* Chicago: University of Chicago Press.

Phrenological head of Gall from the Dundee Art Galleries and Museums and photographed with their kind permission.

Phrenological Head of Gall

Franz Joseph Gall (1758-1828) represents the emergence of medicine and physiology as sources of psychological speculation. From the early nineteenth century, anatomists dissected neural pathways in the brain with increasing precision and these were related to the developing understanding of nerve functioning. These anatomical and physiological discoveries were applied to individual differences in the gross structure of the brain and to disorders of its function due to trauma or disease.

Gall was born in Germany, studied medicine in Strasbourg, and practiced in Vienna, where he gained a reputation as one of the leading neuroanatomists in Europe. In 1791 Gall advocated cortical localization of mental functions; he was the first to draw a clear distinction between the gray matter of the cerebral cortex and the underlying white matter. These advances were described long before his publications on phrenology, with his collaborator Johann Gaspar Spurzheim (1776–1832). However, it is for phrenology—assessing mental characteristics from the external shape of the skull—that Gall is best known. In the early nineteenth century, after losing his post in Vienna for publishing such novel ideas about brain function, he made an enormously successful tour of European capitals (together with Spurzheim) lecturing on and demonstrating phrenology. In Paris phrenology was subjected to examination by a Royal Commission (on which Pinel sat), as had animal magnetism, and with a similar negative conclusion. On the one hand, phrenology became a popular pursuit, developing absurdly specific "cranioscopical inferences" and making extravagent claims which led to its eventual ridicule and demise. On the other hand, Gall's work focused attention on functions carried out in local regions of the brain, in contrast to Flourens's view of its equipotentiality. For example, Gall proposed that the nerve ganglia were hierarchically organized, that the source of behavior was in the cortex, and that different varieties of memory were localized in the frontal cortex, as was the function of speech. "In all my researches, my object has been to find out the laws of organization, and the functions of the nervous system in general, and of the brain in particular. . . . The moral and intellectual dispositions are innate; their manifestation depends on organization; the brain is exclusively the organ of the mind; the brain is composed of many particular and independent organs, as there are fundamental powers of the mind;—these four incontestable principles form the basis of the whole physiology of the brain."

The sculpted head of Gall shown here has phrenological markings on both sides, but those on the left of the original are colored as well as numbered. The head has been oriented to match that of a lithographic portrait of Gall. A slide of the portrait was projected onto the head and photographed so that the facial details of the portrait were superimposed on the model.

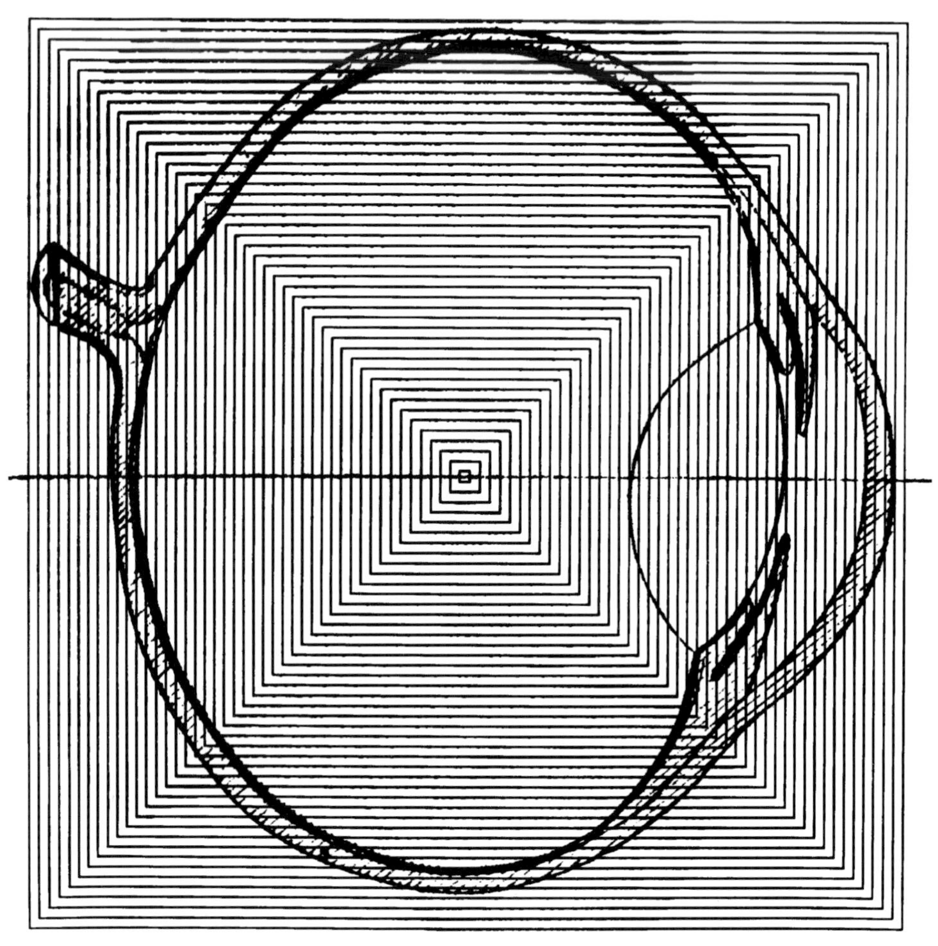

Portrait after an engraving in: Taylor, W. C. 1867. *The National Portrait Gallery of Illustrations and Eminent Persons,* Vol. 2. London: Jackson.

Motif of the eye after an engraving in: Young, T. 1801. On the mechanism of the eye. *Philosophical Transactions of the Royal Society 91*:23–88.

Optometer

Thomas Young (1773–1829) was a physicist and a physician by training, but he was also a philologist and a cryptographer—he commenced the deciphering of the Rosetta stone. In visual science he explained the process of accommodation, and proposed a theory of color vision based on three receptors, sensitive to different regions of the spectrum. His experiments on interference fringes provided support for a wave theory of light in opposition to Newton's corpuscular theory. Descartes had earlier speculated that accommodation occurred as a consequence of variations in the curvature of the crystalline lens, but the alternative of corneal curvature changes was still entertained. In 1801 Young demonstrated that the former interpretation was correct by noting that accommodation persisted when the eye was immersed in water, eliminating corneal refraction. In addition, patients without a lens were unable to accommodate to objects at different distances. He also made detailed measurements of the dimensions of his eyes using an optometer of his own devising. In 1802 he advanced his theory of color vision: "Now, as it is almost impossible to conceive each sensitive point of the retina to contain an infinite number of particles, each capable of vibrating in perfect unison with every possible undulation, it becomes necessary to suppose the number limited, for instance, to the three principal colours, red, yellow, and blue." Later he changed the principal or primary colors to red, green, and violet.

Young was born in Somerset and died in London after a distinguished career covering remarkably wide scientific interests. He was a precocious child who was self-taught in languages and science. He studied medicine at London, Edinburgh, and Göttingen and practiced in London while holding the posts of professor of natural philosophy at the Royal Institution and then foreign secretary of the Royal Society.

Young described the optical aberration of astigmatism, the condition in which lines in different orientations cannot be brought to a focus in the same plane: when one set of lines is sharply focused the other appears blurred, and vice versa. Young measured the astigmatism of his own eye. Regular astigmatism is usually a consequence of the curvatures of optical surfaces in the eye (most commonly of the cornea) not being parts of spheres, but Young attributed it to an asymmetry in his lens. Young's portrait is embedded in a pattern of vertical and horizontal contours which are approximately equally defined. Regular astigmatism will result in one orientation appearing sharper than the other; inclining the head by 90 degrees will reverse the clearly defined contours. The enclosing astigmatic eye is Young's, as it was illustrated in his paper first describing the condition of astigmatism.

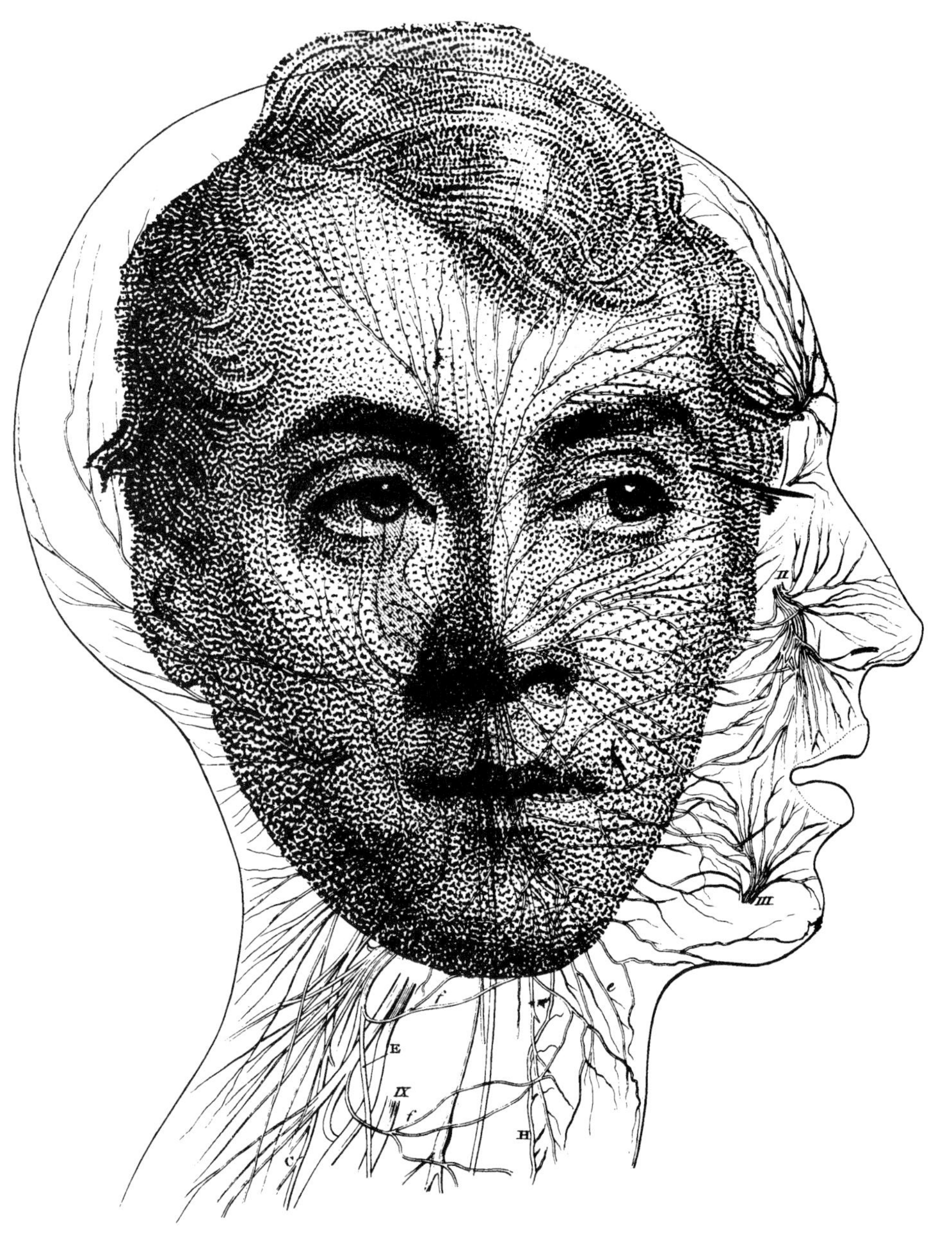

Portrait after a frontispiece engraving in: Bell, G. J., ed. 1870. *Letters of Sir Charles Bell, Selected from His Correspondence with His Brother George Joseph Bell.* London: John Murray.

Motif of the nerves of the head after a drawing by Bell in: Bell, C. 1844. *The Anatomy and Philosophy of Expression as Connected with the Fine Arts;* ed. 3. London: John Murray.

The Nerves of Bell's Head

Charles Bell (1774–1842) has been called the father of physiological psychology. In his privately published *Idea of a New Anatomy of the Brain* (1811) Bell described one of his rare experiments thus: "On laying bare the roots of the spinal nerves, I found that I could cut across the posterior fasciculus of nerves, which took its origin from the posterior portion of the spinal marrow without convulsing the muscles of the back; but that on touching the anterior fasciculus with the point of the knife, the muscles of the back were immediately convulsed. Such were my reasons for concluding that the cerebrum and the cerebellum were parts distinct in function." François Magendie (1783–1855) established in 1822 that the posterior roots are sensory and the anterior roots are motor. This clear evidence for a functional division in the central nervous system was of tremendous import, as much of the subsequent research involved pursuing this division to ever-higher centers. It also provided a physiological basis for localization of function, in accord with Gall's psychological speculations.

Bell traced the course of the nerves from the senses to specific areas of the brain, thereby suggesting a principle of specific nerve energies: "It is provided, that the extremities of the nerves of the senses shall be susceptible each of certain qualities in matter; and betwixt the impression of the outward sense, as it may be called, and the excercise of the internal organ, there is established a connection by which the ideas excited have a permanent correspondence with the qualities of bodies which surround us." In a later paper to the Royal Society he described the muscle or proprioceptive sense and distinguished by experiment the consequences of active and passive eye movements on visual direction.

Bell was born and died in Edinburgh, although he made his mark in London. The portrait shows Bell, aged thirty, shortly after he had moved to London to practice surgery and eventually to establish a medical school. The previous year he had written the third volume of the *Anatomy of the Human Body* (1803), with his oldest brother, John, who was a noted Edinburgh surgeon. His arrival in London was inauspicious, as few knew of his work, but with the publication of his *Essays on the Anatomy of Expression in Painting* (1806), combining his artistic talents and anatomical knowledge, he became widely recognized. The nerves of the head, in which Bell's portrait is shown, was originally drawn by him, and it appeared in the third edition of the book. He demonstrated that the muscles of expression are controlled by the seventh cranial nerve, damage to which can result in what became known as Bell's palsy.

Upper portrait after an engraving in: Wade, N. J., ed. 1983. *Brewster and Wheatstone on Vision.* London: Academic Press.

Lower portrait after an engraving in: *The Illustrated London News* 1868, 52:189.

Motif of stereoscope after a figure in: Brewster, D. 1856. *The Stereoscope. Its History, Theory, and Construction.* London: John Murray.

Philosophical Toys

David Brewster (1781–1868) was a physicist who devised two of the most popular optical instruments of the nineteenth century—the kaleidoscope and the lenticular form of the stereoscope. They were known as philosophical toys, because they combined science with amusement. His principal interest was in the phenomenon of polarization, and he supported Newton's corpuscular theory of light in opposition to Young's wave theory. Brewster wrote on visual as well as physical optics, and his pen, from which he made his living, was applied with polemic and perspicacity to far broader human endeavors. For example, he referred to Bell's experiments on the influence of the eye muscles on visual direction as physiological phantasies, largely because Brewster considered that the seat of vision is in the eye rather than being determined more centrally. He applied the concept of visible direction to a wide variety of phenomena, including stereoscopic vision: objects viewed with two eyes were seen at the intersection of the monocular visible directions. Although he did not add substantially to theory in the context of binocular vision, he did devise, in 1849, the most popular design of stereoscope used in nineteenth-century households. It consisted of a single lens cut in half so that the two half-lenses, when appropriately mounted, acted as magnifiers as well as prisms, fusing adjacent stereophotographs. Brewster also made forays into color vision, suggesting that sunlight was composed of three colors (red, yellow, and blue), and introducing the term *color blindness* into our language. Formerly, it was referred to as Daltonism, after the chemist and physicist John Dalton (1766–1844), who described his own inability to distinguish red from black. Color blindness was preferred because "no person wishes to be immortalized by his imperfection."

Brewster was born in Jedburgh and studied divinity at Edinburgh University. His diffidence when preaching led him to give up the ministry in favor of natural philosophy. He earned his living as an editor of scientific journals and as a prolific writer. His first academic post was as principal at St. Andrews University in 1839, and he later became principal at Edinburgh.

The kaleidoscope is a simple optical instrument involving two plane mirrors inclined at an angle of, for example, 45 or 60 degrees (which can be divided into 360 degrees) and located in a tube. Viewing through one end of the tube multiplies the images of objects at the other. In the case of the upper portrait, the original of which was painted at about the time the kaleidoscope was invented, the face is reflected and rotated successively to give eight images. As with most of Brewster's inventions there was controversy regarding its originality. In the lower illustration, an older Brewster is shown with his lenticular stereoscope.

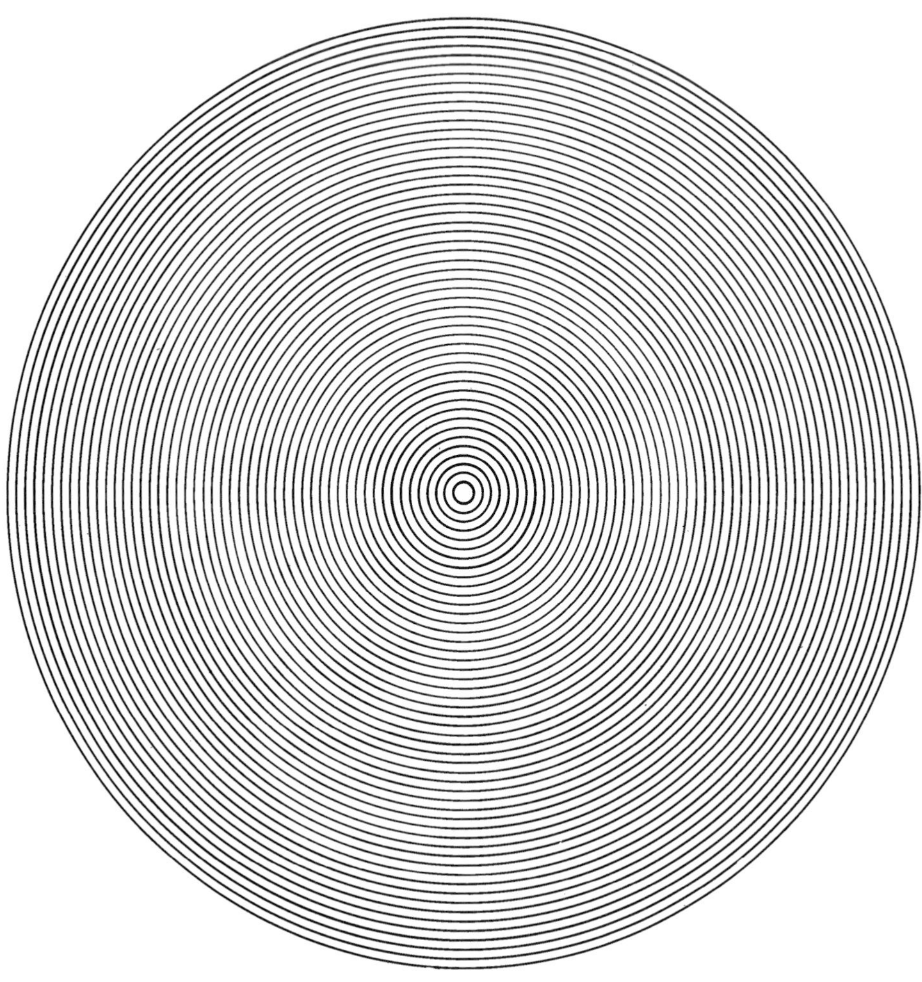

Portrait after a drawing in: Duke-Elder, S., and K. C. Wybar. 1961. *System of Ophthalmology,* Vol. 2. *The Anatomy of the Visual System.* London: Henry Kimpton.

Sehen in subjektiver Hinsicht

Jan Evangelista Purkinje or ***Purkyně*** (1787–1869) has left his mark throughout the body. There are Purkinje cells in the brain, Purkinje fibers around the heart, Purkinje images are reflected from the optical surfaces of the eye, a Purkinje tree can be rendered visible, and at twilight we can experience the Purkinje shift. In the 1820s he wrote two influential books on subjective visual phenomena (*Sehen in subjektiver Hinsicht*) because he believed that "visual illusions reveal visual truths." In his first book (1823) he gave detailed descriptions of phenomena such as afterimages, the visibility of the retinal blood vessels (the Purkinje tree), and the distortions that are produced when viewing regular geometrically periodic patterns, like concentric circles. In his second book (1825) he described the difference in the visibility of colored objects when seen in daylight and twilight—blue objects appear lighter and red ones darker in twilight (the Purkinje shift). He also studied distinct and indistinct (central and peripheral) vision, noting the greater sensitivity to movement in the periphery, but its poorer spatial acuity and color perception. The motion aftereffect was described thus: "One time I observed a cavalry parade for more than an hour, and then when the parade had passed, the houses directly opposite appeared to me to move in the reversed direction to the parade." This phenomenon was related to a variety of vertiginous effects that follow from body movements.

Purkinje's interests in vision were stimulated by reading Goethe's *Theory of Colours* and he was encouraged in his researches by Goethe (to whom his second book is dedicated) because of his use of the phenomenological method. When he gained access to one of the new large achromatic microscopes in 1832 he put his observational skills to good use, as is attested by the Purkinje cells in the brain and the Purkinje fibers in the heart.

Purkinje was born in Bohemia and studied medicine at Prague, where he carried out many experiments with self-administered drugs, considering that such results were more revealing than experiments on animals. Most of his experimental research in both physiology and histology was conducted in Breslau, but at the age of sixty three he was called to the chair of physiology in Prague, where he became one of the most ardent advocates of Czech nationalism.

Purkinje's portrait is partially hidden in a pattern of concentric circles, like one illustrated in his first book on *Sehen in subjektiver Hinsicht;* if the pattern is observed for some seconds the circles themselves will appear to distort, and spokes will seem to radiate from the center and rotate. When the whole pattern is out of focus his face can be seen. Purkinje considered that the distortions were due to the overlap of the image with its afterimage, but it is now known to be caused by transient astigmatic changes in the crystalline lens.

Portrait after frontispiece engraving in: Volkelt, J. 1900. *Arthur Schopenhauer. Seine Persönlichkeit, seine Lehre, sein Glaube.* Stuttgart: Frommanns.

Irrational Man

Arthur Schopenhauer (1788–1860) shared with Hobbes a pessimistic view of human nature, but he posited the source within the individual: he exposed the dark side of humanity. Hobbes saw people at war with one another, whereas Schopenhauer considered that they were at war with themselves. For him, the internal ferment is fueled by irrational motives that far exceed our ability to control them. His is a philosophy of the irrational in contrast to the prevalent rationalism adopted by his predecessors. It is this appeal to the irrational and unconscious that is of such importance in the development of psychology, and his philosophy shares many features with Freud's theories. His views were expressed at an early age in his book *Die Welt als Wille und Vorstellung* (The World as Will and Idea) (1818).

Schopenhauer was influenced by both Goethe and Kant, accepting some of their concepts and rejecting others; he was also inspired by Eastern philosophy. He followed Goethe in developing a theory of color vision. With Kant he accepted that reality (the thing-in-itself) is unknowable, but it consisted of an all-pervading will, of which individual wills are constituent parts. The motive force for the individual will is the struggle to survive. Rather than being under the control of the intellect, rational thought is subservient to the will, which is driven by irrational forces. Life is considered to be a succession of blind impulses, like hunger and sexual desire, that are temporarily satisfied, only to return. Pleasure, the satisfaction of an impulse, is transitory: "No attained object of desire can give lasting satisfaction, but merely a fleeting gratification." Understanding the power of the will only amplifies the suffering it imposes. This dire state of affairs can best be ameliorated by immersion in some activity that is not driven by the will, like art. The power of sexual desire can be reduced, he argued, by leading an ascetic life.

Schopenhauer was born in Danzig and moved to Hamburg at the age of five. He was educated at Göttingen and then Berlin University, where he commenced as a lecturer in 1819. In an act of impressive arrogance he timed his lectures to coincide with those of the eminent philosopher Georg Hegel (1770–1831), intending to lure the latter's students away. The failure of this enterprise resulted in him retiring from academic life and retreating to Frankfurt, where he remained a bachelor for the rest of his life. He wrote that "Marriage is a trap which nature sets for us." In other respects, an ascetic life might have been the best that one could achieve from Schopenhauer's philosophy, but it was not a path that he himself sought to follow.

Schopenhauer's writing is replete with oppositional pairs like life and death, pleasure and pain, love and hate, and his portrait has been transfigured to display this conflict between positive and negative aspects of human endeavor.

Portrait after an engraving in: Haymaker, W., and F. Schiller., eds. 1970. *The Founders of Neurology,* ed. 2. Springfield, Ill.: Thomas.

Extirpator

Marie Jean Pierre Flourens (1794–1867) was a harsh critic of Gall's phrenology, not so much in terms of its psychological speculations as its support of cortical localization based on anecdotal and clinical observation. Flourens provided experimental evidence questioning functional localization in the brain. He was trained in medicine and became renowned for his skill as an experimental physiologist. The technique he introduced was that of extirpation or ablation: the surgical removal of parts of the brain to examine how the remainder functions by studying postoperative behavior. His initial experiments examined extirpation of increasing parts of the cerebellum, said by Gall to be a center for amativeness or sexual responsiveness. The experimental animal (a dog) showed considerable impairment of motor control, but not of amativeness: "He had all his intellectual faculties, all his senses; he was only deprived of the faculty of coordinating and regularizing his movements." Flourens's most productive period was in the 1820s with his experiments on reptiles, birds, and mammals; he rarely made distinctions between the brains of these animals. His principal conclusions were: "1. Despite the diversity of action of each of its parts, the whole nervous system is still a particular system; 2. Independently of the *proper action* of each part, each part has a *common action* with all the others, as have all the others with it." Thus, he viewed the brain as having some degree of localized function, but that it acted as a unit. Moreover, he demonstrated that there is considerable plasticity in the cerebral cortex. Deficits in behavior caused by cortical lesions can recover. Since it was known that brain tissue did not regenerate, this was taken to be evidence that the same functions can be controlled by different parts of the brain. Over a century later, Lashley proposed similar views of the brain's equipotentiality. Gall criticized the extirpation experiments on the grounds that the "deeper and deeper slices" would have severed many cortical and subcortical pathways. This criticism and others of his poor testing methods was well-founded and the ascendancy of Flourens's equipotential views was short-lived.

Flourens was born in southern France and received his medical training at Montpellier University. He then moved to Paris where he was initially an assistant in the Collège de France and eventually became professor. In 1833 he was appointed permanent secretary of the Académie des Sciences and in 1840 he joined "Les Immortels" with his election to the Académie Française. Later in life he was noted for his brief biographies of eminent scientists.

Flourens's portrait is combined with scalpel blades that could be wielded with such precision in conducting experiments by extirpation. "My method consisted in first uncovering the entire brain, and second, looking in this way at the limits of each part, guiding the hand always by the eye, and never making lesions which would cut across the proper limits of each distinct part. In a word, in examining, testing, interrogating one part after another, and always apart from the others."

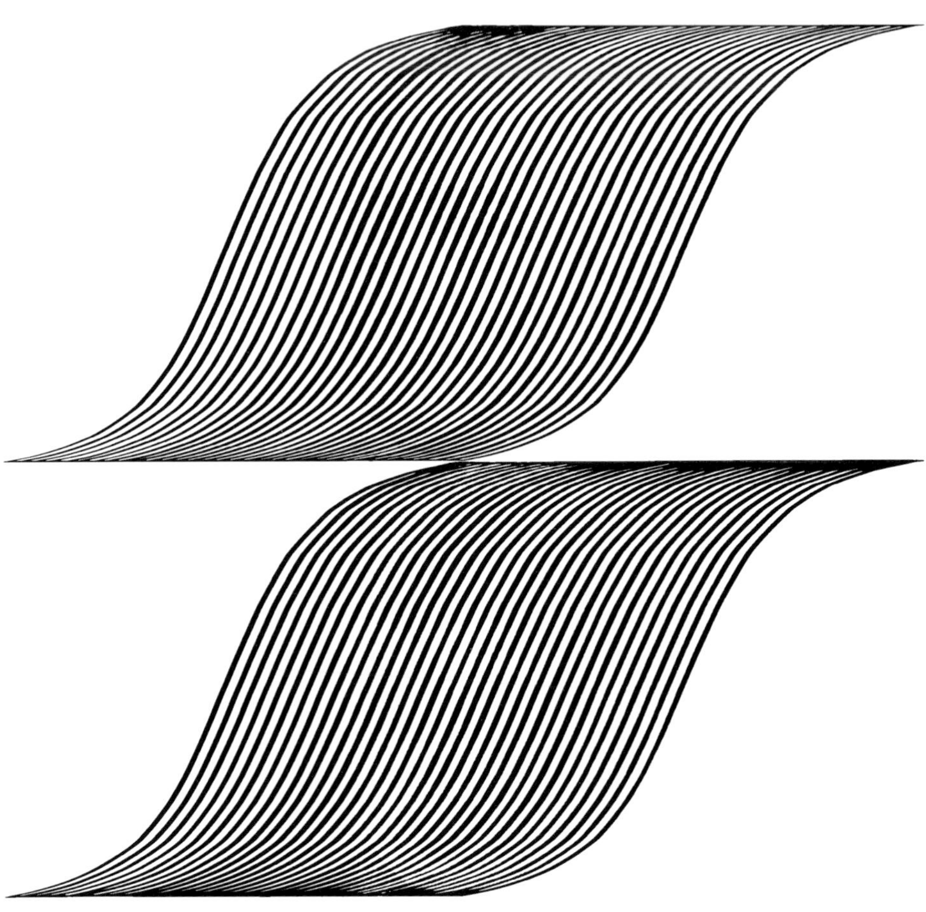

Portraits after frontispiece engraving in: Ross, H. E., and D. J. Murray. 1978. *E. H. Weber: The Sense of Touch.* London: Academic Press.

Weber Fractions

Ernst Heinrich Weber (1795–1878) introduced new methods of measuring sensitivity, establishing perception as an experimental rather than an observational discipline. Working initially with the discrimination of lifted weights, Weber demonstrated that the smallest appreciable difference was a constant fraction of their actual weights. "It appears from my experiments that the smallest difference between two weights which we can distinguish by way of feeling changes in muscle-tension is that difference shown by two weights roughly bearing the relation 39 to 40, i.e. when one is 1/40 heavier than the other." This was so irrespective of the absolute weights compared. Weber further showed that different fractions resulted from passively held weights, visual judgments of the lengths of lines, and auditory discriminations of pitch. That is, a general law of discrimination was proposed that applied to all modalities but with fractions specific to the judgments involved. Weber did not provide a generalized mathematical description of what we now call *Weber's law;* this was left to Fechner. Weber did note that there were clear individual differences in sensitivity, but judgments of a particular individual tended to be constant.

Weber did much more than compare lifted weights. He introduced the use of calipers to measure two-point thresholds on the skin surface and found that sensitivity varied enormously, with greatest sensitivity around the lips and least on the trunk. The magnitude of the thresholds depended on the area of the skin stimulated, which led Weber to introduce the concept of sensory circles—areas on the skin surface that can result in the stimulation of a single peripheral nerve. He developed a method of delayed comparison, varying the interval between presentations of the first and second stimuli: "In this way one can measure and quantitatively express the clarity of the memory for sensations as it decreases from second to second. As we rarely have the opportunity of measuring such mental processes, I commend these experiments to the attention of psychologists." Temperature and kinesthetic sensitivity were also examined in Weber's two books on touch: *De Tactu* (1834) and *Der Tastsinn* (The Sense of Touch) (1846). His work represents a distinct shift in the psychology of perception from philosophy toward physiology, from speculation to experimentation, and from qualitative to quantitative approaches.

Weber was born in Wittenberg where he studied medicine, moving on to take a post at Leipzig University. Two of his younger brothers, Wilhelm Eduard and Eduard Friedrich, made their marks in physics and physiology, respectively, and all three collaborated on the early studies on touch. Ernst Weber held the chairs of anatomy and later of physiology at Leipzig.

Weber's portrait is carried in a motif representing a sequence of psychometric functions—the curves relating the detection of stimulus differences to stimulus intensity. He is portrayed twice close to the upper and lower thresholds for discrimination and it is from such curves that the Weber fraction can be determined.

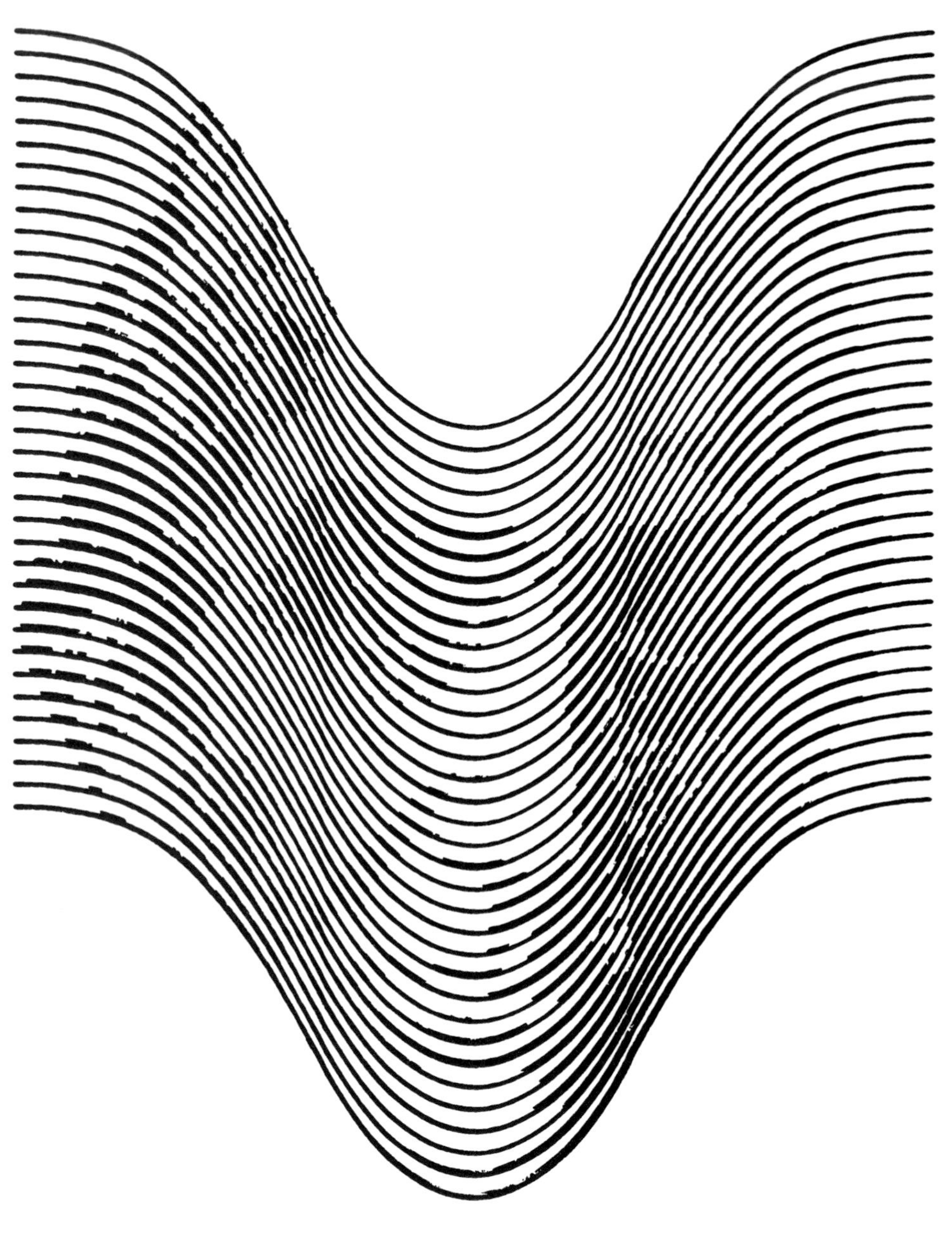

Portrait after an engraving in: Nuttin J. 1961. *Psychology in Belgium.* Louvain: Studia Psychologica.

L'Homme moyen

Lambert Adolphe Jacques Quetelet (1796–1874) has been called the father of social and psychological statistics. Indeed, the term *statistics,* as it is now used, was introduced by him. He applied his training in mathematics and probability initially to physical and then to psychological dimensions of individuals. For example, he utilized published measurements of chest girths of 5,738 Scottish soldiers and noted that their distribution approximated the normal curve—the bell-shaped curve that was developed in the context of games of chance. "Take men of the same age . . . measure them in height, in weight, in strength, or for any other physical quality whatever, or even for an intellectual or moral quality, and you will see these men array themselves . . . in the most regular manner. No matter in what order one takes them, in every age they will fall into numerical classes like the ordinates of the same curve. This law is uniform, and the curve, which I have called *binomial,* is always the same; it is perfectly regular, no matter what test one wishes to apply to human nature." The individual who had characteristics corresponding to the mean of the normal distribution was referred to as *l'homme moyen,* or the average man, although an adequate definition of l'homme moyen required specifying the upper and lower limits as well as the mean of the appropriate dimensions. In his application of the concept to the height of 100,000 French conscripts he noted a discrepancy in the observed and predicted heights and inferred that a number of men had been fraudulently rejected—an early example of the rejection of the hypothesis of chance. He considered that progress in the social and psychological sciences could learn from physics by making a large number of measurements and taking averages. His studies of social statistics, like crimes, suicides, mortalities, and illegitimate births, demonstrated a constancy year by year, and thus an inevitable predictability. He stated: "so long as the same *causes* exist, we must expect a repetition of the same *effects.*" Wundt was later to say that we can learn more from such statistical analyses than we can from philosophy.

Quetelet was born in Ghent and was the first student to receive a doctorate from the university there. His training was in mathematics, which he applied to astronomy. It was on visiting Paris, to learn the new methods of astronomy, that Quetelet was introduced to the theory of probability, which he applied in so many novel areas. He also traveled extensively, visiting observatories, and making contacts with other scientists. He was a catalyst for the organization and communication of scientific ideas. Through his influence, a commission for statistics was founded in Belgium, as was a statistical society in London, and he presided over the first International Statistical Congress in 1853 at Brussels.

Quetelet's portrait is presented in his beloved bell-shaped curve, but it has been inverted so that it provides a better fit to the facial features of the average man.

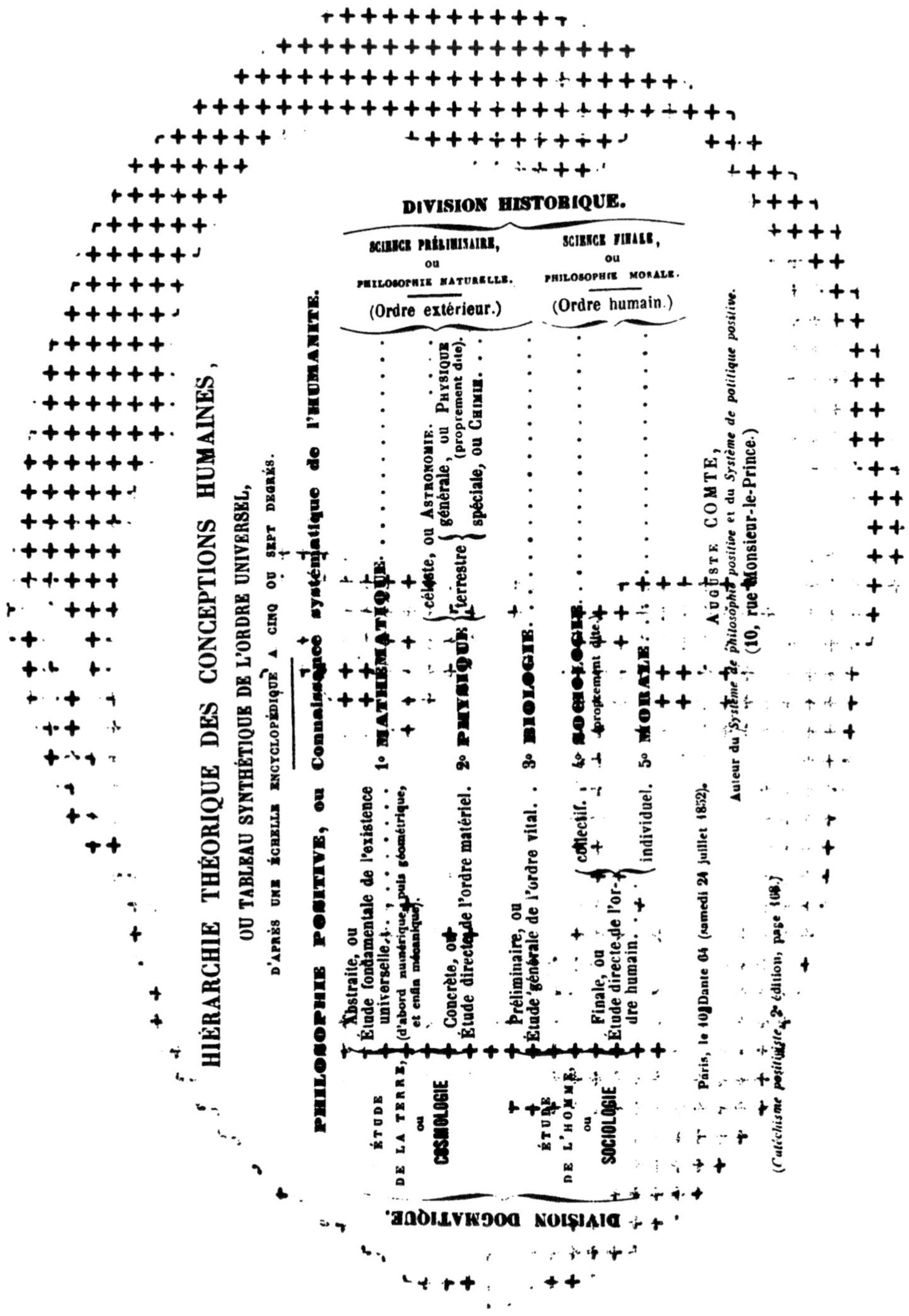

Portrait after frontispiece engraving in: Comte, A. 1968. *Oeuvres d'Auguste Comte,* Vol. 1. Paris: Anthropos.

Motif of text after a table in: Comte, A. 1968. *Oeuvres d'Auguste Comte,* Vol. 11. Paris: Anthropos.

Positivist

Isadore Auguste Marie François Xavier Comte (1798–1857) steered psychology in the social direction, as did Quetelet, but his methods were quite different. Comte coined the term *sociology* and advanced a philosophical creed he called *positivism.* On the one hand, Comte shared with the empiricist philosophers a belief in the primacy of experience, but for him it was public rather than private experience that was paramount. The irreducible element of knowledge was shared or agreed experience; on this science is built, and from it arose positivism. On the other hand, he distrusted the inward analysis of individual experience: "In order to observe, your intellect must pause from activity; yet it is this very activity you want to observe. If you cannot effect the pause you cannot observe; if you do effect it, there is nothing to observe."

Positivism emphasized the public nature of scientific inquiry, so that predictions can be made from established, observable facts. Science was seen as the pinnacle of human endeavor—the third stage of social development. When societies interpreted events in theological or anthropomorphic terms they were at the first stage; there followed a metaphysical stage, where phenomena were considered to be caused by unknown forces. Individuals were said to develop through these stages, too: "each of us is aware, if he looks back upon his own history, that he was a theologian in his childhood, a metaphysician in his youth, and a natural philosopher in his manhood." These considerations led Comte to advocate a hierarchy of sciences, determined by the extent that they still retained metaphysical concepts like forces. Mathematics was placed at the apex, followed by astronomy, physics, chemistry, and biology, with sociology and moral philosophy at the base. Comte's science had much in common with Bacon's, stressing the correlations between phenomena rather than their underlying causes. Experiments served the function of verifying theories rather than generating them. Sociology, or "social physics" as he first called it, differed from the other sciences because it alone was a product of its own history. It was to be studied by an analysis of social institutions and their evolution; the dynamic changes in institutions were examined rather than their static forms. Psychology as such was not included in the scheme of sciences; for Comte psychology was a branch of biology, and he embraced Gall's phrenology as the appropriate method for studying it.

Comte was born in Montpellier and started his university education in Paris, only to be expelled for his political views. His ideas developed as secretary to the socialist philosopher, Comte de Saint-Simon (1760–1825), but their collaboration ended acrimoniously. He never held a permanent academic post and made his meager living by giving public lectures, by writing, and by gifts from admirers. The last phase of his life involved elevating positivism to a religion of humanity, embellished by much of the pomp of the Catholicism he had rejected in his youth.

Comte is represented by symbols that denote his philosophy, and these enclose his hierarchy of the sciences.

Portrait after frontispiece photogravure in: Kunke, J. E. 1892. *Gustav Theodor Fechner (Dr. Mises). Ein deutsches Gelehrtenleben*. Leipzig: Breitkopf & Härtel.

Psychometric Function

Gustav Theodor Fechner (1801–1887) integrated Weber's fraction to found the discipline of psychophysics. Fechner's insight was that the mental and material worlds could be united mathematically in the domains of sensory and stimulus intensities. The new discipline was defined in his *Elemente der Psychophysik* (Elements of Psychophysics) (1860): "Psychophysics should be understood here as an exact theory of the functionally dependent relations of body and soul or, more generally, of the material and the mental, of the physical and the psychological worlds." Fechner distinguished between an outer and an inner psychophysics; the former was concerned with the sensation and stimulus intensities, and the latter with the relation between brain processes and sensations. He realized that experiments in his day would be confined to outer psychophysics, but these were seen as necessary steps toward understanding inner psychophysics. Fechner refined the methods Weber employed to measure difference thresholds and listed three: the method of just noticeable differences (now called the method of limits), the method of right and wrong cases (method of constant stimuli), and the method of average error (method of adjustment). Accepting the validity of Weber's fraction, and naming it Weber's law, he assumed that equal stimulus differences corresponded to equal sensation differences. Sensory magnitude could be assigned values according to the number of just noticeable differences above the absolute threshold. Starting from the absolute threshold the stimulus intensities corresponding to successive difference thresholds could be calculated, if the Weber fraction is known, and plotted. The curve is logarithmic, and it can be expressed mathematically: sensory magnitude is proportional to the logarithm of stimulus magnitude—the lawful relationship that bears Fechner's name. In his eighth decade Fechner applied his quantitative approach to the study of beauty and founded the subject of experimental aesthetics.

Fechner was born near Halle and received a medical training at Leipzig University, where Weber lectured, though he never practiced medicine. After graduation Fechner was more attracted to physics than physiology, later lecturing and conducting research on electricity at the University of Leipzig. He also undertook a series of experiments on subjective colors and on the visibility of long-lasting afterimages. These latter probably resulted in a temporary blindness, accompanied by a protracted depression, which led to his resignation from the chair of physics at Leipzig in 1840. After several years of isolation he returned to his earlier philosophical speculations, and eventually found a unity between his physical and philosophical views. Fechner began writing satirical and speculative pamphlets under the pseudonym of Dr. Mises when he was a medical student, and continued in this vein throughout his life; they reflected a continuing mental conflict between his scientific materialism and his philosophical pantheism.

The curves in which Fechner is just noticeable are a transformation of those that encompassed Weber: they, too, represent psychometric functions and Fechner's portrait is to be found in the area of uncertainty.

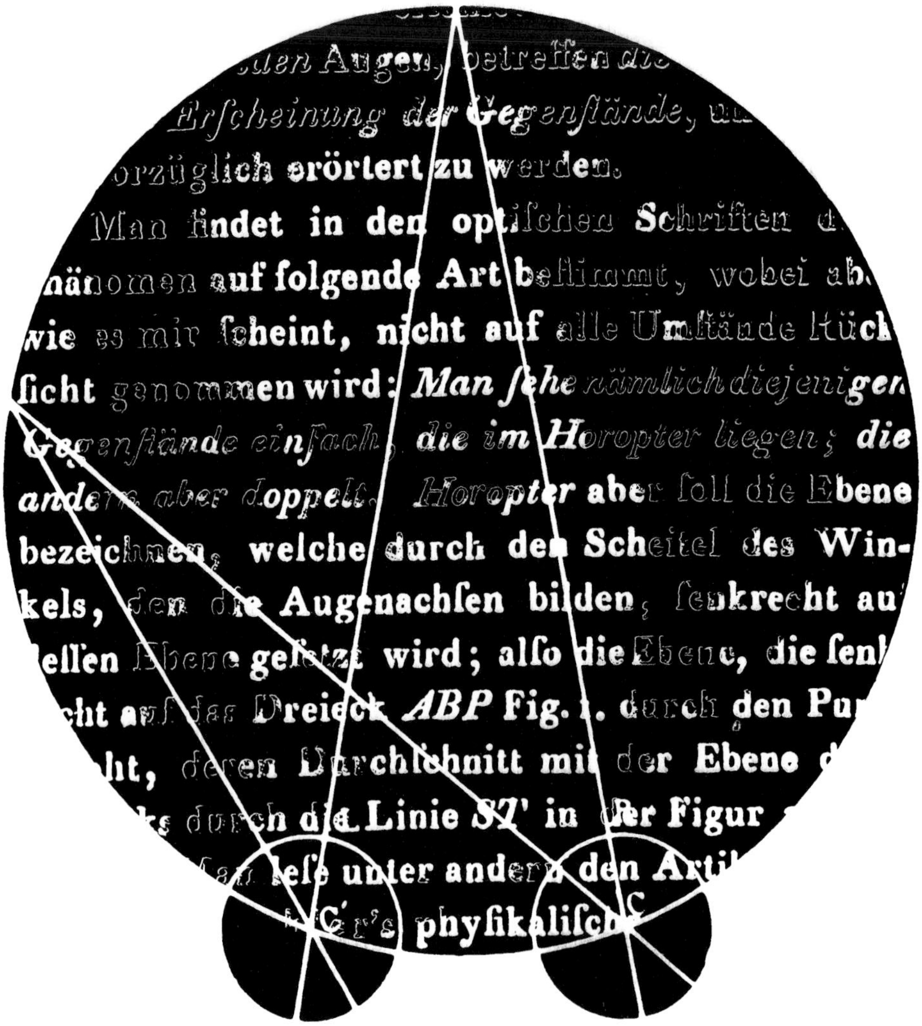

Portrait after a painting in: Polyak, S. 1957. *The Vertebrate Visual System.* Chicago: University of Chicago Press.

Motif of text after: Vieth, G. U. A. 1818. Über die Richtung der Augen. *Annalen der Physik und Chemie 58*:233–255.

Motif of binocular circle after a figure in: Wheatstone, C. 1838. Contributions to the physiology of vision—Part the first. On some remarkable, and hitherto unobserved, phenomena of binocular vision. *Philosophical Transactions of the Royal Society, 128*:371–394.

Vieth-Müller Circle

Johannes Peter Müller (1801–1858) formulated a doctrine of specific nerve energies to account for the qualitative differences in experience provided by the senses. Like most doctrines this one was not new; Bell had stated a similar principle and Young's three color theory contained the same concept. Nonetheless, it was enunciated in the greatest detail and with most authority by Müller in his *Handbuch der Physiologie des Menschen* (Handbook of Human Physiology) (1833, 1840). The doctrine states that we are not directly aware of external objects, but only of the activity of our nerves, and that the five sensory nerves can each yield only a particular experience. "The nerve of each sense seems to be capable of one determinate kind of sensation only, and not of those proper to the other organs of sense; hence one nerve of sense cannot take the place and perform the functions of the nerve of another sense."

Müller's *Handbuch* established him as the leading systematist and teacher of his day and was used as a standard text for decades. It brought together a wealth of detail about comparative anatomy and physiology, in addition to many original observations. It also united clinical practice with experimental physiology. Earlier, in 1826, Müller had published two books on vision: one on comparative physiology in which he gave detailed descriptions of eye movements, and the other on subjective visual phenomena of the type described by Purkinje. A few years later he carried out experiments on frogs that confirmed the status of the reflex and also established the Bell-Magendie law beyond dispute.

Müller was born in Koblenz and studied medicine at the University of Bonn. In 1833 he was called to the chair of physiology at Berlin. Müller placed great emphasis on observation and thoroughness in conducting empirical research. Not surpisingly, he attracted the ablest students to Berlin, of whom Helmholtz was one; these were to overturn the vitalism that Müller himself continued to believe in.

Müller's initial work on binocular vision was described in his *Zur vergleichenden Physiologie des Gesichtssinnes* (Studies on the Comparative Physiology of Vision) (1826). Prior to the invention of the stereoscope it was considered that binocular single vision followed from stimulation of corresponding points on the two retinas. With binocular fixation on one point, the region of space at which corresponding retinal points will be stimulated is called the horopter. Gerhard Ulrich Anton Vieth (1763–1836) and Müller provided independent geometrical descriptions of the horopter, in 1818 and 1826, respectively, and it became known as the Vieth-Müller circle. The concept was introduced to English readers by Wheatstone. Here Müller's portrait is embedded in text from Vieth's paper, and both are enclosed within Wheatstone's representation of the binocular circle.

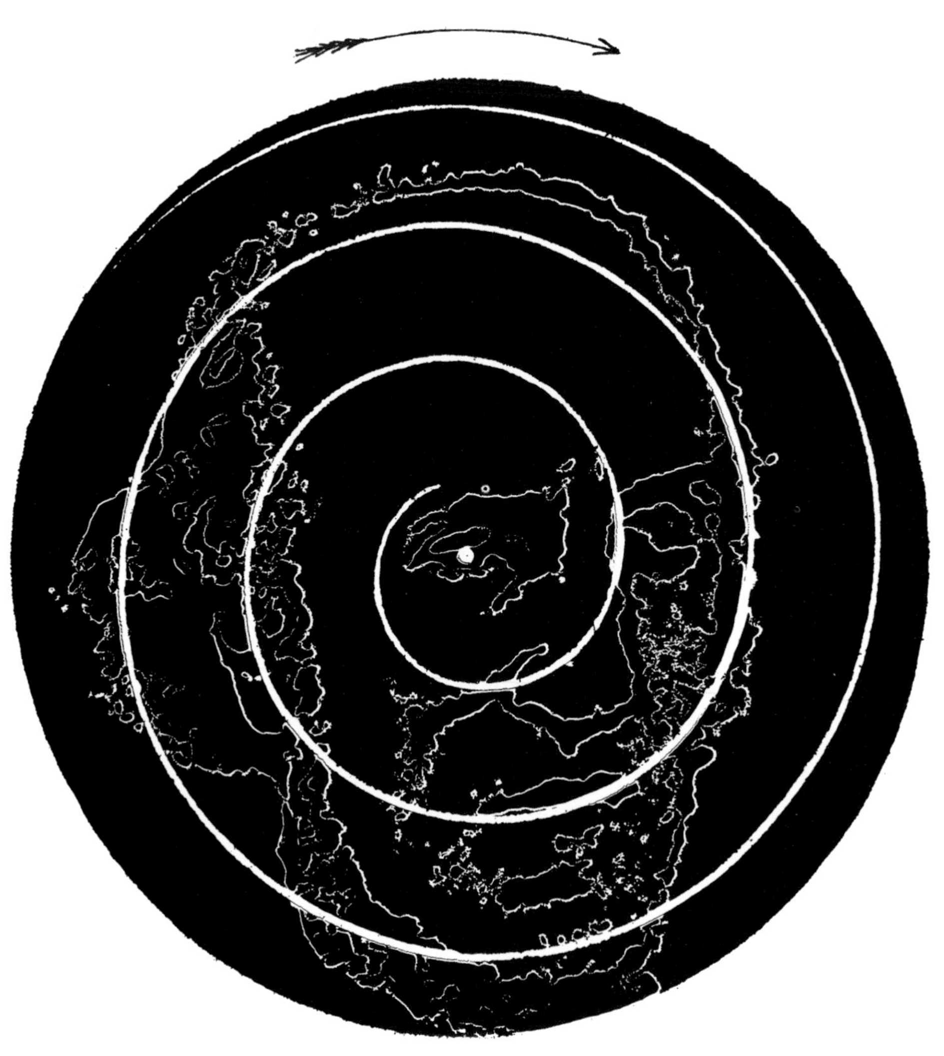

Portrait after an engraving in: Nuttin, J. 1961. *Psychology in Belgium.* Louvain: Studia Psychologica.

Motif after a figure in: Plateau, J. 1850. Vierte Notiz über neue, sonderbare Anwendungen des Verweilens der Eindrücke auf die Netzhaut. *Annalen der Physik und Chemie 80*:287–292.

Plateau Spiral

Joseph Antoine Ferdinand Plateau (1801–1883) was a pioneer in the study of visual persistence. In 1832 he invented a means of presenting stimuli briefly and in sequence (the phenakistoscope) to yield apparent motion. At about the same time similar devices were invented independently in Vienna (the stroboscope) and in Bristol (the daedaleum), and these philosophical toys are the forerunners of motion pictures. The phenakistoscope consisted of a disk with slits at regular intervals around its circumference paired with a sequence of slightly different designs, like a dancing figure; when the disk is rotated the designs are exposed in sequence through the slits and the figure appears to move. Plateau also conducted experiments on the motion aftereffect using the spiral pattern in which his portrait is presented: "When one rotates the disc in the direction of the arrow for sufficiently long, but not until the eyes are tired, and then turns to another object, e.g., the face of a person, one sees a remarkable phenomenon: namely, it appears as if the head of the person shrinks. If the disc is rotated in the opposite direction the effect is reversed: the head appears to expand." These were the first systematic experiments on the motion aftereffect, and the Plateau spiral became the principal stimulus used to study motion aftereffects in the latter half of the nineteenth century. Plateau carried out his studies of visual persistence and motion aftereffects before his ill-advised experiment on afterimages which resulted in his subsequent blindness: he was temporarily blinded after looking at the sun for 20 seconds in order to generate a long lasting afterimage, and he became permanently blind in 1842. Despite this handicap he continued to work on a range of subjective visual phenomena until shortly before his death. Toward the end of his life he published a series of annotated bibliographies of works on subjective vision from antiquity until the end of the eighteenth century.

Plateau was born in Brussels and became professor of physics and astronomy at the University of Ghent in 1834. His father was an artist, and he conducted a number of significant studies using colors. When colors are presented briefly and in succession their apparent intensity is proportional to the time of presentation. This photometric relationship is now known as the Talbot-Plateau law, as it had earlier been formulated in a less precise way by William Henry Fox Talbot (1800–1877), the pioneer of the negative process in photography. On the basis of experiments with painters mixing grays to appear midway between specified white and black papers, Plateau proposed a power function as an alternative to Fechner's logarithmic law. He also showed that accidental colors (afterimages) mixed with colored stimuli and with one another according to the laws of color mixture.

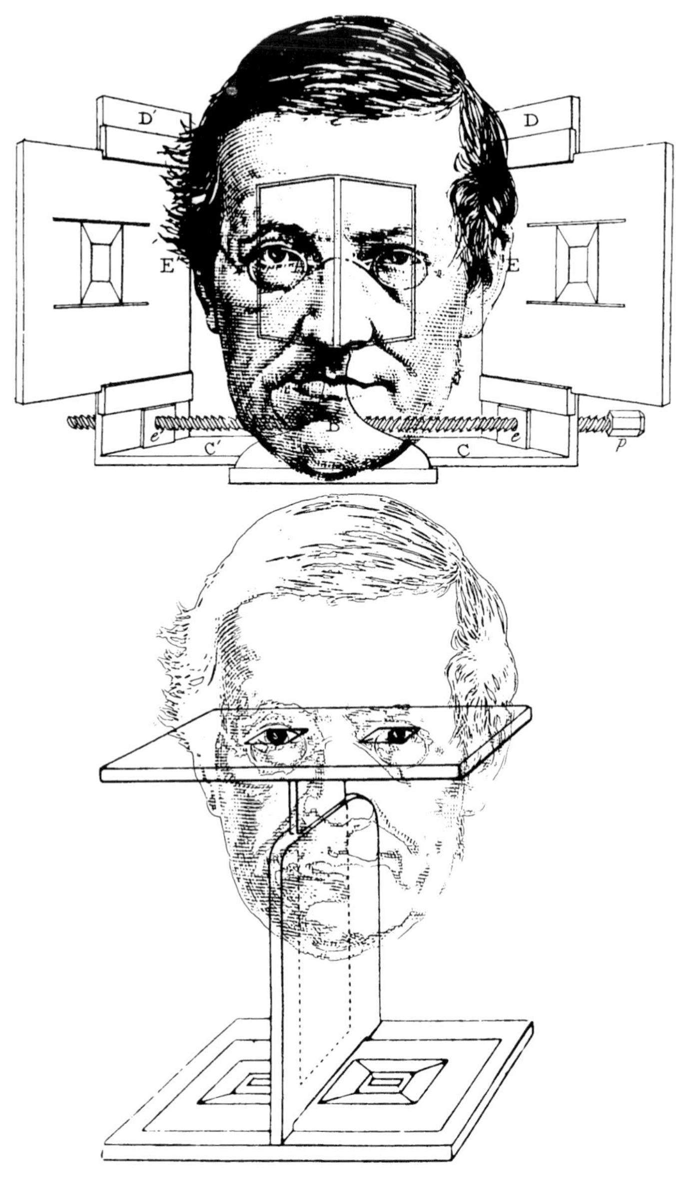

Portraits after an engraving in: *The Illustrated London News.* 1868, *52*:145.

Motif of mirror stereoscope after a figure in: Wheatstone, C. 1838. Contributions to the physiology of vision—Part the first. On some remarkable, and hitherto unobserved, phenomena of binocular vision. *Philosophical Transactions of the Royal Society 128*:371–394.

Motif of prism stereoscope after a figure in: Wheatstone, C. 1852. Contributions to the physiology of vision—Part the second. On some remarkable, and hitherto unobserved, phenomena of binocular vision. *Philosophical Transactions of the Royal Society 142*:1–17.

Stereoscopist

Charles Wheatstone (1802–1875) invented an instrument (the stereoscope) that not only transformed the vision of pictures but also the picture of vision. He made his first stereoscope in 1832, although he did not publish his description of the experiments conducted with it until 1838. Before the stereoscope, binocular single vision was analysed in terms of visual directions and the Vieth-Müller circle; any points outside the circle would be seen as double. Wheatstone demonstrated, with the aid of suitably paired figures mounted in the stereoscope, that singleness and depth followed stimulation of slightly disparate retinal points. "The appearances, which are by this simple instrument rendered so obvious, may be easily inferred from the established laws of perspective; . . . Yet they seem to have escaped the attention of every philosopher and artist who has treated of the subjects of vision and perspective." The stereoscope opened the way to studying vision with the precision that physicists had applied in their domain: variables like retinal disparity, retinal size, accommodation, and convergence could be studied in isolation in order to determine their role in depth perception. The stereoscope was quickly adopted as a valuable tool in the study of vision, particularly in Germany. Wheatstone himself made several different models of the stereoscope and he also invented a pseudoscope, in which the retinal disparities were reversed, resulting in a conflict between different cues for depth. He was quick to appreciate the advantage of a marriage between photography and the stereoscope, and encouraged Talbot to make stereophotographs for him.

Wheatstone was born in Gloucester. He was appointed to the chair of experimental philosophy at King's College, London, at the age of 32, and held the post for the rest of his life. He invented a number of musical instruments, the most popular of which was the concertina. He is best known for his work in electricity, measuring its velocity and devising a bridging means of measuring resistance. He also devised an electromagnetic chronoscope. In the 1820s he published work on visual persistence, and constructed a philosophical toy which traced beautiful patterns—called the kaleidophone, after Brewster's kaleidoscope. He précised Purkinje's books on subjective visual phenomena and published a translation anonymously. Brewster in his turn devised a lenticular stereoscope after seeing Wheatstone's mirror model demonstrated at a meeting of the British Association. However, Brewster and Wheatstone were fierce anatgonists, and their public dispute over the invention of the stereoscope, aired in the correspondence columns of *The Times,* reflected nineteenth-century science at its most acrimonious.

Wheatstone is portrayed twice, with his mirror and prism stereoscopes.

We may now inquire how it is that a frown should express the perception of something difficult or disagreeable, either in thought or action. In the same way as naturalists find it advisable to trace the embryological development of an organ in order fully to understand its structure, so with the movements of expression it is advisable to follow as nearly as possible the same plan. The earliest and almost sole expression seen during the first days of infancy, and then often exhibited, is that displayed during the act of screaming; and screaming is excited, both at first and for some time afterwards, by every distressing or displeasing sensation and emotion,—by hunger, pain, anger, jealousy, fear, &c. At such times the muscles round the eyes are strongly contracted; and this, as I believe, explains to a large extent the act of frowning during the remainder of our lives. I repeatedly observed my own infants, from under the age of one week to that of two or three months, and found that when a screaming-fit came on gradually, the first sign was the contraction of the corrugators, which produced a slight frown, quickly followed by the contraction of the other muscles round the eyes. When an infant is uncomfortable or unwell, little frowns—as I record in my notes—may be seen incessantly passing like shadows over its face; these being generally, but not always, followed sooner or later by a crying-fit. For instance, I watched for some time a baby, between seven and eight weeks old, sucking some milk which was cold, and therefore displeasing to him; and a steady little frown was maintained all the time. This was never developed into an actual crying-fit, though occasionally every stage of close approach could be observed.

Portrait after a photograph in: Irvine, W. 1955. *Apes, Angels, and Victorians. A Joint Biography of Darwin and Huxley.* London: Weidenfeld & Nicolson.

Motif after text in: Darwin, C. 1872. *The Expression of the Emotions in Man and Animals.* London: John Murray.

The Expression of Darwin's Emotions

Charles Robert Darwin (1809–1882) revolutionized the life sciences with the publication of *The Origin of Species* in 1859. He had a distinguished scientific ancestry: his grandfather, Erasmus, proposed that all species evolved from a common source, and his father, Robert, was a physician who conducted experiments on the visibility of afterimages. Charles provided the evidence for a mechanism to account for evolution. The theory built upon the fact of variability in all organisms. Some variations can affect the fitness for survival and reproduction, particularly in the event of any environmental changes. Those individuals that are better fitted to new conditions will have a greater chance of producing offspring, a process of natural selection that was not considered to be purposive. "This preservation of favourable individual differences and variations, and the destruction of those which are injurious, I have called Natural Selection, or the Survival of the Fittest." He pursued the consequences of these ideas to human behavior, particularly in *The Descent of Man* (1871) and in *The Expression of the Emotions in Man and Animals* (1872), thus laying the foundation for comparative psychology. In the former he argued that the rudiments of human mental processes are evident in animals, and in the latter he noted the similarity of human facial expressions and gestures to those of animals. Darwin also stressed the universality of emotional expressions in human groups.

Darwin spoke highly of Bell's book on the anatomy of expression, and drew upon it in his own. Darwin's own books are sparsely illustrated, and then they tend use pictures from other books rather than drawings made specifically for them. The text presented here describes an expression, frowning, that is often encountered in the portraits and photographs of Darwin, and indeed is evident in the portrait shown. In the text he mentions the observations he made on his own children. He had earlier made a detailed record of his firstborn's development from a few days to over two years of age, and these were published in the journal *Mind* in 1877; they implicitly suggest that the development of the individual mirrors the evolution of species. Evolutionary theory transformed biology and it was a motive force in defining a distinct brand of American psychology.

Darwin was born in Shrewsbury and had an undistinguished record as a student. He studied medicine at Edinburgh, but found the sight of blood distasteful, and so left to study for the ministry at Cambridge, but spent his time pursuing his interests in botany and zoology. In 1831 Darwin set forth as naturalist on the five-year voyage of the survey ship H.M.S. *Beagle* during which he collected most of the evidence that was to support his later theory of evolution. He was reluctant to publish his theory because of the predictable theological controversy it would generate, but he was persuaded to do so after receiving a letter from Alfred Russel Wallace (1823–1913) who had derived a similar theory independently.

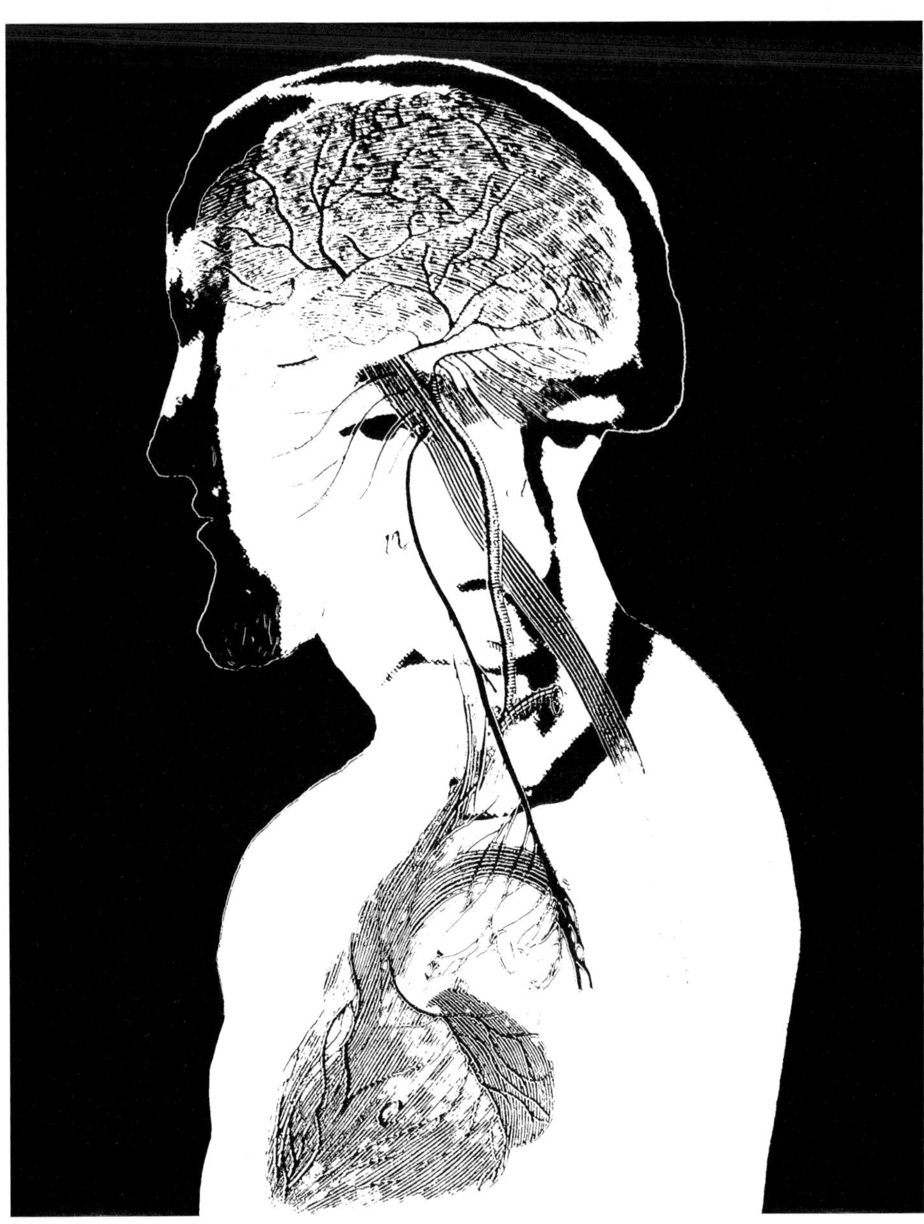

Portrait after an engraving in: Duke-Elder, S. 1968. *System of Ophthalmology,* Vol. 4. *The Physiology of the Eye and of Vision.* London: Henry Kimpton.

Motif after a diagram in: Bernard, C. 1866. *Leçons sur les propriétés des tissus vivants.* Paris: Baillière.

Milieu Intérieur

Claude Bernard (1813–1878) introduced the concept of the *milieu intérieur*—the regulatory function that the nervous system applies to the stability of internal secretions and tissues. It anticipated the notion of homeostasis, introduced by Walter Cannon (1871–1945) in 1932, which has been at the heart of many psychological theories of learning and motivation. In his experimental studies of salivation, Bernard came close to describing classical conditioning: "Taking a fasting horse, you expose the duct of the parotid gland on the side of the jaw; you open the duct, and no saliva flows. If you then show the horse some oats or, even better, if you do not show him anything but make a motion which indicates to the animal that you are going to feed him, immediately a jet of saliva flows continuously from the parotid duct." A quarter of a century later Pavlov proposed a process for such conditioning, using similar experimental techniques. The range of Bernard's experimental research was vast, being concerned initially with digestion and its nervous control, and extending to the whole of experimental physiology and its philosophical underpinnings. His influence on physiology, both through his teaching and his many textbooks, was far-reaching. His studies of control mechanisms in the vascular system led him to propose a more holistic view of physiology: he stated that "systems do not exist in Nature, but only in men's minds." He rejected the prevalent approach of comparative physiologists who emphasized species differences, proposing a general physiology which "does not seek to grasp the differences that separate beings, but the common points that unite them." Bernard was also sceptical about the use of averages in the study of complex systems, favoring the presentation of results from the "most perfect experiment" as a reflection of the true state of affairs.

Bernard was born near St. Julien on the Rhône and was to return there frequently from his laboratories in Paris to ponder over his physiological discoveries. He came late to the study of medicine and was greatly influenced by François Magendie, with whom he collaborated and who turned his interests away from medicine and toward experimental physiology. Bernard succeeded Magendie at the Collège de France and later a special chair of physiology was created for him at the Sorbonne. As a young man he moved to Paris to pursue a literary career. Despite being directed away from literature his scientific writing resulted in his election to the Académie Française.

Bernard is shown within a diagram of the nerves connecting the heart and the brain, taken from one of his textbooks. This book represented his approach to physiology by emphasizing the unity of living processes rather than focusing on species differences: he sought "to return to the elementary condition of the vital phenomenon, a condition that is identical in all animals."

Maar is dan ten opzichte der psychische processen iedere quantitatieve behandeling uitgesloten? Geenszins! Een gewichtige factor scheen voor meting vatbaar: ik bedoel den tijd, die tot eenvoudige psychische processen wordt gevorderd. Voor de beslissing der vraag, of wij recht hebben, het in 't algemeen bewezen verband voor bijzondere gevallen toe te passen, met andere woorden, of we mogen aannemen, dat aan de verscheidenheid van ieder bijzonder gevoel, van iedere bijzondere voorstelling, van iedere uiting van den wil eene absoluut corresponderende verscheidenheid in de werking der hersenen is verbonden, schijnt de bepaling van dien tijd niet zonder gewicht. Sedert langen tijd stelde ik mij voor, daartoe pogingen te doen. In de zitting der Koninklijke Academie van wetenschappen van 24 Junij 1865 gaf ik een overzicht der eerste, onder medewerking van den Heer de Jaager en van eenige andere leerlingen der Utrechtsche Hoogeschool, dienaangaande verkregen uitkomsten, die daarop uitvoeriger werden medegedeeld in de dissertatie van den Heer de Jaager: over den *physiologischen tijd der psychische processen*. Het denkbeeld tot deze proeven, zoo als trouwens de voorrede vermeldt, was van mij uitgegaan, de gevolgde methoden waren door mij aan de hand gegeven, en de proeven werden in het physiologisch laboratorium verricht en door mij bestuurd. Omstreeks denzelfden tijd gaf ik, met aanwijzing der methoden, een overzicht der verkregen uitkomsten in eenige populaire voordrachten, te Utrecht en elders gehouden.

Portrait after frontispiece photogravure in: Bowman, W. 1891. Obituary of F. C. Donders. *Proceedings of the Royal Society of London* 49:vii–xxiii.

Motif after text in: Donders, F. C. 1869. Over de snelheid van psychische processen. *Nederlandsch Archief voor Genees- en Natuurkunde* 4:117–145.

Donders' See

Frans Cornelis Donders (1818-1889) introduced reaction time as a measure of mental processing. In 1865 he presented a paper to the Royal Netherlands Academy of Sciences outlining his initial experiments on timing mental processes. A more elaborate report was published in 1868, and again in 1869 (from which the text opposite is taken). Donders began his paper by lamenting the difficulty of applying the rigor of physiology to the study of mental processes. "But will all quantitative treatment of mental processes be out of the question? By no means! An important factor seemed to be susceptible to measurement: I refer to the time required for simple mental processes. For answering the question whether we are entitled to apply the generally proved relation to special cases—in other words, whether we may assume that there is an absolute correspondence between diverse functions in the brain and the diversity in each particular sensation, each private mental picture, each expression of the will—it seems that the determination of that duration of time is not without importance." Donders was aware of Helmholtz's measurements of the velocity of nerve conduction, and the durations of simple response times. "The idea occurred to me to interpose into the process of physiological time some new components of mental action. If I investigated how much time this would lengthen the physiological time, this would, I judged, reveal the time required for the interposed term." The expression "reaction time" was introduced in 1873 by Sigmund Exner (1846–1926), and Donders distinguished between various types: a-type was to single stimuli, b-type was to several stimuli, and c-type was to one but not to an alternative stimulus. Donders's c reaction times are longer than a or b. Much of the early research in Wundt's laboratory was concerned with confirming Donders's extensive work on reaction times.

Donders was trained in medicine at Utrecht and his abiding interests were in physiology. He became engaged in ophthalmology almost by accident, when he translated a book from German to Dutch, repeating many of the experiments reported in it. He became professor of ophthalmology at the University of Utrecht in 1852. Donders wrote extensively on anomalies of refraction and accommodation, considering the latter to be a consequence of pupillary contraction. Donders's law states that the eyes always assume the same orientation in a particular position no matter what pattern of movements were taken to reach it.

Although his main research was concerned with vision, Donders's impact on psychology has been a consequence of his use of reaction time as an index of cognitive functioning. His portrait is presented in text that differs in clarity: it is intentionally difficult to accommodate to the peripheral text, while the more clearly defined central region defines Donders's face.

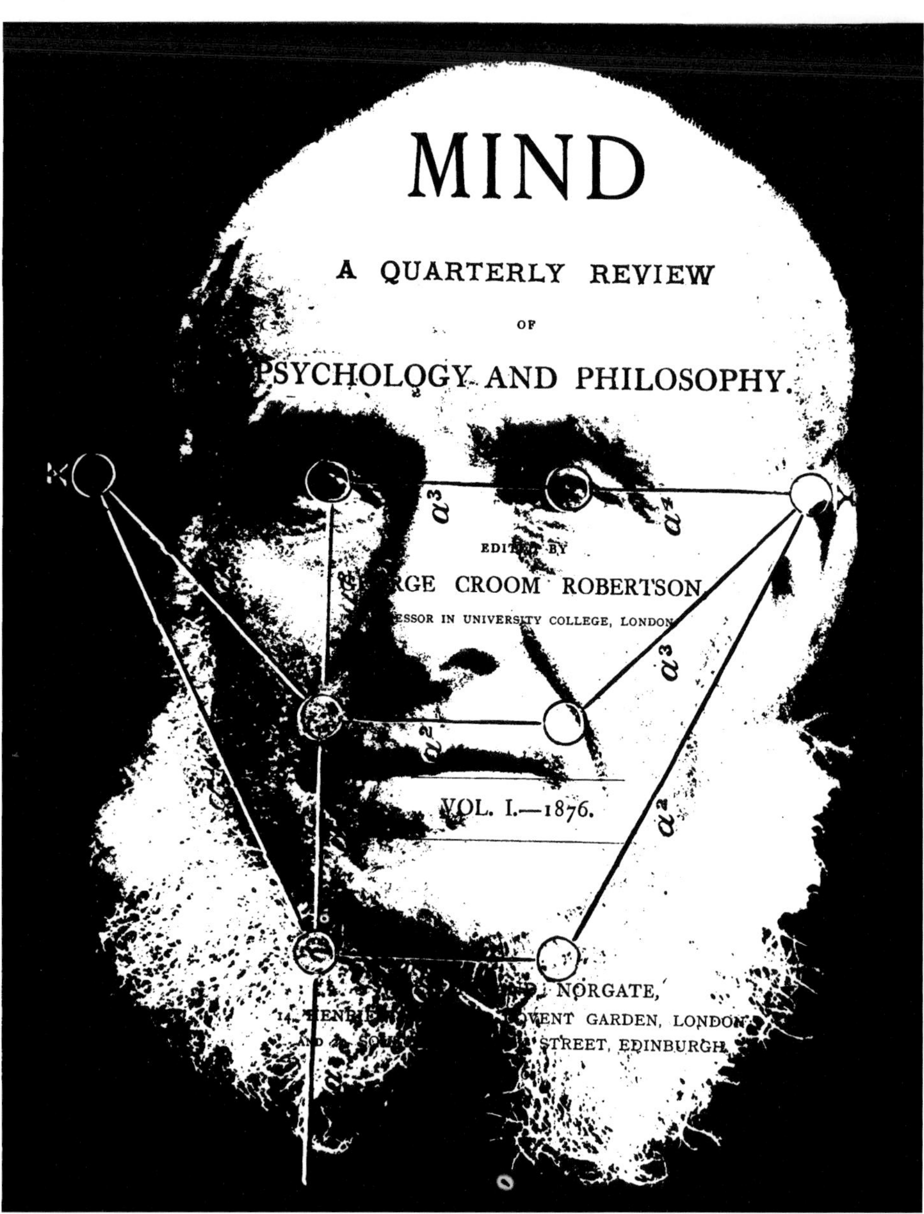

Portrait after a photograph in: Bain, A. 1904. *Autobiography.* London: Longmans, Green.

Text motif after the title page of the first issue of *Mind.*

Motif after a diagram of a neural model in: Bain, A. 1873. *Mind and Body. The Theories of Their Relation.* London: Henry King.

Alexander Bain (1818–1903) wrote two textbooks on psychology that provided the prototypes for subsequent writers; he also founded in 1876 the first journal, *Mind,* concerned principally with psychological issues. Bain integrated sensory-motor physiology with philosophy to espouse an independent discipline of psychology "conceiving that the time has now come when many of the striking discoveries of Physiologists relative to the nervous system should find a recognised place in the Science of Mind." He extended the union to higher mental processes and voluntary action, emphasizing the importance of sensory feedback in the control of movement: "In treating of the Senses, besides recognising the so-called muscular sense as distinct from the five senses, I have thought proper to assign to Movement and the feelings of Movement a position preceding the Sensations of the senses; and have endeavoured to prove that the exercise of active energy originating in purely internal impulses, independent of the stimulus produced by outward impressions, is a primary fact of our constitution." In stressing the motor component of perception he was the harbinger of behaviorism: "action is a more intimate and inseparable property of our constitution than any of our sensations, and in fact enters as a component part into every one of the senses." He also appreciated that those actions connected with the alleviation of pain or the increase of pleasure would occur with greater frequency.

The Senses and the Intellect (1855) and *The Emotions and the Will* (1859) became the standard texts for psychology until James's *Principles* appeared three decades later. In addition to his texts on psychology, Bain wrote books on English grammar, ethics, logic, rhetoric, and phrenology.

Bain was born in Aberdeen, and was essentially self-educated. He studied philosophy at Marischal College, Aberdeen, and taught moral and mental philosophy there for the next five years. He returned to Aberdeen University in 1860, as professor of logic, after a period in London lecturing and living off his pen. The illustration reflects the importance of Bain's *Mind,* which was initially edited by one of his former students; it also incorporates a model of neural processing designed by Bain to give differential output with input of varied intensities. That is, he proposed a connectionist account of learning: "I can suppose that, at first, each one of the circuits would affect all others indiscriminately; but that, in consequence of two of them being independently made active at the same moment (which is the fact in acquisition), a strengthened connexion or diminished obstruction would arise between these two, by a change wrought in the intervening cell-substance; and that, afterwards, the induction from one of these circuits would not be indiscriminate, but select; being comparatively strong toward one, and weaker toward the rest."

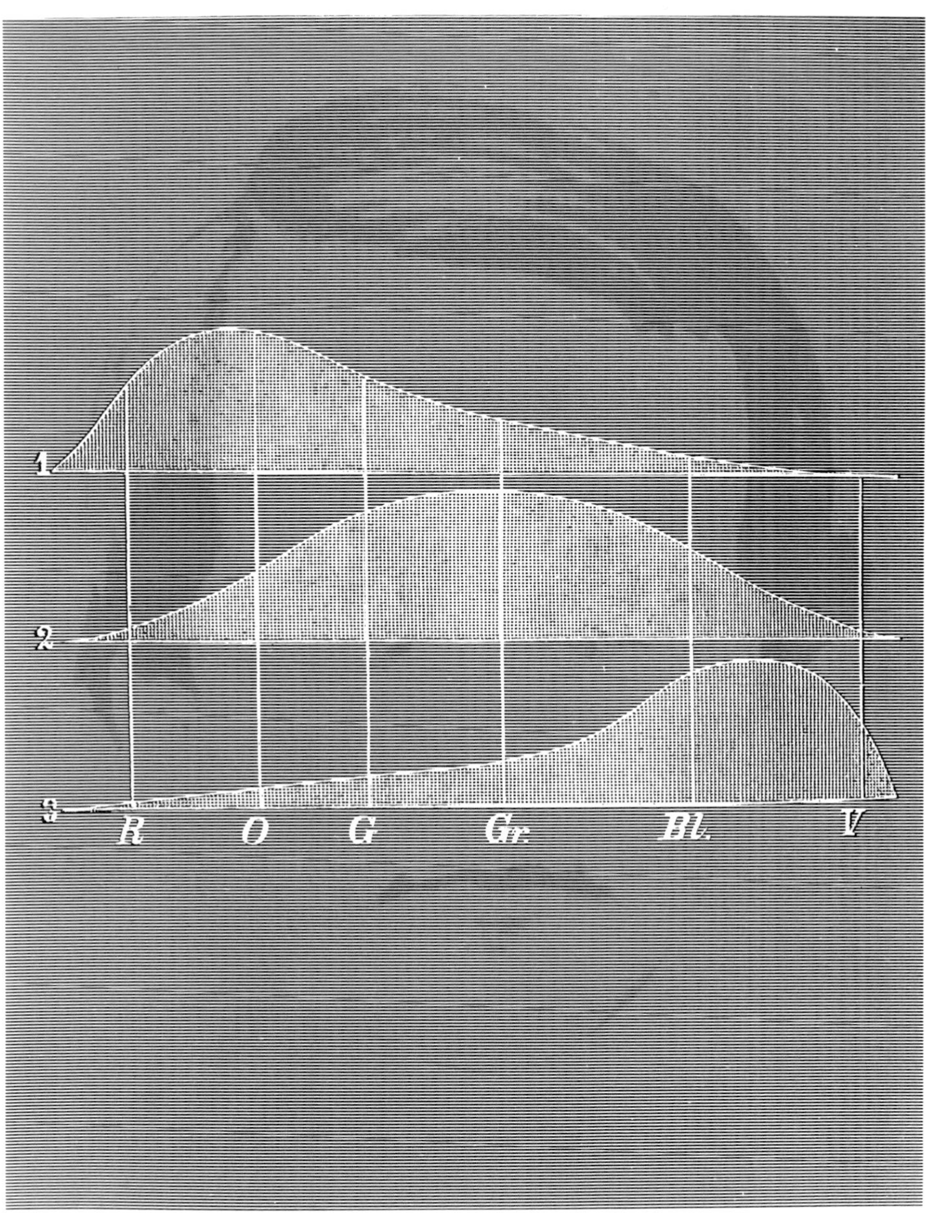

Portrait after a daguerreotype in: Koenigsberger, L. 1902. *Hermann von Helmholtz,* Vol. 1. Braunschweig: Vieweg.

Motif after a diagram in: Helmholtz, H. von. 1896. *Handbuch der physiologischen Optik,* ed. 2, revised. Hamburg: Voss.

Young Helmholtz

Hermann Ludwig Ferdinand von Helmholtz (1821–1894) established the law of conservation of energy in both the physical and biological domains; he measured the speed of nerve transmission, and made numerous contributions to vision and audition. The range of his scientific researches was enormous, and he made these accessible to a wide public through his Popular Lectures on Scientific Subjects. He studied physiology under Müller, but he was to provide the evidence to replace vitalism with mechanism. Moreover, contrary to Müller's assertions, Helmholtz demonstrated that nerve conduction is not instantaneous. His initial experiments were carried out with a neuromuscular preparation from the frog, but similar results were obtained from reaction time experiments with humans. By stimulating the skin on the toe or thigh and requiring subjects to respond as quickly as possible, estimates of conduction velocity could be derived by subtraction; the values were between 50 and 100 meters per second.

Helmholtz was born in Potsdam and displayed a keen interest in physics as a boy; economic necessity led him to study medicine (with an army scholarship) at Berlin. On release from the army, he took up an academic career, being called to the chair of physiology at Königsberg in 1849, and thereafter to Bonn, Heidelberg, and Berlin. While at Königsberg he invented the ophthalmoscope and measured the speed of nerve transmission. The second and third volumes of his monumental *Handbuch der physiologischen Optik* (Handbook of Physiological Optics) were published during his tenure in Heidelberg; the three volumes appeared separately in 1856, 1860, and 1866, and then together in 1867. The first volume concerned physical optics; the second, the physiology of vision; and the third was on visual perception. His analysis of perception drew more heavily on British empiricism than on the Kantian philosophy prevalent in Germany. Helmholtz adopted Berkeley's concept of unconscious inference to account for the way in which we learn to see and how common perceptions can arise from varied patterns of stimulation: "The sensations of the senses are tokens for our consciousness, it being left to our intelligence to learn how to comprehend their meaning." This position was supported by many experiments, particularly with the stereoscope: "The invention of the stereoscope by Wheatstone made the difficulties and imperfections of the Innate Theory of sight much more obvious than before, and led to another solution which approached much nearer the older view, and which we call the *Empirical* Theory of Vision." Color vision was treated in the second volume: Helmholtz extended Young's hypothesis that color could be perceived through the action of three mechanisms, and he presented three speculative curves showing the respective wavelength sensitivities of nerves with these specific energies.

A youthful Helmholtz, aged 26, is shown in combination with the curves depicting the analysis of white light into its three components.

Portraits after photographs in: Forrest, D. W. 1974. *Francis Galton. The Life and Work of a Victorian Genius.* London: Paul Elek.

Face Recognition

Francis Galton (1822–1911) was an inveterate measurer who embarked on a natural history of human perception and performance. He measured intelligence and mental imagery, and introduced the methods of word association and of twin studies. In addition, he introduced fingerprinting as a method of identifying individuals; invented the weather map; and assessed both the beauty of women and the boredom of lectures. His impact was most keenly felt in the area of individual differences. Not only did he appreciate that differences could be measured but he also devised a means for comparing them. This was perhaps his most lasting achievement. Rather than comparing the measures themselves they could be related in terms of their variability. This insight arose from his analysis of hereditary genius. Galton was a cousin of Charles Darwin, and was greatly influenced by the theory of evolution. He developed an early interest in personal differences of mental function, linking them both with sensory discrimination and with reaction time. He combined the Darwinian concepts of variability and adaptation with his mathematical leanings to measure individual differences in behavior, culminating in his Anthropometric Laboratory (1884) at which thousands paid to have their physical and mental characteristics measured. Galton proposed that mental abilities were normally distributed in the population after the manner of Quetelet's bell-shaped curves for height and weight, and that they were inherited. He sought support for the importance of nature over nurture (terms he introduced in this context) by asking eminent scientists to complete questionnaires. It was in considering these data in 1888 that Galton "first clearly grasped the important generalization that the laws of heredity were solely concerned with deviations expressed in statistical units." This was supported by the analysis of data collected from earlier laborious measurements of the dimensions of sweet pea seeds over two generations; he found that the offspring mean reverted to the mean of the population and he tried to devise a measure of this reversion (or regression).

Galton was born in Birmingham, where he commenced his medical studies. They were not completed because he developed an interest in mathematics, which he studied at Cambridge, and because his father died leaving him a comfortable inheritance. He became a gentleman scientist in the tradition of Victorian England, with the financial independence to pursue a life of exploration, writing, and experimental inquiry. Although he never held a university post he did endow a chair of eugenics (the belief that the most important human characteristics are inherited) to the University of London, and he was a cofounder of the journal *Biometrika.*

Galton experimented with composite photography as well as with photographing the face from different viewpoints. Composites were produced by photographing a number of persons (initially criminals) on a single plate. He noted that "the special villainous irregularities . . . have disappeared, and the common humanity that underlies them has prevailed." The full-face and profile views of Galton superimposed here were originally taken in Bertillon's laboratory in Paris when Galton was 71.

Portrait after an engraving in: Polyak, S. 1957. *The Vertebrate Visual System.* Chicago: University of Chicago Press.

Motif after a diagram of the brain in: Broca, P. 1888. *Mémoires sur le cerveau de l'homme et des primates.* Paris: Reinwald.

Broca's Area

Pierre Paul Broca (1824–1880) provided evidence from clinical examination and autopsies to support cerebral localization of function. He was initially influenced both by comparative anatomy and by Gall's speculations on cortical localization. Such evidence was not new but Broca's views were treated with greater seriousness by the scientific community because he was not as tainted by phrenology. Gall had described the case of a patient with a lesion of the anterior left lobe of the brain, who lost his memory for names. Other cases were to follow, but Broca's was the most timely. In 1859 he was involved in founding the first Anthropological Society at Paris, and this was the platform from which his most noted work was delivered. During one of the early meetings of the society arguments about the relation of brain volume to intelligence led to discussions of brain localization and speech. At that time Broca treated a patient suffering from loss of speech, referred to as aphemia by Broca and later as aphasia. The patient was known as Tan since this was the only utterance he made, but he was able to understand speech. Tan died one week later and his brain, which was exhibited at the next meeting of the society, was found to have a cavity in the left frontal lobe. A second patient with similar symptoms had "a profound, but accurately circumscribed lesion of the posterior third of the second and third frontal convolutions." This is now referred to as Broca's area or Broca's convolution. Broca provided a more intricate analysis of language than simply localizing it in a particular part of the brain, as had the phrenologists: "The nature of that faculty and the place to which it should be assigned in the cerebral hierarchy could give rise to some hesitation. It is only a kind of memory and have the individuals who have lost it, lost only, not the memory of the words but the memory of the procedure which one has to follow in order to articulate the words?" Despite disputes regarding the priority of Broca's discovery and the extent of the lesions in his patients, the link forged between language and cortical location proved very fruitful, and led others, like Carl Wernicke (1848–1905), to relate the receptive aspects of language to more posterior locations in the left hemisphere.

Broca was born near Bordeaux and spent most of his life in Paris, where he became professor of clinical surgery. In the last year of his life he was elected to the Senate as a representative for French science.

Broca was a prolific writer and published over 500 scientific papers, as well as several books. He is shown in a diagram of Broca's area, taken from an illustration in one of his own books on the brain.

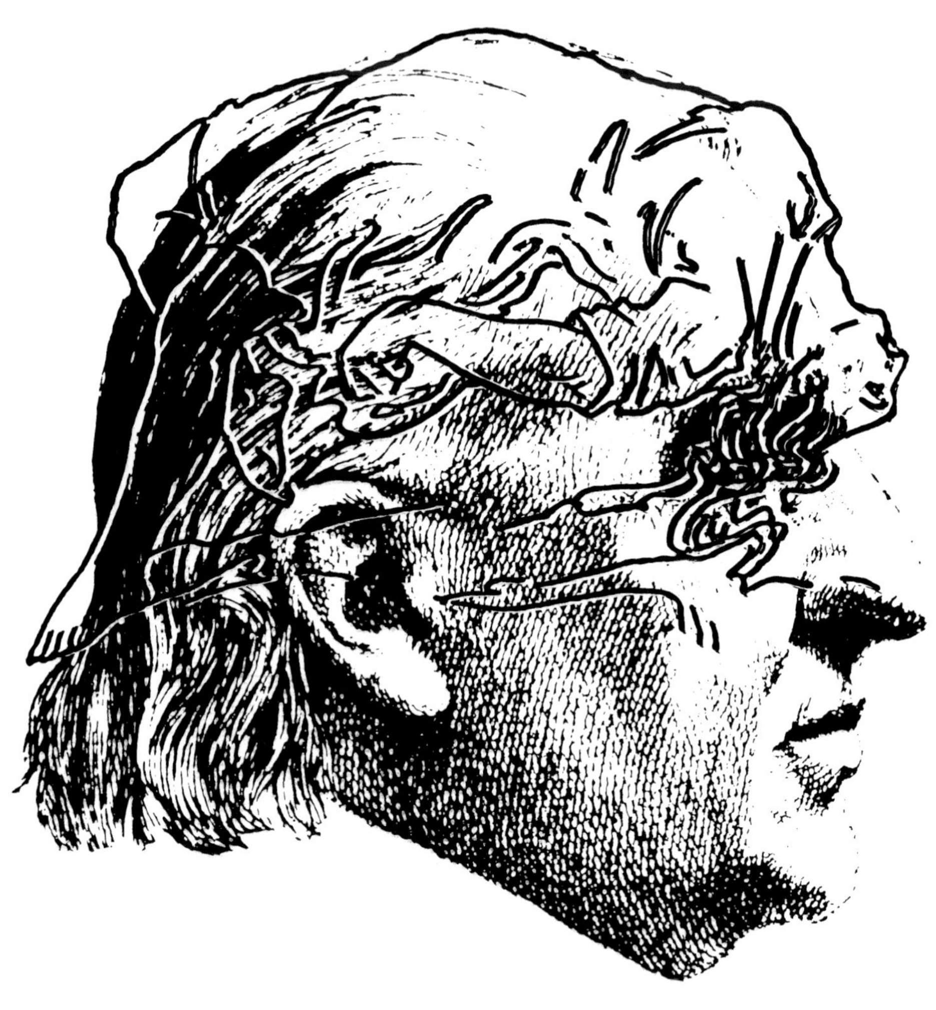

Portrait after frontispiece engraving in: Charcot, J. M. 1892. *Oeuvres complètes de J. M. Charcot. Leçons sur les maladies du système nerveux.* Paris: Baittaille.

Motif after a drawing of a hysterical patient adopting *l'arc de cercle* in: Charcot, J. M., and P. Richer. 1887. *Les Démoniaques dans l'art.* Paris: Delahaye et Lecrosnier.

L'Arc de Cercle

Jean Martin Charcot (1825–1893) was an established neurologist who lent respectability to the study of hypnosis. Mesmer's animal magnetism had been made partially acceptable in medical circles by Braid's use of it as an anesthetic, under the name of hypnosis. Its study had continued in Nancy, where Hippolyte Bernheim (1840–1919) had hypnotized a wide range of patients, often alleviating their symptoms. Bernheim considered that all persons were susceptible to hypnotism but to varying degrees, and that suggestion was a valuable aid to healing. This psychological interpretation was opposed by Charcot, who linked hypnosis to hysteria. Hysteria was taken to be an organic condition even though there was no evidence to support it: "We have here unquestionably one of those lesions which escape our present means of anatomical investigation, and which, for want of a better term, we designate *dynamic* or *functional* lesions." He argued that only hysterical patients could be hypnotized. Charcot classified different types of hysteria (traumatic and major) and he described the hypnotic stages through which his hysterical patients passed—lethargy, catalepsy, and somnambulism. He eventually conceded that Bernheim's interpretation was more sustainable than his own.

Charcot was born in Paris, where he spent most of his life. He opted for a career in medicine after contemplating life as an artist; he studied at the hospital which Pinel had transformed from a prison, the Salpêtrière. Later, in the same institution, he occupied the first chair of diseases of the nervous system ever created. Again like Pinel, he was a highly skilled clinician who added greatly to the classification of nervous diseases. He was also a gifted teacher who demonstrated the art of diagnosis with patients in the presence of his students. His lectures became celebrated and attracted students from around the world. Freud attended for four months in 1885–1886; he was greatly influenced by Charcot and held him in very high regard. Charcot was, with Broca, a staunch supporter of cerebral localization, and he dealt with aphasia at length in his lectures. He related clinical symptoms to brain autopsies and developed the clinical-anatomical method.

Charcot's portrait is shown together with a drawing of a hysterical patient in a classic posture—*l'arc de cercle.* It is the same hysterical crisis that is represented in the famous painting by Brouillet, "A Clinical Lecture at the Salpêtrière," in which Charcot demonstrates hypnosis to a group of students. Moreover, a drawing in the upper left background of the lecture room displays a patient in this same posture. It is likely that the repeated demonstration of the same patient passing through the same hypnotic states in a room with adequate visual guidance for mimicry was one of the factors that led Charcot to his erroneous conclusions about hypnosis and hysteria.

Portrait after a photograph in: Duke-Elder, S. 1968. *System of Ophthalmology,* Vol. 4. *The Physiology of the Eye and of Vision.* London: Henry Kimpton.

Motif after a diagram of retinal structure in: Polyak, S. 1957. *The Vertebrate Visual System.* Chicago: University of Chicago Press.

Physiologist of the Retina

Hermann Rudolf Aubert (1826–1892) was one of the towering figures of physiological optics, alongside Helmholtz and Hering. In 1865 he published his *Physiologie der Netzhaut* (Physiology of the Retina), which clarified much of the terminology in physiological optics as well as adding substantially to its body of knowledge. Aubert defined vision as "the faculty by which light is perceived as such and gradations in its intensity are appreciated." He introduced the concept of adaptation and distinguished it from accommodation, which terms had previously been used interchangeably: accommodation referred to the adjustment of the eye to focus on objects at different distances, whereas adaptation denoted the adjustment of vision to the intensity of light. He systematically plotted the time courses of light and dark adaptation, calibrating the intensity of the light source with an episcotister of his own invention; he measured his own thresholds for detecting light at regular intervals throughout almost two hours in darkness. His work on indirect or peripheral vision was of signal importance in attaching differences in function to the receptors of the retina: he found that visual acuity diminished toward the periphery of the retina and that color vision was restricted to regions surrounding the fovea. He also demonstrated that the sensitivity to color in peripheral vision was dependent upon the background against which they were seen: colors on black backgrounds could be seen farther into the periphery than those on white. In the following year, 1866, anatomists related these differences in function to the distribution of rods and cones in the retina which led to the formulation of what later became known as duplicity theory. Aubert made accurate estimates of detection and difference thresholds for light intensity and for motion perception. The detection of motion in darkness was ten times poorer than its detection relative to a stationary visible background. With a light observed in isolation, "sometimes a person is absolutely sure of seeing motions when no objective motions are present"; he called this an autokinetic sensation. In 1861 he described how a vertical line in an otherwise dark room appears to be tilted in the opposite direction to the head when the latter is inclined—now called the Aubert phenomenon. Aubert's principal concern was with space perception and he established that visual acuity is better for near than for far objects (the Aubert-Förster phenomenon) and that the velocity of a moving target is underestimated when it is tracked (the Aubert-Fleischl phenomenon).

Aubert was born in Frankfurt-am-Main and studied medicine at the University of Berlin. He taught at the University of Breslau and occupied the chair of physiology at the University of Rostock from 1865 until his death.

Aubert is shown in the detailed anatomy of the retina, and that structure in its turn is enclosed within the letters spelling its name.

Portrait after an engraving in: Nuttin, J. 1961. *Psychology in Belgium.* Louvain: Studia Psychologica.

Delboeuf Illusion

Joseph Rémi Leopold Delboeuf (1831–1896) examined such diverse topics as psychophysics, the analysis of dreams, and hypnosis. He maintained an interest in vision throughout his academic life, and an illusion he initially described in 1892 bears his name. The Delboeuf illusion involves the misperception of the sizes of equivalent circles when one encloses a smaller circle and the other is enclosed by a larger one: the enclosed circle appears larger. His interpretation of the illusion bore similarities to Bain's motor approach to perception: he considered that perceived size was a function of eye movements, and that the illusion configuration could influence the ways the eyes moved. Delboeuf was encouraged in his psychophysical work by Plateau, and he went on to introduce the concept of sense-distance—the equivalence of suprathreshold stimulus differences. This removed a problem with Fechner's methods as it allowed sense-differences to be ranked. The concept has proved basic to subsequent measurements of sensation.

In 1866, when he moved to Liège, Delboeuf's psychophysical research was replaced by an observational analysis of dreams. He used dreams to examine the interplay between memory and perception, and was among the first to appreciate their psychological significance. Later, in 1885, he studied hypnotism with Charcot at the Salpêtrière, while Freud was there. Delboeuf was less than convinced by the experiments he witnessed, and considered that some of the hypnotic effects were a consequence of the patients' knowledge of what was expected of them. Moreover, he suggested that the hypnotist had both an influence on, and was influenced by, the hypnotic subject: most hypnotists adopted the procedures that had first proved successful in hypnotising subjects. His subsequent interpretations of hypnotic phenomena were more closely allied to Bernheim's at Nancy, whom he visited in 1888, than to Charcot's, and he appreciated the importance of speech in the whole process. Not only did Delboeuf treat patients using hypnosis but he also confronted them with their symptoms. He concluded that the hypnotist "puts the subject back into the state in which his trouble manifested itself and combats with the spoken word the same trouble, but in a state of rebirth." Freud was to use a similar technique later and to adopt a similar interpretation.

Delboeuf obtained doctorates in philosophy and in mathematics from the University of Liège, and continued his researches on geometry at Bonn, where he also became acquainted with German experimental psychology. He was appointed professor of philosophy at the University of Ghent, where he commenced his research on psychophysics. He met most of the leading psychologists of his day and he was described by William James as an excellent teacher. His portrait is combined with a variant of the size-contrast illusion that bears his name: the ellipses matching the frames of his spectacles are the same size, but appear unequal due to the ellipses surrounding or surrounded by them.

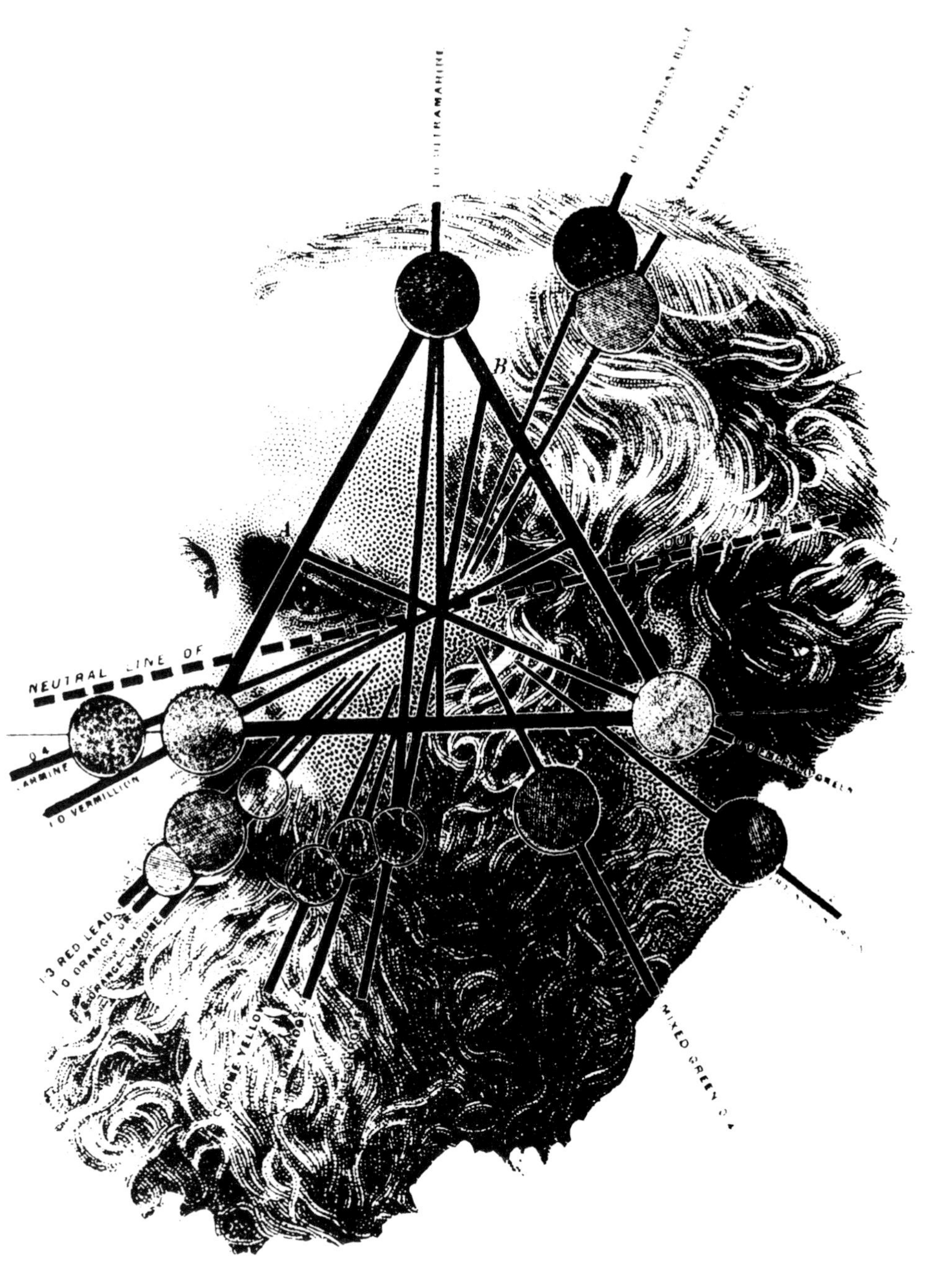

Portrait after a frontispiece engraving in: Maxwell, J. C. 1890. *The Scientific Papers of James Clerk Maxwell,* Vol. 1. W. D. Niven, ed. Paris: Hermann.

Motif after a color triangle in: Campbell, L., and W. Garnett. 1882. *The Life of James Clerk Maxwell.* London: Macmillan.

Colour Mixer

James Clerk Maxwell (1831–1879) rendered the investigation of color vision a quantitative science and applied it to the analysis of anomalies in color perception. He revived Young's three-color theory, as did Helmholtz, but provided a more complete defense of it. The essential difference between their approaches was that Maxwell appreciated that subtraction as well as addition was required in order to produce all colors from three primaries. Moreover, Helmholtz had argued that the three-color mechanism acted at the level of the specific nerve energies, whereas Maxwell, like Young, contended that there were three different color receptors. Support for this derived from his studies of color-defective persons, who could be classified according to the color receptors that were absent or anomalous.

Maxwell introduced the method that has become standard in experiments on color mixing: "The coloured paper is cut into the form of discs, each with a small hole in the center, and divided along a radius, so as to admit of several of them being placed on the same axis, so that part of each is exposed." When the device, often called Maxwell's disk, is rotated rapidly, the colors combine: "I have found by independent experiments, that the colour produced by fast spinning is identical with that produced by causing the light of the different colours to fall on the retina at once." Later, smaller disks were added so that comparisons could be made during rotation. Most color-defective persons could match any color with only two of the primaries. The resulting equations led to the proposal of a three-dimensional color solid, with variables that would now be called hue, saturation, and intensity. The location of white in the color solid was of critical importance: hue was determined by the angular position with respect to white, and saturation by the distance from white. Maxwell considered that color was the province of physics rather than phenomenology: "I think there is a good deal to be learned from the names of colours; not about colours, of course, but about names."

Maxwell was born in Edinburgh and studied physics at its university followed by mathematics at Cambridge. He held posts at Aberdeen and London universities before his appointment, in 1871, as foundation professor of experimental physics at Cambridge. He commenced his color experiments at Edinburgh and returned to them throughout his life. In 1861 he demonstrated the first color photograph to a meeting at the Royal Institution. Separate photographs of a tartan ribbon were taken through red, green, and blue filters and projected through similar filters.

The color triangle had its origins in Young's work, but it was subsequently modified by Maxwell. He is portrayed in combination with a diagram illustrating the chromatic relations of colored papers; ultramarine, vermilion, and emerald-green occupy the corners.

Portrait after frontispiece photogravure in: König, E. 1901. *W. Wundt. Seine Philosophie und Psychologie.* Stuttgart: Fromanns.

Motif after a photograph of the Institut für experimentelle Psychologie in: Meischner, W., and E. Eschler. 1979. *Wilhelm Wundt.* Cologne: Pahl-Rugenstein.

The Institution of Psychology

Wilhelm Maximilian Wundt (1832–1920) founded the first Institut für experimentelle Psychologie at Leipzig in 1879. This event is often taken as marking the onset of psychology as an independent discipline. Wundt called his experimental approach to the study of conscious experience *physiological psychology*, and his text bearing that title, first published in 1874, was widely adopted as expressing the new psychology. Like Bain, he sought to unite physiology and psychology: "The present work shows by its very title that it is an attempt to bring together two sciences which have for a long time followed very different paths although they are concerned with almost one and the same subject matter, that is, with human life."

Wundt was born near Mannheim and received a medical education at Heidelberg. He later returned to Heidelberg to become an assistant in physiology to Helmholtz, and there published his first book *Beiträge zur Theorie der Sinneswahrnehmungen* (Contributions to a Theory of Sense Perception) (1862), which provided an outline of the course he considered the new psychology should follow. In 1875 he moved to Leipzig, where both Weber and Fechner were still active; on his arrival Wundt had some difficulty in persuading the authorities that he required space for his apparatus and for conducting experiments, but his arguments prevailed. The institute had limited facilities for formal laboratory experiments on psychophysics and reaction time, but it did attract enthusiastic students, and in 1881 he founded a new journal, *Philosophische Studien*, in which the results could be published.

Wundt wrote voluminously on many branches of psychology; Boring estimated that throughout his academic life his published output was, on average, 700 words a day. His views changed during the many revisions of his books, and so the later editions often contrasted with earlier ones. He distinguished between the mediated experience available to the physical sciences and the immediate experience investigated by psychology. His use of introspection to study the latter resulted in the proposal that sensations and feelings were the elements of consciousness. Sensations could be combined to yield perceptions, but for these to influence behavior they required attention: the voluntary control of attention to focus on aspects of perception was termed *apperception*. It was the active role played by attention that could rearrange perceptions to form a creative synthesis. Feelings were described in terms of three oppositional features: pleasantness-unpleasantness, strain-relaxation, and excitement-calm. Wundt was an empiricist and an associationist interested in the universal aspects of conscious experience; the application of psychology to real-world issues held little appeal for him.

His portrait is presented within an outline of the building that housed the original Institut für experimentelle Psychologie (which was previously the university prison) in 1879. It was increased in size four years later, and the university built a new institute in 1896 to Wundt's design.

Portrait after a photograph in: Duke-Elder, S. 1968. *System of Ophthalmology,* Vol. 4. *The Physiology of the Eye and of Vision.* London: Henry Kimpton.

Hering Grid

Karl Ewald Konstantin Hering (1834–1918) represented the phenomenological and nativist tradition in studying perception, which was contrasted to Helmholtz's empiricist approach, and the two men were often locked in conflict. His work in vision concerned space perception, color vision, and contrast phenomena. Hering based his opponent-process theory on color appearances rather than on mixing lights of different wavelengths. Like Maxwell, he believed that much could be learned from color names, but in contrast Hering considered that they would be useful in understanding color perception. He adopted the procedure of presenting colored papers to observers and asking them to name the colors from which they were mixed. Red, green, blue, and yellow were not said to be mixtures of any other colors. He also examined simultaneous and successive color contrast phenomena. Together, these led him to propose a theory of color vision based on three oppositional pairs: red-green, blue-yellow, and white-black. He speculated that there are three retinal pigments that are either built up or broken down by light to yield the six elements. Modern color theory has shown both Helmholtz and Hering to be correct in principle but wrong in detail: the initial stage involves three cone pigments (not three kinds of fibers) the signals from which combine neurally (not in the action of the pigments) to produce opposing pairs of red-green, blue-yellow, and black-white.

In the area of space perception Hering utilized the concept of local sign, proposed by Rudolf Hermann Lotze (1817–1881); each retinal point was considered to have a local sign for height, width, and depth. This conflicted with Helmholtz's emphasis on learning to interpret the retinal signals, largely via information from eye movements. Hering did investigate binocular eye movements and argued that the two eyes move as a single unit: his law of equal innervation states that when one eye moves the other moves with equal amplitude and velocity, either in the same or the opposite direction. Eye movements were also implicated in visual direction: "For any given two corresponding lines of direction, or visual lines, there is in visual space a single visual direction line upon which *appears* everything which *actually lies* in the pair of visual lines." The center of visual direction was called the cyclopean eye.

Hering was born in Altgersdorf, a small village in Saxony. He graduated in medicine from the University of Leipzig in 1858, but pursued an academic rather than a medical career. He succeeded Purkinje as professor of physiology at the University of Prague, returning to Leipzig in 1895.

One of the contrast phenomena he described has been named after him—the Hering grid. It consists of an array of white squares on a black background, and illusory light gray dots can be seen in the intersections of the black lines. Some of the black lines are slightly thicker than others and these define the low-contrast portrait of Hering.

Portrait after a photograph in: Runes, D. G. 1959. *Pictorial History of Philosophy.* New York: Philosophical Library.

Mach Bands

Ernst Mach (1838–1916) developed a positivist approach to science and, following in the paths of Berkeley and Hume, he argued that all sciences reduce to sensations. He was convinced that "the foundations of science as a whole, and of physics in general, await their next greatest elucidations from the side of biology, and especially from the analysis of sensations." In his *Beiträge zur Analyse der Empfindungen* (translated as The Analysis of Sensations) (1886) he stated: "Thing, body, matter, are nothing apart from their complexes of colors, sounds, and so forth—nothing apart from their so-called attributes," and these should be studied by introspection. Accordingly, Mach's positivism differed from that of Comte, who abhored introspection. However, they shared the Baconian distrust of theorizing, which allowed error to intrude in science.

Mach defined a new area of form perception by correlating the appearance of contours with physical variables. In studying the complexes of sensations that are involved in the perception of forms, Mach prepared the ground for the Gestalt psychologists. However, one striking contrast phenomenon could not be defined so readily: a uniform gradient of luminance from light to dark does not appear uniform: a light band flanks the light border while a dark band is visible to the side of the dark border. These are now called Mach bands and he described them mathematically in terms of the second derivative of luminance change: "What we *see* are not differential coefficients, which is an intellectual affair, but only the *direction* of the curve-elements, and the *declination* of the direction of one curve-element from that of another." Mach produced the gradients by rotating simply drawn, radiating figures on a disk. They can also be seen in drawings of repetitive ramplike lines tapering gradually from thick to thin. The phenomenon has been utilized intuitively by artists for centuries to enhance the visibility of borders that would be difficult to see otherwise. Earlier, in 1875, he had published a book on the perception of bodily rotation and on the basis of his experimental results proposed a hydrodynamic theory of semicircular canal function that is still generally accepted.

Mach was born in Moravia, then part of Austria, and obtained a doctorate in physics at the University of Vienna. He was appointed professor of physics at the University of Prague in 1867; at that time Hering was professor of physiology, though their analyzes of sensations differed radically. Mach returned to Vienna in 1895 to become professor of the history and theory of the inductive sciences. Mach's portrait can be dimly defined within the light and dark bands that surround him: the design was drawn to match the borders of his head, the details of which can be discerned from afar. Some artistic license has been taken in defining the facial features since they are not, strictly speaking, due to Mach bands, but they can be seen with an adequate analysis of the sensations.

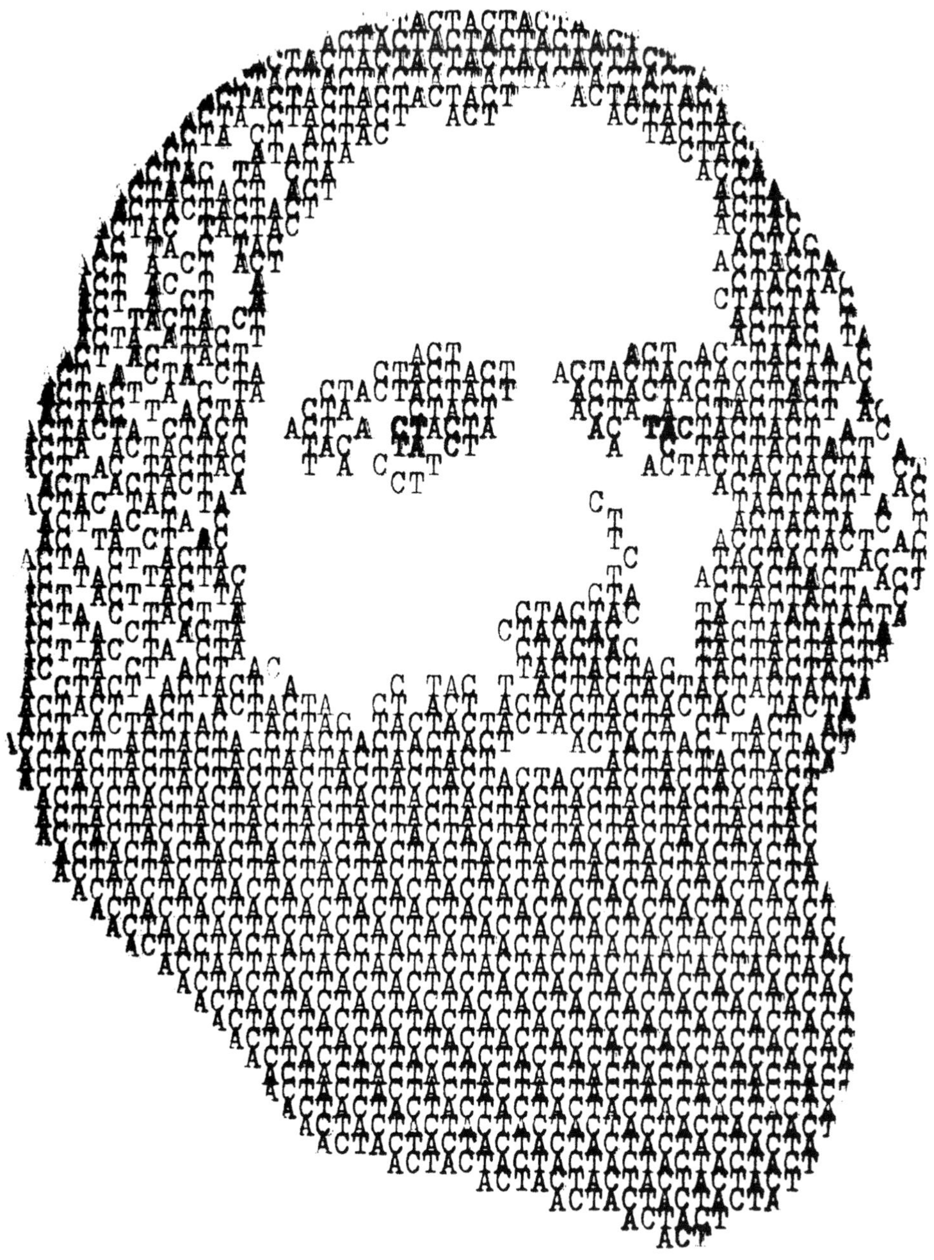

Portrait after a photograph in: Kantor, J. R. 1969. *The Scientific Evolution of Psychology,* Vol. 2. Chicago: Principia.

Act Psychologist

Franz Brentano (1838–1917) replaced Wundt's psychology, which examined the contents of conscious experience, with a theory emphasizing the active nature of all psychological phenomena. The data of psychology were taken to be mental acts, which were intentionally directed to external objects. Three classes of mental act were distinguished: perceiving, judging, and feeling. He considered that phenomenology rather than experiment was the appropriate method to study mental acts; the mind was able to contemplate its own activity, since one act could be the object of another. Although he called his approach empirical, it was not experimental; he saw little difference between philosophy and psychology. He commenced his *Psychologie vom empirischen Standpunkt* (Psychology from an Empirical Standpoint) (1874) by stating: "The title which I have given this work characterizes both its object and its method. My psychological standpoint is empirical: experience alone is my teacher. . . . Our most urgent need in psychology is not the variety and universality of the tenets, but rather the unity of the doctrine. Within this framework we must strive to attain what first mathematics and then physics, chemistry, and physiology have already attained, i.e. a core of generally accepted truths capable of attracting to it contributions from all other fields of scientific endeavor." His desire to establish absolute truths placed him in the philosophical line stemming from Aristotle. His attack was not only on the atomistic theory of Wundt but also on his associationism. He provided a dynamic and holistic psychology for which there were many ready adherents, including Mach. Among his students were Christian von Ehrenfels (1859–1932), who developed the concept of Gestalt qualities, and Edmund Husserl (1859–1938), who extended phenomenology into the philosophical domain. Brentano's ideas were adopted by others in Germany and Austria who investigated more complex psychological processes than were countenanced in Wundt's laboratory, and they are said to have influenced Freud.

His research was not devoid of quantitative experiments. He conducted several studies of the Müller-Lyer illusion, measuring its magnitude with variation of the fin angle. He proposed a theory for orientation illusions generally, suggesting that acute angles are perceptually enlarged and obtuse angles reduced. He also modified the Müller-Lyer configuration by replacing the fins by square elements and by removing the lines between the fins.

Brentano was born in Marienbad on the Rhine and moved to Bavaria at an early age. He was trained for the Catholic priesthood and, before he was ordained, obtained a doctorate in philosophy from the University of Tübingen. He eventually left the church and was appointed professor of philosophy at the University of Vienna in 1874. His importance to psychology lies primarily in the influences he had on others. He published relatively little, certainly in comparison to Wundt, but he sowed the seeds that would later blossom into the Gestalt movement.

Brentano is represented in the letters of the name given to his psychology; it requires an intentional mental act on behalf of the perceiver to recognize him.

Another variety of the psychologist's fallacy is the assumption that the mental state studied must be conscious of itself as the psychologist is conscious of it. The mental state is aware of itself only from within; it grasps what we call its own content, and nothing more. The psychologist, on the contrary, is aware of it from without, and knows its relations with all sorts of other things. What the thought sees is only its own object; what the psychologist sees is the thought's object, plus the thought itself, plus possibly all the rest of the world. We must be very careful therefore, in discussing a state of mind from the psychologist's point of view, to avoid foisting into its own ken matters that are only there for ours. We must avoid substituting what we know the consciousness is, for what it is a consciousness of, and counting its outward, and so to speak physical, relations with other facts of the world, in among the objects of which we set it down as aware. Crude as such a confusion of standpoints seems to be when abstractly stated, it is nevertheless a snare into which no psychologist has kept himself at all times from falling, and which forms almost the entire stock-in-trade of certain schools. We cannot be too watchful against its subtly corrupting influence.

Summary. To sum up the chapter, Psychology assumes that thoughts successively occur, and that they know objects in a world which the psychologist also knows. *These thoughts are the subjective data of which he treats, and their relations to their objects, to the brain, and to the rest of the world constitute the subject-matter of psychologic science.*

Portrait after frontispiece photograph in: James, H., ed. 1920. *The Letters of William James,* Vol. 2. London: Longmans, Green.

Motif after text in: James, W. 1890. *The Principles of Psychology,* Vol. 1. New York: Holt.

Pragmatist

William James (1842–1910) cast a pragmatic eye over psychology and presented his views in *The Principles of Psychology;* its two volumes were published in 1890 after twelve years of preparation. The *Principles* summarized the state of psychology in a literary style that was both informative and accessible: it assayed the substance of psychology unfettered by excessive jargon. "This book, assuming that thoughts and feelings exist and are vehicles of knowledge, thereupon contends that psychology when she has ascertained the empirical correlation of the various sorts of thought or feeling with definite conditions of the brain, can go no farther—can go no farther, that is, as a natural science. . . . This book consequently rejects both the associationist and the spiritualist theories; and in this strictly positivist point of view consists the only feature of it for which I feel tempted to claim originality." His pragmatism consisted of evaluating concepts in terms of their usefulness. In addition to providing a comprehensive reevaluation of mental life, he introduced both novel terms (like the stream of consciousness) and theories: his theory of emotion stressed that perception leads to bodily reactions which then induce feelings of emotion. Nonetheless, James was disparaging of his own efforts, e.g., his excellent chapter on space perception is described in the preface as "a terrible thing," and he doubted whether any author "can hope to have many readers for fourteen hundred continuous pages from his own pen."

James was born in New York City and educated in a variety of schools throughout America and Europe. He considered becoming an artist, but was steered toward science. He obtained a medical degree from Harvard University and taught physiology there for a short time. He developed a taste for psychology during visits to Germany, where he was exposed to the new psychology of Wundt as well as the mechanistic physiology of Helmholtz and his contempories. In 1875 he established a laboratory in Harvard for conducting psychological experiments, but James is not noted for his experimental work. He was a popular teacher, but few of his students achieved eminence in psychology. He was familiar with the European theories of the new psychology, but his main theoretical mark was to support a general pragmatism, which was enunciated in the *Principles.* James is often contrasted with Wundt: each was popular in his own country, but they did not think too highly of one another. James considered that Wundt's work boring, while Wundt described the *Principles* as literature rather than psychology.

James's commonsense approach to consciousness is evident in the text in which he is embedded, taken from the chapter "The Methods and Snares of Psychology." The greatest snare is the "confusion of his own standpoint with that of the mental fact about which he is making his report."

Portrait after a photograph in: Strachey, J. 1955. *The Standard Edition of the Complete Psychological Works of Sigmund Freud,* Vol. 2. London: Hogarth Press.

Motif after a photograph of Anna O in: Ellenberger, H. F. 1970. *The Discovery of the Unconscious. The History and Evolution of Dynamic Psychiatry.* London: Allen Lane.

Anna-lyst

Josef Breuer (1842–1925) interested Freud in hysteria by discussing one of his cases with him. However, before his limited excursion into the study of mental illness Breuer had earned an independent reputation in physiology and medicine. In his work with Hering, on the reflex regulation of respiration, he discovered what is now known as the Hering-Breuer reflex. Receptors in the lungs respond to the extent of stretching and signal this to the brain via the vagus nerve, setting in train a feedback control of respiration. In 1875, following this research, he established, simultaneously with Mach and the Edinburgh chemist Alexander Crum Brown (1838–1922), the function of the semicircular canals. During head rotation the endolymph in the canals displaces receptors in the ampulla, signaling angular accelerations and exerting control over posture and eye movements. Breuer also distinguished between the canal receptors and the otolith organs of the vestibular system, which detected orientation with respect to gravity.

Anna O (Bertha Pappenheim, 1860–1936) is perhaps one of the most celebrated patients in psychology; her case was very complex and, despite Breuer's acute powers of observation, was probably made more so as a consequence of its retrospective reconstruction. Breuer treated Anna O from 1880 until 1882, and described four phases through which her mental illness passed. All involved two distinct states of consciousness. During the late evening she was rational, whereas during the day she suffered from paralyses and contractures, ocular disturbances, speech difficulties, and hallucinations. The transition between the two conditions took place in the late afternoon. She then went into a spontaneous hypnotic state from which she emerged with an almost normal second personality. Breuer found that her symptoms could be relieved (although not permanently removed) by talking in great detail about the origins and appearances of each of them. This constituted Breuer's *talking cure.* During induced hypnosis Breuer would sometimes "ask her to concentrate her thoughts on the symptom we were treating at the moment and tell me the occasions on which it had appeared. The patient would proceed to describe in rapid succession and under brief headings the external events concerned and these I would jot down" to be discussed later. Anna's case, together with others treated by Freud, was published in their *Studien über Hysterie* (Studies on Hysteria) (1895); the theoretical chapter was written by Breuer, who can be credited with linking neuroses to unconscious processes and with developing a technique to render the unconscious processes conscious. Although it is not known how, Anna O recovered from her neurosis and embarked on an active life supporting social and religious causes.

Breuer was born in Vienna, studied medicine at its university and had a thriving medical practice there; Freud was one of his patients. Most of his experimental work was conducted at his practice—even his experiments on vestibular function in pigeons. Breuer is depicted in combination with two views of Anna O reflecting her dual personality.

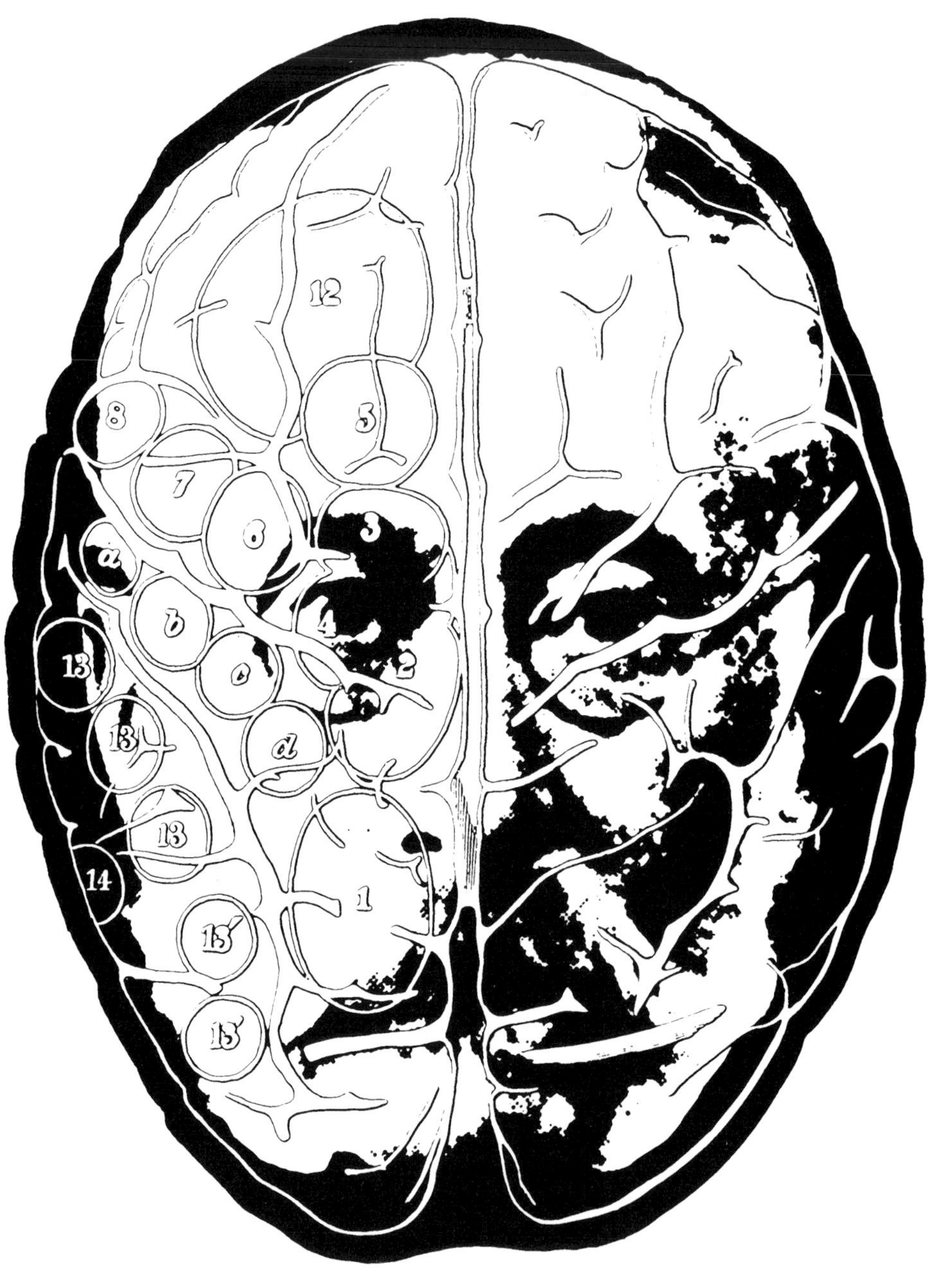

Portrait after a photograph in: Haymaker, W., and F. Schiller. eds. 1970. *The Founders of Neurology,* ed. 2. Springfield, Ill.: Thomas.

Motif after a diagram of the brain in: Ferrier, D. 1876. *The Functions of the Brain*. London: Smith, Elder.

Brain Stimulator

David Ferrier (1843–1928) electrically stimulated the brains of many species and mapped areas of the cortex: "the whole brain is regarded as divided into sensory and motor regions . . . a scientific phrenology is regarded as possible." The long-held view that the brain was unaffected by direct stimulation had been overturned by Gustav Theodor Fritsch (1838–1927) and Eduard Hitzig (1838–1907) in 1870. They galvanically stimulated the exposed brains of unanesthetized dogs and found specific precentral areas that resulted in muscular contractions: they divided the cortex into two parts—motor and not motor. Thus a new physiology, based on cortical localization, was being established at around the time of the new psychology. "The discovery of new methods of investigation opens up new fields of inquiry, and leads to the discovery of new truths. The discovery of the electrical excitability of the brain by Fritsch and Hitzig has given a fresh impetus to researches on the functions of the brain, and throws new light on many obscure points in cerebral physiology and pathology."

The involvement of certain cortical regions in motor control had been proposed by John Hughlings Jackson (1835–1911) on the basis of his studies of epilepsy and these, too, were the stimulus for Ferrier's investigations. In 1873 he commenced a series of experiments on anesthetized frogs, pigeons, guinea pigs, rabbits, cats, dogs, and monkeys in which he applied faradic stimulation to localized areas of the cortex; he also carried out ablations of the same areas. These demonstrated large species differences, and pointed to the dangers of extrapolating as broadly as Flourens had done. Most attention was paid to stimulation of monkey cortex, and Ferrier described his results in *The Functions of the Brain* (1876), which was dedicated to Jackson. Precise movements of muscle groups followed localized stimulation in the precentral area, sensory defects resulted from more posterior ablation, and lesions in the frontal cortex disturbed intelligent behavior: "The removal of the frontal lobes causes no motor paralysis, or other evident physiological effects, but causes a form of mental degradation, which may be reduced in ultimate analysis to loss of the faculty of attention."

Ferrier was born in Aberdeen and studied classics and philosophy at its university, where he came under Bain's influence. After a year at Heidelberg he studied medicine at Edinburgh University. He was appointed professor of forensic medicine at King's College Hospital, London, and later occupied the specially created chair of neuropathology. He was a founding editor of the journal *Brain* in 1878, and was instrumental in planning the first surgical removal of a tumor from a human brain. Ferrier is represented in a drawing of the human brain that is marked with the motor map of monkey cortex: the numbers specify localized movements with the letters representing movement areas for the hand and wrist.

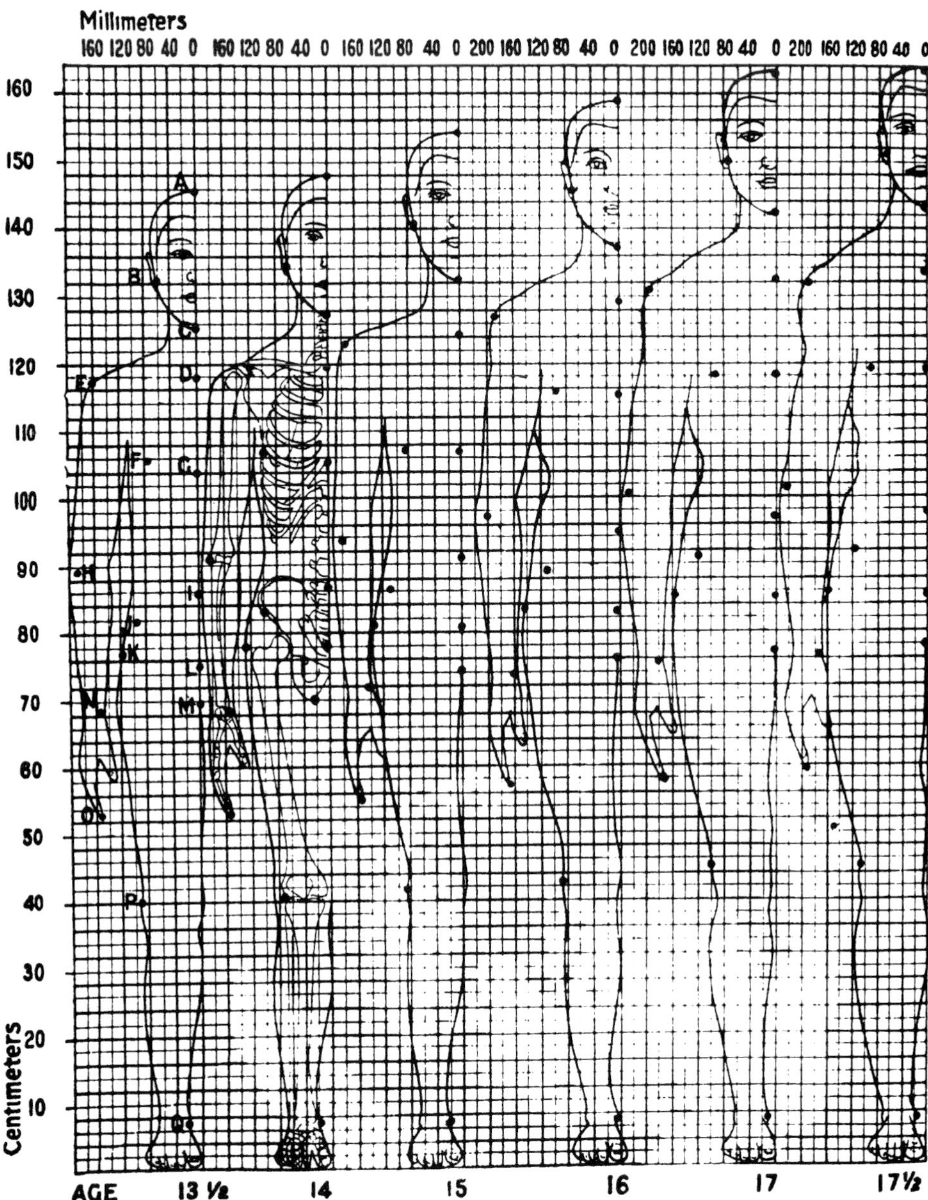

Portrait after a photograph in: Sanford, E. C. 1924. Granville Stanley Hall 1846–1924. *American Journal of Psychology* 35:313–321.

Motif after a figure in: Hall, G. S. 1904. *Adolescence. Its Psychology and Its Relation to Physiology, Anthropology, Sociology, Sex, Crime, Religion and Education*, Vol. 1. New York: Appleton.

The Adolescence of Psychology

Granville Stanley Hall (1844–1924) brought a functionalist approach to the developing psychology in America and added to its organs and organization. His concern was with the functions that mental processes served in everyday adaptations to life. He had been greatly influenced by Darwin's theory of evolution, and his principal research interest was in growth and development. His convictions are clearly stated in his *Adolescence* (1904): "The genetic ideas of the soul which pervade this work are new in both matter and method, and that if true they mark an extension of evolution into the psychic field of the utmost importance." Later he wrote a book on *Senescence* (1922). However, it was his organizational skills that had the greatest bearing on the growth of psychology.

Hall was born near Ashfield, Massachusetts, and was educated for the church but realized that it was not his calling. He pursued independent study of philosophy and physiology in Germany (where he met Fechner) before returning to the United States in 1871. He became acquainted with his contemporary William James at Harvard, and obtained a doctorate for work on space perception from that university. He then visited Germany again, where he worked with Wundt (as his first American student) and also with Helmholtz. Some time after his return, Hall was appointed professor of psychology at Johns Hopkins University and later became the first president of Clark University, although his tenure was turbulent: his plans for a grand university on the German scale did not accord with those of its benefactor. In 1887, while at Johns Hopkins he founded the first journal in English devoted solely to psychology—the *American Journal of Psychology*. Its establishment was bizarre. Hall was given a donation of $500 to found a journal of experimental psychology on the donor's unstated understanding that it was to be concerned with psychical research! Hall founded other journals: the *Pedagogical Seminary* (which later became the *Journal of Genetic Psychology*) in 1893, and the *Journal of Applied Psychology* in 1915. Another notable establishment was that of the American Psychological Association in 1892, and he was its first president, serving a second time in 1924. In 1909 he invited both Freud and Jung to America in celebration of Clark's twentieth anniversary. Freud's lectures were published in the *American Journal of Psychology*, thus awakening a wider audience to psychoanalysis. Hall was an influential teacher and Clark produced the majority of American doctorates in psychology in the final decade of the last century. Despite Hall's exposure to the experimental psychology and physiology of his day, he did not conduct many experiments after his move to Clark.

Hall's portrait is incorporated with his figure showing the growth of the whole body in *Adolescence*.

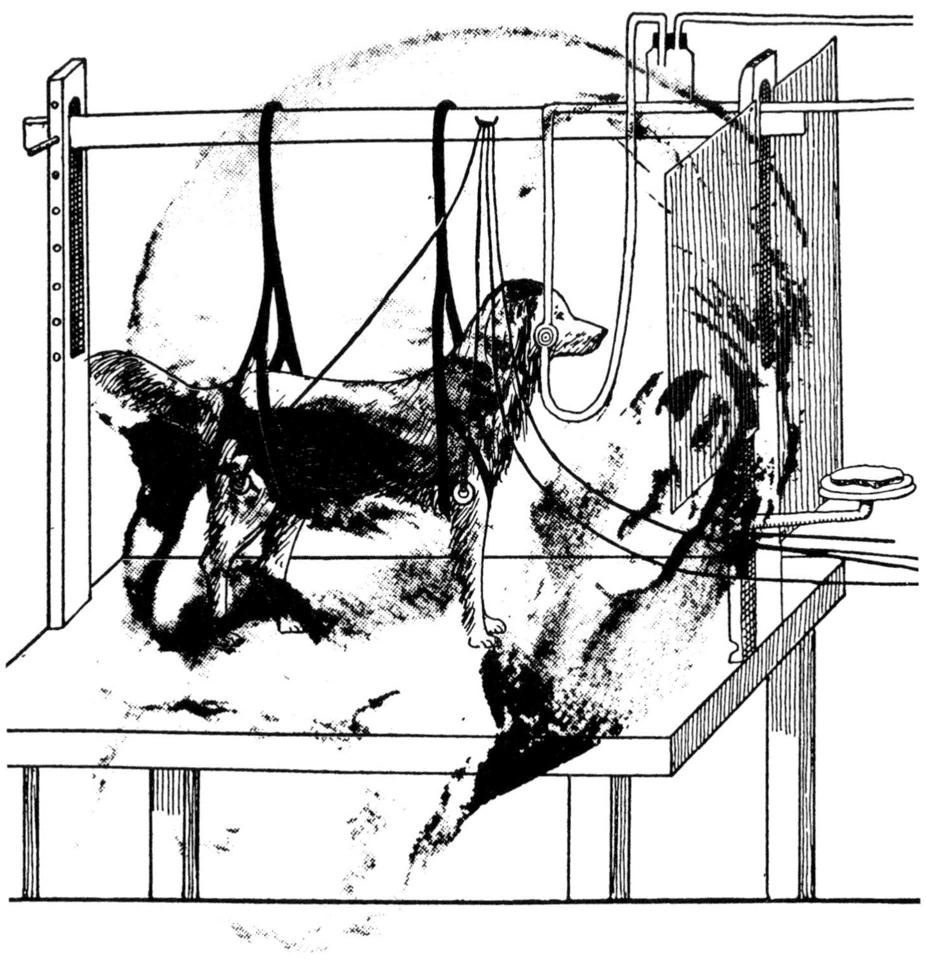

Portrait after frontispiece drawing in: Pavlov, I. P. 1928. *Lectures on Conditioned Reflexes. Twenty-five Years of Objective Study of the Higher Nervous Activity (Behaviour) of Animals.* W. H. Gantt, trans. London: Martin Lawrence.

Motif after a diagram of conditioning apparatus in the same book.

Pavlov's Dog

Ivan Petrovich Pavlov (1849–1936) extended the concept of reflexes into the psychological domain. His lifelong interest was in the digestive process, and his study of internal secretions during digestion won him the Nobel Prize for medicine in 1904. His last three and a half decades were spent investigating an incidental observation made during his early experiments—that dogs started salivating in anticipation of food (or dilute acid applied to the tongue) rather than upon ingestion. "Psychical excitation, i.e., the action of a substance at a distance, is exactly the same as when it is in the mouth. It is absolutely the same in all respects. Depending on the kind of food shown to the dog, whether dry or liquid, edible or absolutely inedible, the salivary gland functions in exactly the same way as when these substances are introduced into the mouth." He investigated these "psychical secretions" by pairing a neutral stimulus (like a bell) with food, and measuring the amount of saliva secreted. Following many pairings salivation occurred to the neutral stimulus alone and Pavlov called this *conditioning:* food was the unconditional stimulus and the bell was the conditional stimulus; salivation to the food was an unconditioned reflex, whereas that to the bell was a conditional reflex.

Pavlov was dismissive of the psychology of his day; he referred to his fellow neurophysiologist Charles Scott Sherrington (1857–1952) as a dualist, and to Janet and Köhler as animists. He interpreted conditioning in terms of excitation and inhibition in the higher nervous system rather than employing any mentalistic concepts. However, his systematic experiments on conditioning have reverberated throughout psychology, not only in learning theory but also in the clinical domain (with his studies on inducing experimental neuroses) and in personality and the study of temperament. "All these experiments clearly bring out the fact that a development of a chronic pathological state of the hemispheres can occur from one or other of two causes: first a conflict between excitation and inhibition which the cortex finds itself unable to resolve; second the action of extremely powerful and unusual stimuli."

Pavlov was born in Rayazan in central Russia. He studied medicine in St. Petersburg and later became director of the Medical Military Academy there. He was an indefatigable researcher who paid little attention to the everyday necessities; his wife even bought his shoes for him. "I have received all that can be demanded of life: the complete realization of the principles with which I began life. I dreamed of finding happiness in intellectual work, in science—and I found it."

Pavlov is shown together with detail of the apparatus he used for studying conditioning in dogs; in this instance, the unconditioned stimulus was electrical stimulation of the skin.

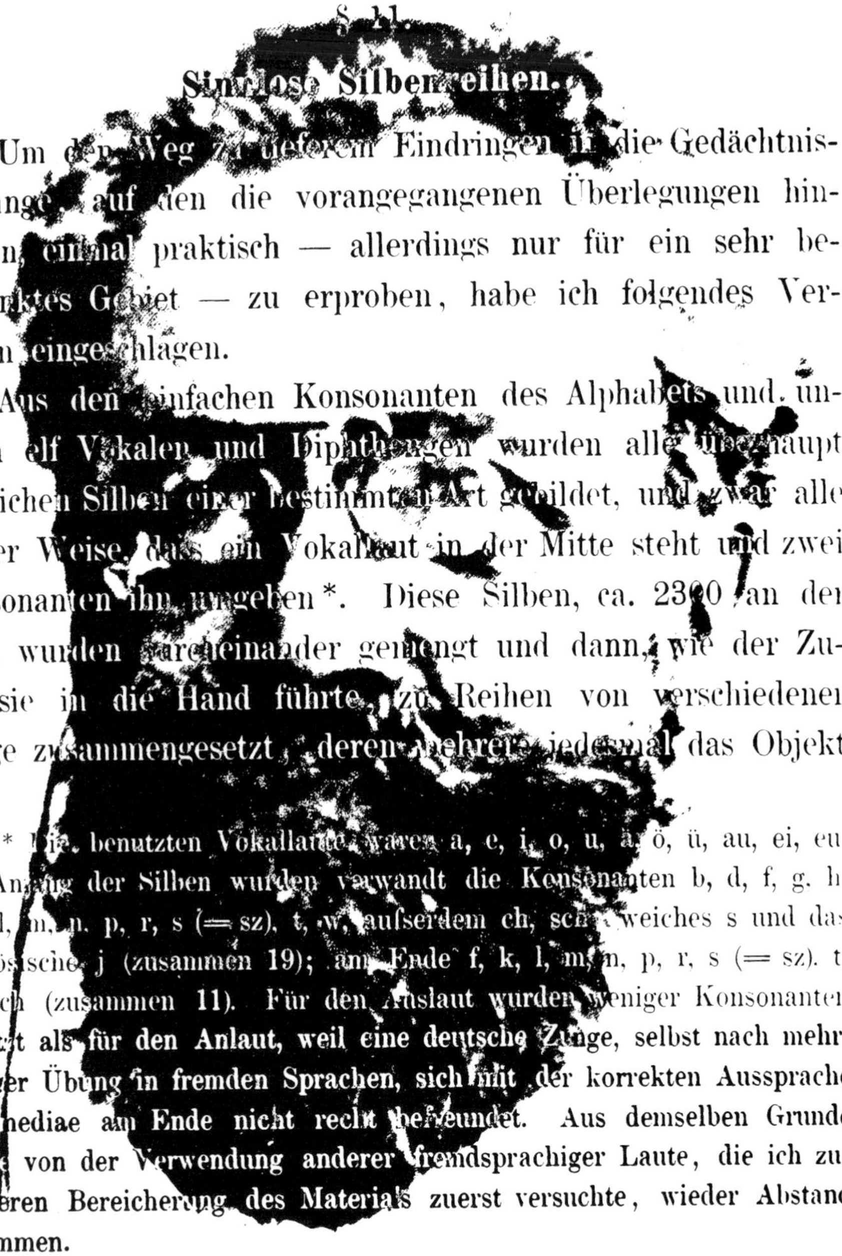

§ 11.

Sinnlose Silbenreihen.

Um den Weg zu tieferem Eindringen in die Gedächtnisvorgänge, auf den die vorangegangenen Überlegungen hinweisen, einmal praktisch — allerdings nur für ein sehr beschränktes Gebiet — zu erproben, habe ich folgendes Verfahren eingeschlagen.

Aus den einfachen Konsonanten des Alphabets und unseren elf Vokalen und Diphthongen wurden alle überhaupt möglichen Silben einer bestimmten Art gebildet, und zwar alle in der Weise, dafs ein Vokallaut in der Mitte steht und zwei Konsonanten ihn umgeben*. Diese Silben, ca. 2300 an der Zahl, wurden durcheinander gemengt und dann, wie der Zufall sie in die Hand führte, zu Reihen von verschiedener Länge zusammengesetzt, deren mehrere jedesmal das Objekt

* Die benutzten Vokallaute waren a, e, i, o, u, ä, ö, ü, au, ei, eu. Am Anfang der Silben wurden verwandt die Konsonanten b, d, f, g, h, j, k, l, m, n, p, r, s (= sz), t, w, aufserdem ch, sch, weiches s und das französische j (zusammen 19); am Ende f, k, l, m, n, p, r, s (= sz), t, ch, sch (zusammen 11). Für den Auslaut wurden weniger Konsonanten benutzt als für den Anlaut, weil eine deutsche Zunge, selbst nach mehrjähriger Übung in fremden Sprachen, sich mit der korrekten Aussprache der mediae am Ende nicht recht befreundet. Aus demselben Grunde wurde von der Verwendung anderer fremdsprachiger Laute, die ich zur gröfseren Bereicherung des Materials zuerst versuchte, wieder Abstand genommen.

Portrait after a photograph in: Schultz, D. P., and S. E. Schultz. 1987. *A History of Modern Psychology,* ed. 4. San Diego: Harcourt Brace Jovanovich.

Motif after text in: Ebbinghaus, H. 1885. *Über das Gedächtnis. Untersuchungen zur experimentellen Psychologie.* Leipzig: Duncker & Humblot.

Memory Man

Hermann Ebbinghaus (1850–1909) invented a quantitative method of studying learning. "In the realm of mental phenomena, experiment and measurement have hitherto been chiefly limited in application to sense perception and to the time relations of mental processes. By means of the following investigations we have tried to go a step farther into the workings of the mind and to submit to an experimental and quantitative treatment the manifestations of memory. The term, memory, is to be taken here in its broadest sense, including Learning, Retention, Association and Reproduction."

Ebbinghaus was trained in philosophy and might have remained in that discipline but for the chance discovery on a visit to London of an old copy of Fechner's *Elements of Psychophysics.* He sought to apply the rigor of the psychophysical methods to the study of memory. The then current methods of introspection were of little assistance in this regard, and new techniques were required. The one he invented was the use of nonsense syllables. He made up approximately 2,300 consonant-vowel-consonant sequences, which could be randomly sorted into lists of varying length. The nonsense syllables reduced (but did not eliminate) the meaningfulness of the individual items; they could be learned to some criterion and then recalled and relearned at some later time. "The aim of the tests carried on with these syllable series was, by means of repeated audible perusal of the separate series, to so impress them that immediately afterwards they could voluntarily just be reproduced. This aim was considered attained when, the initial syllable being given, a series could be recited at the first attempt, without hesitation, at a certain rate, and with the consciousness of being correct." With himself as the sole subject, Ebbinghaus established fundamental principles of learning and retention, including the forgetting curve, and that slight increases in the amount of material to be learned results in large increases in learning time (now referred to as the Ebbinghaus law).

Ebbinghaus was born in Barmen; he received a training in the humanities at the universities of Bonn, Halle, and Berlin before obtaining a doctorate in philosophy at Bonn. He then studied independently for seven years before being appointed to a post at the University of Berlin. One year after publishing his book on memory he set up a psychological laboratory there, and he opened another at Breslau in 1894. He was cofounder of the *Zeitschrift für Psychologie und Physiologie der Sinnesorgane* in 1890, and his textbook *Grundzüge der Psychologie* (Principles of Psychology) (1897) was very popular and ran to three editions. Despite these diverse influences on psychology, it is his research on forgetting for which he is remembered.

The text in which Ebbinghaus's portrait is embedded is taken from his book *Über das Gedächtnis* (On Memory) (1885), where the use of nonsense syllables is first described.

Portrait after a photograph in: Murchison, C., ed. 1932. *A History of Psychology in Autobiography,* Vol. 2. Worcester, Mass.: Clark University Press.

Motif after a drawing in: Morgan, C. L. 1900. *Animal Behaviour.* London: Arnold.

Lloyd Morgan's Canon

Conwy Lloyd Morgan (1852–1936) issued a canon of parsimony to guide interpretations of animal behavior: "In no case may we interpret an action as the outcome of the exercise of a higher psychical faculty, if it can be interpreted as the outcome of the exercise of one which stands lower in the psychological scale." Following Darwin's lead, biologists had studied behavior in a multitude of species and related it to their position on the phylogenetic scale. One source of such anecdotal descriptions was George John Romanes (1848–1894) who imputed varying degrees of reason to animals: "With regard to Romanes' collection of anecdotes, psychologically interesting in its way, I felt, as no doubt he did, that not on such anecdotal foundations could a science of comparative psychology be built." Morgan's counter to anecdotalism was a more keenly observed anecdote regarding the ability of his fox terrier to lift a latch on a gate. "The way in which my dog learnt to lift the latch of the garden gate, and thus let himself out, affords a good example of intelligent behaviour. . . . Now the question in any such case is: How did he learn the trick? In this particular case the question can be answered, because he was carefully watched. . . . In this case the lifting of the latch was unquestionably hit on by accident, and the trick was only rendered habitual by repeated association in the same situation of the chance act and happy escape. Once firmly established, however, the behaviour remained constant throughout the remainder of the dog's life." He referred to the initial activity of his dog as trial-and-error learning, and argued that apparently intelligent behavior can only be understood if its development has been investigated.

Morgan was born in London and studied engineering at the Royal School of Mines and biology at the Royal College of Science in London. Most of his academic career was at the University of Bristol, where he held the chair of zoology and geography, and later that of psychology and ethics. He visited the United States in 1896 and while at Harvard he was instrumental in guiding Thorndike's research on learning. Morgan's book *An Introduction to Comparative Psychology* (1894) essentially defined the area that was to adopt that name: "My central object in this work is to discuss the relation of the psychology of man to that of the higher animals. . . . A secondary object . . . is to consider the place of consciousness in nature, the relation of psychical evolution to physical and biological evolution, and the light which comparative psychology throws on certain philosophical problems." Following his retirement from Bristol he taught at Clark and Harvard universities. Morgan's portrait, with his long, flowing beard, is presented together with a drawing of his fox terrier lifting the latch of the garden gate.

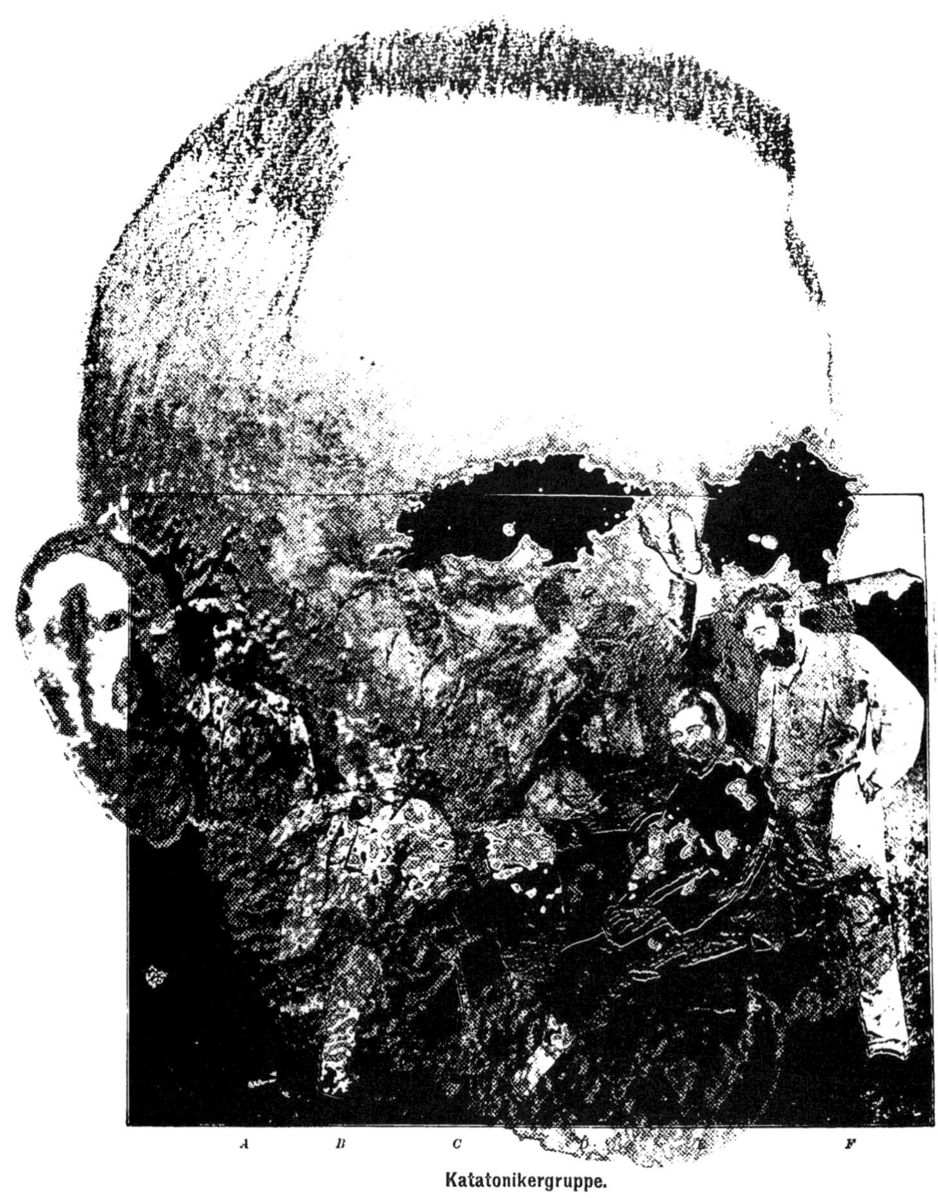

Portrait after a photograph in: Zilboorg, G., and G. W. Henry. 1941. *A History of Medical Psychology.* New York: Norton.

Motif after a photograph in: Kraepelin, E. 1899. *Psychiatrie. Ein Lehrbuch für Studierende und Aertze,* Vol. 2. *Klinische Psychiatrie,* ed. 6. Leipzig: Barth.

Nosologist

Emil Kraepelin (1856–1926) brought a considerable degree of order to the classification of mental disorders. His nosology was initially presented in *Psychiatrie. Ein Lehrbuch für Studierende und Aertze* (Psychiatry. A Textbook for Students and Physicians) (1883) and it developed through its later editions. It was based on the accumulation of large numbers of case histories and their statistical analysis and it has provided a model for later classifications. Kraepelin's approach resulted in a closer alignment of psychiatry with medicine generally because many categories of mental illness were treated in disease terms. That is, they were considered to be organic disorders of the brain that could be classified, had a developmental course, and were often assumed to be incurable. The contrast between Kraepelin's theories and treatments of psychoses and those Freud adopted for neuroses was marked. The principal innovation of Kraepelin's system was the distinction between the psychotic states of manic-depression and dementia praecox. His lectures consisted of demonstrating to his students patients who fell into the various categories; he would describe their physical conditions, their medical histories, psychological symptoms, and then classify their mental states. For example: "Experience shows that this condition is very characteristic of an entirely different disease [from melancholia], to which we will give the name *maniacal-depressive insanity*. . . . This disease generally runs its course in a *series of isolated attacks*, which are not uniform, but present either states of depression of the kind described or characteristic states of excitement. . . . The isolated attacks are generally separated by longer or shorter intervals of freedom." With regard to a patient who was withdrawn, listless, and lacking affect, he reported: "We have a *mental and emotional infirmity* to deal with, which reminds us only outwardly of the states of depression previously described. This infirmity is the incurable outcome of a very common case history, to which we will provisionally give the name *Dementia Praecox*." He also listed melancholia, general paralysis of the insane, catatonia, paranoia, hysteria, alcoholism, morphinism, cocainism, and others. Eugen Bleuler (1857–1939) later challenged the assertion that dementia praecox (insanity of adolescence) was incurable, presenting cases in which the patients had recovered. He changed its name to schizophrenia and stressed the breakdown of associations as its fundamental feature.

Kraepelin was born in Mecklenburg. He studied medicine at the universities of Würzburg and Leipzig, and was later called to the chair of psychiatry at Dorpat, then Heidelberg, and later at Munich. He was impressed by Wundt's psychology, and worked in his laboratory on the effects of drugs on behavior. Kraepelin remained a close associate of Wundt, and his concern with the disruption of attentional control in psychoses reflected Wundt's influence, as did his application of association techniques. He found that alcohol and fatigue increased associations of habit and decreased mental associations, resembling disorders of thought in psychosis.

Kraepelin can be seen in the company of a group of catatonic patients.

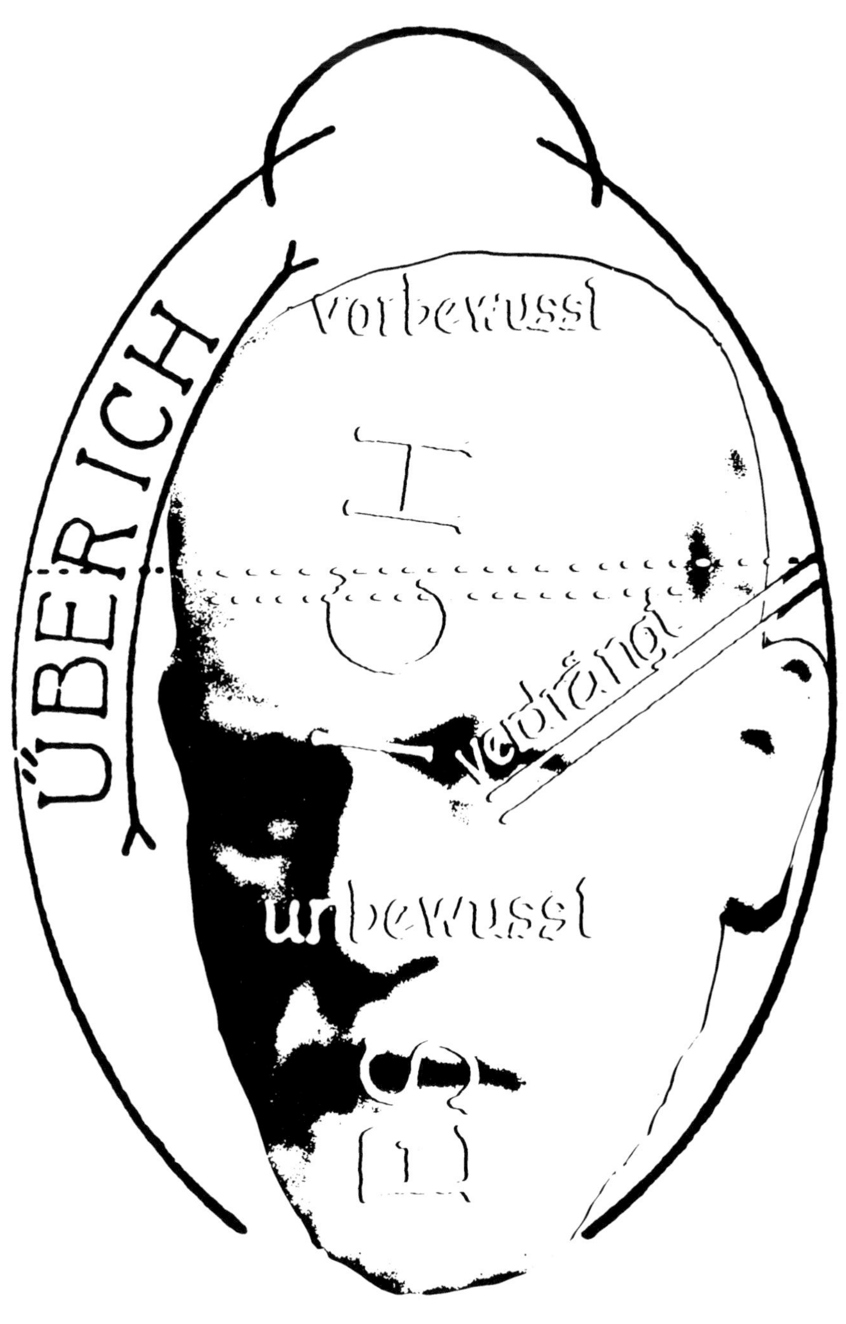

Portrait after a frontispiece photograph in: Freud, S. 1955. *The Standard Edition of the Complete Psychological Works of Sigmund Freud,* Vol. 18. J. Strachey, trans. London: Hogarth Press.

Motif after a model of mental motivation in: Freud, S. 1933. *Neue Folge der Vorlesungen zur Einführung in die Psychoanalyse.* Vienna: Internationaler Psychoanalytischer Verlag.

Ichonoclast

Sigmund Freud (1856–1939) established psychoanalysis as a treatment of neuroses, and developed a theory of mind that emphasized unconscious motivation. He challenged many of the intellectual icons of his day, particularly those associated with infantile sexuality and personality development. Freud devised numerous neologisms that are now part of the fabric of our language. Perhaps his greatest impact has been on the popular conception of psychology rather than on the subject itself. His methods in psychopathology displayed his neurological training in disguise, and his theoretical concepts indirectly reflect his exposure to the mechanistic neurophysiology of his day. Most concepts in Freudian theory have a long and well-defined heritage, but Freud assembled and reassembled them in novel ways.

Freud's interests in hysteria were stimulated by discussing Anna O's case with Breuer and in Paris working with Charcot. Freud continued his investigations with Breuer in Vienna, and his analysis of other cases convinced him that sexual conflicts lay at the basis of hysteria. Hypnosis was not effective for all patients, and he developed Breuer's talking cure into the method of free association. Patients lay on a couch and were instructed to say whatever came into their mind, without any selection or censorship. The method was taken to expose, indirectly, repressed memories and desires. These could also emerge in dreams, the interpretations of which assumed great importance in Freud's theory of unconscious (*unbewusst*) motivation: he described dreams as "disguised fulfilments of repressed wishes." Three forces and their interactions fashioned behavior, and he once displayed these in graphical form: the id (*Es*) represents unconscious, biological desires which are partially repressed (*verdrängt*) by the superego (*Überich*); a resolution is achieved by the preconscious (*vorbewusst*) ego (*Ich*), which also interacts via the senses with the real world (indicated by the small bump on the top of the diagram). These concepts were initially formulated in 1923, although the diagram did not appear until ten years later. The portrayal of Freud is derived from a photograph taken at the same time (1922) that this theory of mind was proposed, and he is enclosed within it.

Freud was born in Freiberg, Moravia, and moved to Vienna while still a young boy. He studied medicine at the University of Vienna, in the course of which he attended classes in philosophy given by Brentano, but the greatest influence on him was the physiologist Ernst Brücke (1819–1892). He was a prize pupil in neurology, gaining a small grant to visit Charcot in 1885, thereby changing his life and the course of abnormal psychology. Freud's band of ardent acolytes were not without their disagreements, particularly over the importance of infantile sexuality.

Portrait after a photograph in: Day, R. H., and H. Knuth. 1981. The contributions of F C Müller-Lyer. *Perception 10*:126–146.

Illusionist

Franz Carl Müller-Lyer (1857–1916) produced a novel figure which resulted in errors of space perception. In the Müller-Lyer illusion, "the arms of an acute angle appear shorter and those of an obtuse angle longer than equally long arms of a right angle." Müller-Lyer illustrated some variations on this simple arrangement and many others have been devised making this the most studied geometrical illusion. He did examine some aspects of the illusion systematically; the effect of arm angle and arm length were manipulated, and he did relate the distortion to angle interaction in the natural environment. Were it not for the simple line drawings he published in 1889 few psychologists would know his name, although he later made an impact on sociology.

The study of geometrical-optical illusions reflected the Zeitgeist of late nineteenth century psychology, and many of the now familiar configurations bear the names of psychologists of that period. There are Brentano and Ebbinghaus variants of the Müller-Lyer illusion; Delboeuf, Helmholtz, Hering, Münsterberg, Titchener, and Wundt spatial illusions; Mach investigated some brightness illusions; and Hall examined illusions of motion. Illusion figures could have been drawn at any time in the preceding two millenia, but they required a theoretical focus. Visual illusions represented the independence that psychology had won from physiology. Enough was known of the dioptrics of the eye to satisfy physiologists that the projected dimensions of the figures onto the retina were not distorted, hence the effects must be a consequence of higher processes which were not accessible to physiological inquiry, and belonged to the domain of the new psychology. Geometrical-optical illusions were interpreted in terms of eye movements (Delboeuf, Wundt), angle expansion effects (Brentano), the operation of perspective, and confusions between parts of the display. Müller-Lyer favored the last: "The lines are judged to differ in length because the judgment takes not only the lines themselves into consideration, but also, unintentionally, some part of the space on either side."

Müller-Lyer was born in Baden-Baden and studied medicine at the universities of Strasbourg, Bonn, and Leipzig, and psychology and sociology at the universities of Berlin, Vienna, Paris, and London. Among his teachers were the physiologist Emil Du Bois-Reymond (1818–1896) and Charcot. From 1888 he settled in private practice in Munich and wrote extensively on sociology. His major influence was Comte and he developed a method he called phaseological: "This method divides the history of human culture and civilization into periods or *phases.* On comparing these distinct phases one with another, the investigator perceives *lines of evolution,* i.e. trends which persist throughout each phase, and which reveal to us the direction of culture and progress."

A graphically embellished variant of the illusion is shown here: the black horizontal lines are of equal length, but the upper one appears longer. The portrait of Müller-Lyer is contained within the design, with the horizontal lines bisecting his eyes and mouth.

Portrait after frontispiece drawing in: Pearson, E. S. 1938. *Karl Pearson. An Appreciation of Some Aspects of His Life and Work.* Cambridge, England: Cambridge University Press.

Pearson's r

Karl Pearson (1857–1936) laid the foundations for modern statistics. He explored the mathematical basis for correlation, expressing the relationship between two variables by a single coefficient, and he established a test for the goodness-of-fit between observed and theoretical distributions (chi-square). He was a mathematician who applied his skills to the domain of biology, and was one of the original biometricians. His aim was to enlist statistical studies of variation to support the Darwinian theory of evolution. In 1898 he was awarded the Darwin Medal by the Royal Society, of which he was a fellow. Philosophically he was a positivist in the mold of Hume and Mach (indeed, Mach's *The Analysis of Sensations* is dedicated to Pearson), believing that causation was merely correlation in time. His philosophy was expressed in *The Grammar of Science* (1892): "*The classification of facts, the recognition of their sequence and their relative significance is the function of science,* and the habit of forming a judgment upon these facts unbiassed by personal feeling is the characteristic of what may be termed the scientific frame of mind. . . . *The unity of all science consists alone in its method, not in its material.*" Galton encouraged Pearson in his biometrical endeavors, and in 1896 the latter derived a more convenient equation for computing the former's correlation, which was denoted by *r*. Pearson referred to *r* as the Galton function or coefficient of correlation, but it is now called the product-moment correlation coefficient. The journal *Biometrika* was founded by Galton and Pearson in 1901 and Pearson edited it. Pearson was Galton's biographer.

Pearson was born in London and studied mathematics at Cambridge University, where Maxwell was one of his teachers. He then went to Germany, where he indulged his eclectic interests, attending lectures ranging from physics to metaphysics. His love of German science and literature was perhaps the basis for his adoption of the Germanic Karl in preference to his given name Carl. On his return to England he studied law but never practiced it. He was appointed professor of applied mathematics and mechanics at University College, London in 1884, and his most influential work in statistics was conducted in the decade that spans the turn of the century. It was inspired both by the publication of Galton's *Natural Inheritance* (1889) and by his zoologist colleague Walter Frank Raphael Weldon (1860–1906). In 1911 a bequest from Galton endowed a chair of eugenics at the University of London with the request that it first be offered to Pearson, who accepted it. This continued a link between biometrics and eugenics that was initiated by Galton's *Hereditary Genius* and would be extended by Fisher, though Pearson and Fisher became bitter rivals.

Pearson is here defined graphically by the letter *r* representing the product-moment coefficient of correlation that results from applying his procedures. His rueful prediction that he would be remembered mainly by a symbol or an equation proved correct.

Profile portraits after a frontispiece photograph in: Binet, A., and T. Simon. 1916. *The Development of Intelligence in Children.* E. S. Kite, trans. Baltimore: Williams & Wilkins.

Portrait of Binet testing a child after a photograph in the same book.

Intelligence Tester

Alfred Binet (1857-1911) introduced new methods of testing intelligence. In 1905, at the request of the French government, he devised (with Théodore Simon, 1873–1961) a test for measuring the intelligence of children, particularly aimed at distinguishing those of subnormal from normal intelligence. "The fundamental idea of the method is the establishment of what we shall call a measuring scale of intelligence. This scale is composed of a series of tests of increasing difficulty, starting from the lowest intellectual level that can be observed, and ending with that of average normal intelligence. Each group in the series corresponds to a different mental level." He had earlier carried out informal tests of sensory acuity and reaction time (in the Galton tradition) on his own daughters, and he considered that these were inappropriate indices of intelligence—measures of memory, attention and comprehension seemed better. The first test consisted of 30 items which were presented in increasing order of difficulty. It was revised and extended in 1908: "Our principal conclusion is that we actually possess an instrument which will allow us to measure the intellectual development of young children whose age is included between three and twelve years. This method appears to us practical, convenient and rapid." The ratio of mental to chronological age to yield an intelligence quotient, or IQ, was introduced in 1912 by William Stern (1871–1938), and it was adopted by Lewis Madison Terman (1877–1956) in developing the Stanford-Binet scale in 1916.

Binet was born in Nice and received his education in Paris; although he was trained in law, like Pearson he did not practice it. He developed an interest in psychology from independent reading, particularly of the British associationists, and obtained a post with Charcot with whom he worked for eight years. In his initial publications on hypnotism Binet claimed that perceptual effects could be magnetically shifted from one side of the body to the other. Delboeuf pointed out that the subjects were well aware of the experimenter's expectations and that this was the basis for the results. Binet eventually acceded to this criticism: "One of the principal and constant causes of error . . . is suggestion, that is, the influence of the operator by his words, gestures, attitudes and even silences, on the subtle and alert intelligence of the person whom he has put in the somnambulistic state."

Binet worked at the first psychological laboratory in France (at the Sorbonne) and became its director in 1894. A year later he was a cofounder of *L'Année Psychologique*. Binet did not consider that the complexity of intelligence could be captured by a simple ratio; while he did not introduce the concept of IQ he sowed the seeds of its invention. This is reflected in the portrayals of Binet, where the letters are not fully formed, but required his insights for their inception.

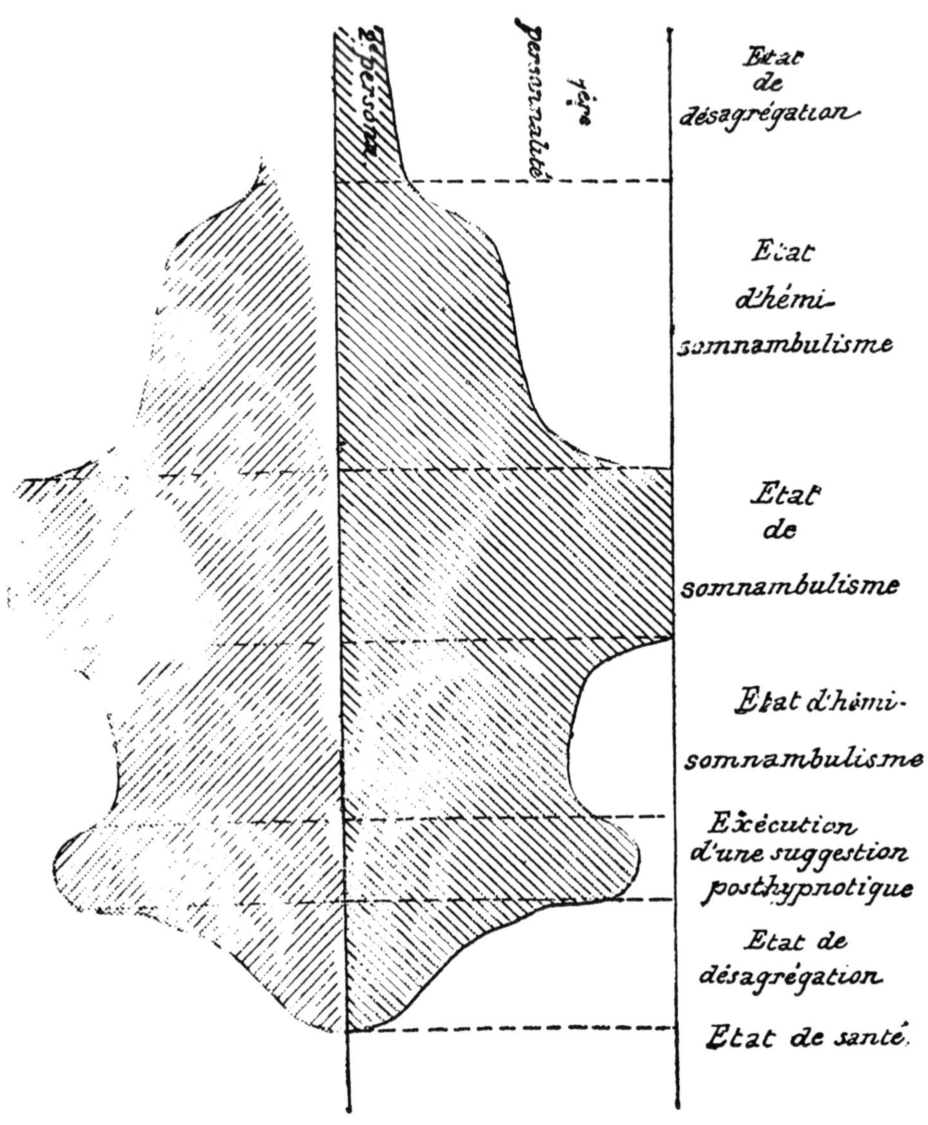

Portrait after a drawing in: Murchison, C., ed. 1930. *A History of Psychology in Autobiography,* Vol. 1. Worcester, Mass.: Clark University Press.

Motif after a figure in: Janet, P. 1889. *L'Automatisme psychologique. Essai de psychologie expérimentale sur les formes inférieures de l'activité humaine.* Paris: Baillière.

Psychopathologist

Pierre Marie Felix Janet (1859–1947) studied the neuroses and developed a method of treating them called psychological analysis. Concepts like the subconscious and *l'idée fixe* (obsessional ideas) were coined by him: "The *idée fixe* of the hysteric is *subconscious.* This term should not lead to any philosophical quarrels. It is not a question of deciding that the mind is, or is not, divisible. The term subconscious expresses simply the fact that the patient sometimes can, and other times cannot express his obsessive idea." He distinguished between the neurotic states of hysteria and psychasthenia, a distinction that was to influence Jung's categories of extroverted and introverted personalities. Janet's psychological analysis was similar to that developed independently by Delboeuf, and later by Freud. It initially consisted of returning the patient (in the following case of Marie) by suggestion to the traumatic effects that precipitated the neurosis: "I was able to efface the idea only by a singular means. It was necessary to bring her back by suggestion to the age of thirteen years, to put her back into the initial conditions of the delirium, and then to convince her that her [menstrual] period had lasted three days and had not been interrupted by any unfortunate accident."

Janet was born in Paris, was educated at its university, and spent most of his life in that city. His early psychological interests were focused by his hypnotic treatment of a celebrated clairvoyant and hysteric called Léonie, and other patients. For this work, published as *L'Automatisme Psychologique* (Psychological Automatism) (1889), he received his doctor of letters. This came to Charcot's notice and he appointed Janet director of the newly formed experimental psychology laboratory at La Salpêtrière, although Charcot died soon after Janet's appointment. For Janet hypnosis was a psychological rather than a physiological phenomenon. Indeed, his study of the early history of the magnetizers led him to realize the likely causes of Charcot's erroneous interpretations of hysterical behavior. In 1902, in competition with Binet, Janet was elected to the most prestigious post in French psychology—professor of experimental and comparative psychology at the Collège de France. He gave annual lectures on different subjects and published extensively until his retirement in 1935, but his elevation did remove him from the sources of his inspiration—his patients. He was a cofounder and editor of the *Journal de Psychologie Normale et Pathologique* in 1904.

Janet's ideas were very similar to those advanced by Freud, and they evolved in the first decades of this century. However, as Freud's influenced waxed, Janet's waned, partly because he did not attract such dedicated disciples and partly because his work was not translated into English. His wan portrait is split into two states, corresponding to the dissociation of the personality during hypnosis, as it was illustrated in his first book.

Portrait after a photograph in: Hilgard, E. R. 1987. *Psychology in America. A Historical Survey.* San Diego: Harcourt Brace Jovanovich.

Motif after a figure in: Münsterberg, H. 1897. Die verschobene Schachbrettfigur. *Zeitschrift für Psychologie* 15:184–188.

Displaced Chessboard Figure

Hugo Münsterberg (1863–1916) applied psychology to a wide range of activities—from industry to law courts to life in general. Of psychology he said: "It started in the narrow circles of the philosophers, and it is now at home wherever mental life is touched. The historian strives today for psychological explanation, the economist for psychological laws; jurisprudence looks on the criminal from a psychological standpoint; medicine emphasises the psychological value of its assistance; the realistic artist and poet fight for psychological truth; the biologist mixes psychology in his theories of evolution; the philologist explains the languages psychologically; and while aesthetical criticism systematically coquets with psychology, pedagogy seems ready even to marry her." It was in the areas of forensic and industrial psychology that his influence was greatest. Indeed, the origins of forensic psychology are to be found in *On the Witness Stand* (1909) which emphasized the unreliability of many legal procedures, from eyewitness testimony to interrogation. *Psychology and Industrial Efficiency* (1913) sought to determine by experiment the best possible conditions for work, through personnel selection and vocational guidance. He wrote many popular books like *Psychology and the Teacher* (1909) and he edited *Subconscious Phenomena* (1909), which included a chapter by Janet. In his own chapter, Münsterberg drew on his "practical studies in hypnotism, hysteria, automatic writing and similar abnormalities. . . . To acknowledge that the subconscious is found only through constructions in the service of explanation does not detract from its scientific reality; the core of the earth is of the same logical type. But such acknowledgement does imply that the only correct question is this: which of the many constructions of the not-conscious causes is most useful for the explanation of the known facts?"

Münsterberg was born in Danzig. He studied psychology under Wundt at Leipzig before completing a medical degree at Heidelberg. Although he worked with Wundt he did not agree with his interpretation of voluntary action and adopted a theoretical position more closely aligned to that of James. James, who had been impressed by Münsterberg's *Beiträge zur experimentellen Psychologie* (Contributions to Experimental Psychology) (1889), invited him to direct the psychological laboratory at Harvard in 1892. He was elected president of the American Psychological Association in 1899 and his presidential address was on psychology and history.

Münsterberg was a complex figure, displaced from his native Germany and never truly accepted in his adopted America; his affection for his homeland was treated as unpatriotic with the outbreak of World War I, and he was even denied an obituary fitting for such a distinguished figure. Ironically, despite his training in Germany, he reflected a very practical approach to psychology that was radical even for many of his American colleagues. He is portrayed in the context of an illusion he described: the parallel lines are apparently displaced because of the positioning of the black squares.

Upper portrait after a photograph in: Murchison, C., ed. 1930. *A History of Psychology in Autobiography,* Vol. 1. Worcester, Mass.: Clark University Press.

Lower portrait after a photograph in: Kimble, G. A., M. Wertheimer, and C. L. White, eds. 1991. *Portraits of Pioneers in Psychology.* Hillsdale, N.J.: Erlbaum.

Paired-associate

Mary Whiton Calkins (1863–1930) devised the method of paired-associates for studying human learning in 1896. It was developed independently a few years later by Georg Elias Müller (1850–1934) at the University of Göttingen. Calkins appears to have been unaware of Ebbinghaus's work with nonsense syllables, but she was similarly stimulated by a desire to understand the laws of association. Her method consisted of pairing colors with numerals: "A color was shown for four seconds, followed immediately by a numeral, usually black on a white ground, for the same time. After a pause of about eight seconds, . . . another color was shown, succeeded at once by a second numeral, each exposed for four seconds. The pause of eight seconds followed, and the series of 7, 10 or 12 pairs of quickly succeeding color and numeral was continued in the same way. At the close a series was shown of the same colors in altered order, and the subject was asked, as each color appeared, to write down the suggested numerals if any such occurred." She varied the factors of frequency, recency, primacy, and vividness and found that frequency was the most important for memory. As she noted later, the method would be taken as more important than the result; initially it was called the method of right associates and later, paired-associates. She had earlier worked on dreams, waking herself by alarm clock and recording their content; she concluded that dreams were rarely about significant events in life. Around the turn of the century her interests shifted toward a science of self: "Self-psychology has three basal conceptions: that of the self, that of the object, and that of the self's relation or attitude toward its object." This aspect of her psychology was introspectionist and she vehemently criticized behaviorism, but she did try to reconcile structuralism and functionalism.

Calkins was born in Hartford, Connecticut. She studied at Smith College after which she was appointed lecturer at Wellesley College, where she spent almost all her academic life. Special arrangements were made for her to attend seminars given by James at Harvard, as it, like most other universities at that time, did not admit women graduate students. She established a psychological laboratory at Wellesley and continued working at Harvard with Münsterberg. Her work on paired-associates was presented for her doctorate at Harvard but, despite its strong recommendation by the professors, the university authorities were not prepared to award the degree to a woman. She survived this slight, continued her research at Wellesley, and was elected president of the American Psychological Association in 1905; in 1918 she was elected president of the American Philosophical Association. A pair of portraits of Calkins are associated with these significant numerals.

Portrait after a frontispiece photograph in: Flügel, J. C. 1946. Charles Edward Spearman, 1863–1945. *British Journal of Psychology* 37:1–6.

Spearman's g *and* s

Charles Edward Spearman (1863–1945) applied the correlational method to assess the reliability of mental tests and proposed a two-factor theory of intelligence. "There emerges the concept of a hypothetical *general* and purely *quantitative* factor underlying all cognitive performances of any kind. Such a factor as this can scarcely be given the title of 'intelligence' at all; being evoked to explain the correlations that exist between even the most diverse sorts of cognitive performance, it does not deserve a name appropriate to any particular sort. On this view, accordingly, the name is commonly written in inverted commas, or else replaced by the simple letter *g*." Spearman used the correlational approach to study intelligence and he found high correlations between the scores of the same children on different items of intelligence tests. He proposed that the performance on all tasks was based on some general level of intelligence that was differently weighted according to the specific task tackled, rather than a set of separate capacities for memory, attention, comprehension, and reasoning, as Binet thought. This led to a theory of intelligence involving a general factor (*g*) underlying all performance, and specific factors (*s*) relating to particular types of intellectual task: "But if, thus, the totality of cognitive operations is served by some general factor in common, then each different operation must necessarily be further served by some *specific* factor peculiar to it." Spearman was the founding father of factor analysis, but he conducted this research before the modern methods of factor analysis had been developed. He is also noted for devising a technique for measuring correlations between ranked data—the Spearman rank-order correlation. Despite this association with statistical procedures and his appreciation of their benefits, Spearman was cautious about their application: he referred to statistics as being a good servant but a bad master. In addition to his books *The Nature of Intelligence* (1923) and *The Abilities of Man* (1927) he wrote a two-volume history, *Psychology down the Ages* (1937).

Spearman was born in London, where he spent most of his life. Uncertain of the direction his career should take he followed Descartes's example of military service but later described it as the mistake of his life. He went on to obtain a thorough grounding in psychology in Germany, working with Oswald Külpe (1862–1915) in Würzburg and G. E. Müller in Göttingen, as well as with Wundt in Leipzig. On his return to England in 1907 he directed the small laboratory of experimental psychology at University College, London; he was appointed professor of mind and logic in 1911 and he became the first professor of psychology in 1928. His greatest influences were Wundt's introduction of the experimental method to psychology and Galton's approach to measurement. Spearman's moustachioed portrait retains the military bearing of his early career in the army. His portrait is defined by specific factors (*s*) that distinguish him from the general background (*g*).

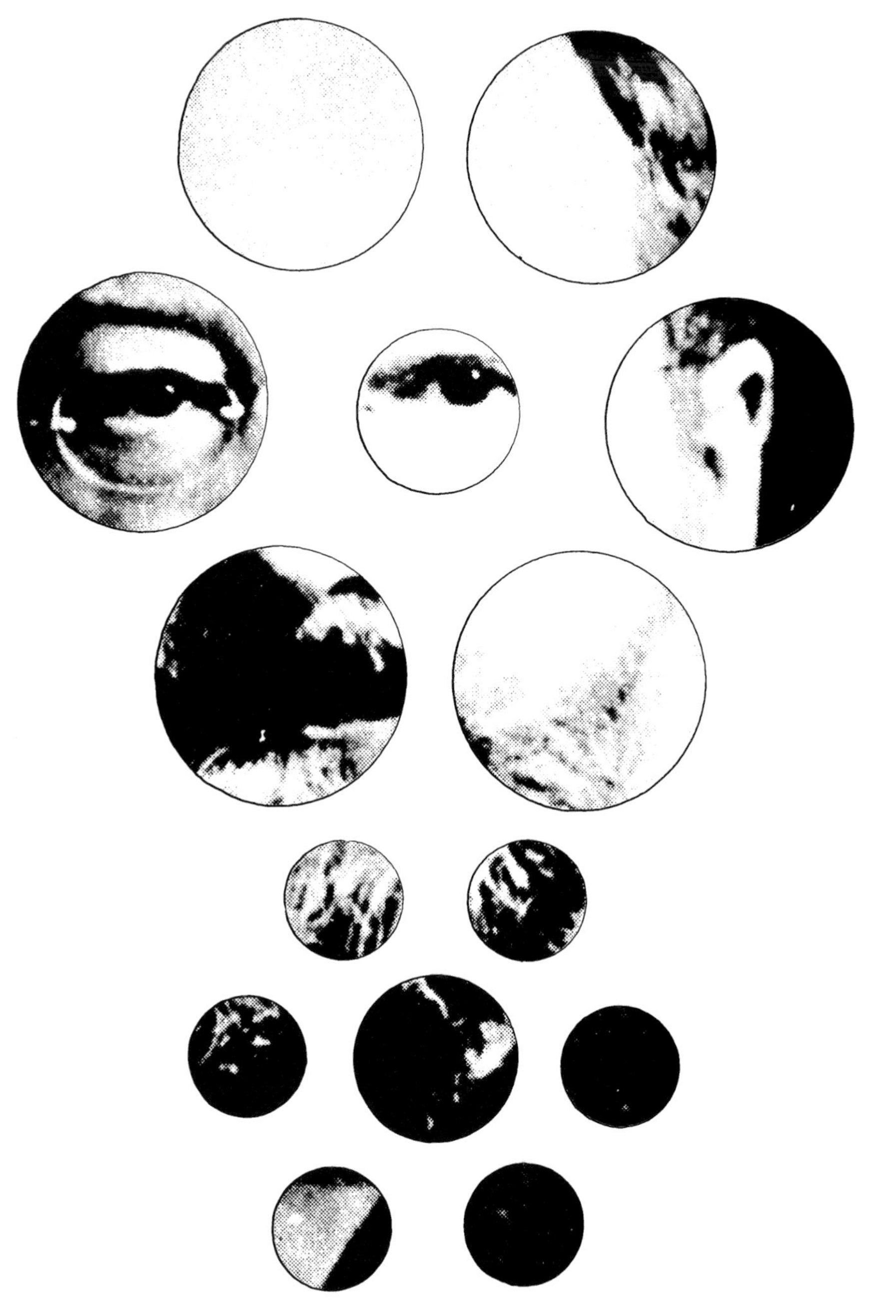

Portrait after a photograph in: Schultz, D. P., and S. E. Schultz. 1987. *A History of Modern Psychology,* ed. 4. San Diego: Harcourt Brace Jovanovich.

Motif after a figure in: Titchener, E. B. 1901. *Experimental Psychology. A Manual of Laboratory Practice,* Vol. 1. *Qualitative Experiments. Part 1. Student's Manual.* New York: Macmillan.

Structuralist

Edward Bradford Titchener (1867–1927) employed introspection to uncover the structures of human consciousness. He followed in the path of his mentor, Wundt, but he placed more emphasis on the elements of consciousness and their combination by association. "Just as experimental psychology is to a large extent concerned with problems of structure, so is 'descriptive' psychology, ancient and modern, chiefly occupied with problems of function." He was scathing of those he considered to be functional theorists, like James and Brentano, because: "It cannot be said that this functional psychology, despite what we might call its greater obviousness to investigation, has been worked out with as much patient enthusiasm or with as much scientific accuracy as has the psychology of mind structure." In defining structuralism Titchener gave the name to the movement, functionalism, that was to replace it. His distrust of explanations based on unobservable events owed much to Mach's positivism.

The elements of consciousness were, according to Titchener, sensations, images, and affections. These elements could be isolated by a method of introspection that excluded the use of object names, because describing the meaning of objects introduced "stimulus error." Most of his experimental work was directed at the analysis of sensations, which had the attributes of quality, duration, intensity, extensity, and clearness. Sensations could be combined by association, rather like Locke's mental chemistry, to yield perceptions. Ideas and emotions derived from associations of images and affections, respectively.

Titchener was born in Chichester and studied classics at Oxford University, where he first came into contact with Wundt's psychology. His two years in Wundt's laboratory had a profound effect on his life, both in terms of the personal contacts he made and his approach to psychology. He met Frank Angell (1857–1939) in Leipzig who, on his return to America, invited Titchener to Cornell University. Titchener took the post in 1892, becoming professor in the following year on Angell's move to Stanford University. Like Münsterberg, Titchener never really adapted to life in the New World, nor did he integrate himself into institutions of American psychology, although he did edit the *American Journal of Psychology* from 1921 until shortly before his death. He tried to foster European ideas and ideals in his adopted country. His department at Cornell was run with Teutonic precision and he translated German books into English. At times this was a frustrating enterprise because Wundt often completed a new edition of a book before Titchener had completed translating the earlier edition.

Elements of Titchener's portrait are shown in the circles of the size-contrast illusion bearing his name. It is closely related to the Delboeuf illusion and consists of two equal circles surrounded by larger and smaller ones: the upper circle appears smaller than the lower one.

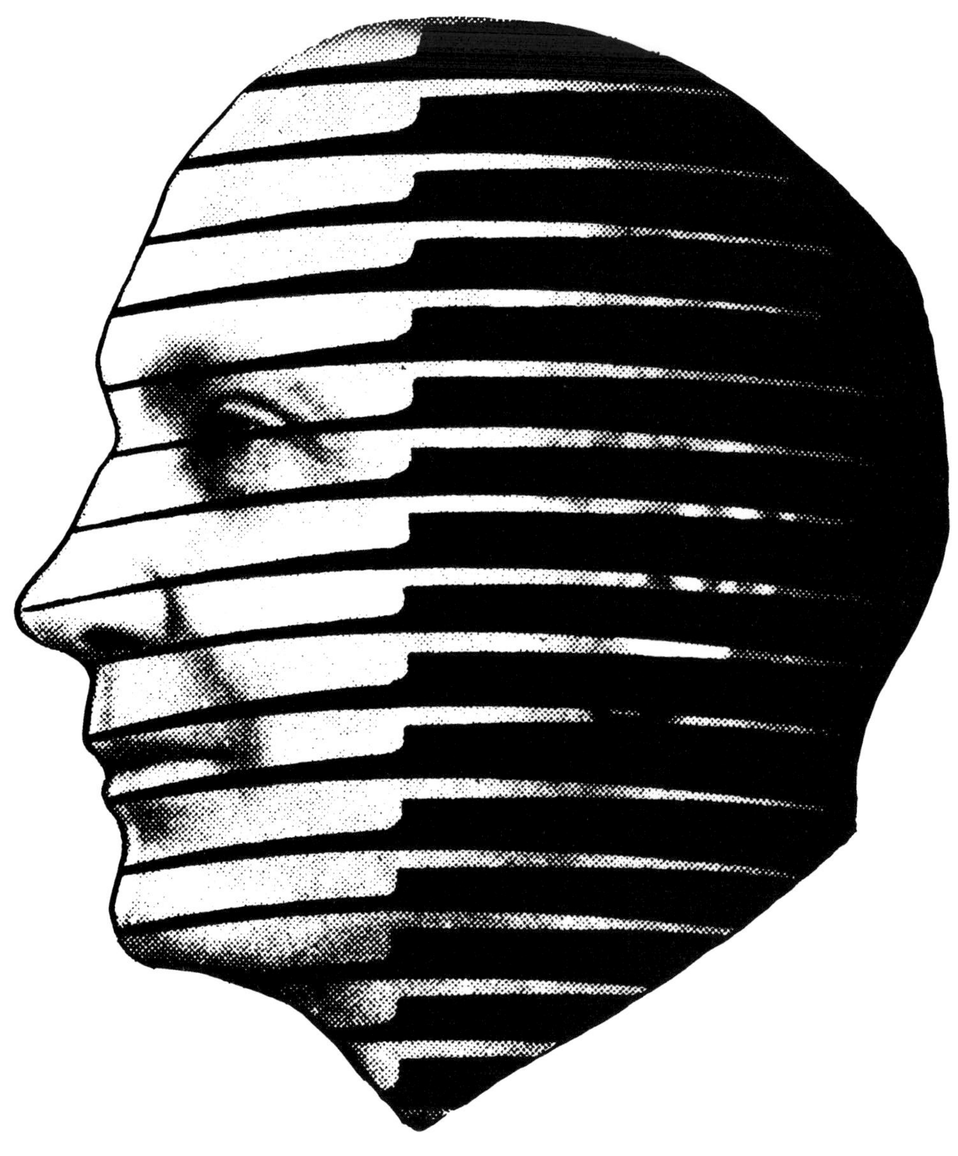

Portrait after a photograph in: Murchison, C., ed. 1932. *A History of Psychology in Autobiography,* Vol. 2. Worcester, Mass.: Clark University Press.

Motif after a figure in: Woodworth, R. S. 1901. On the voluntary control of the force of movement. *Psychological Review,* 8:350–359.

Dynamic Psychologist

Robert Sessions Woodworth (1869–1962) called his brand of functionalism "dynamic psychology," although he tried to avoid alignment with particular schools of thought. His book *Dynamic Psychology* (1918) was a reaction to the theories of Titchener, Watson, and McDougall and in it he adopted "a position that should be independent and yet have room for all genuine psychological efforts." He examined motivation and placed great importance on the contribution the organism makes to behavior. "Motivation has always seemed to me a field of study worthy to be placed alongside performance. That is, we need to know not only what the individual can do and how he does it, but also what induces him to do one thing rather than another and to put so much energy into what he does." He drew a distinction between mechanism and drive—between the performance of a task and the motivation for it. Among his books are *Contemporary Schools of Psychology* (1931) and *Experimental Psychology* (1938). The latter was used as a standard text until it was revised in 1954, and in it Woodworth's hopes for the subject were expressed: "The prospect was attractive to some psychologists, discontented with the endless disputations of the schools and eager to get down to questions which could be settled by an appeal to the facts of observation. . . . Today we are inclined to claim for experimental psychology a scope as wide as that of psychology itself, while admitting that we do not know exactly how to subject some of the biggest problems to a rigorous experiment. Until these problems are attacked experimentally, they will not be solved." The biggest problems were said to be in child and abnormal psychology. Woodworth lectured and wrote on a wide range of psychological issues; his introductory text *Psychology: A Study of Mental Life* (1921) was extremely popular.

Woodworth was born in Belchertown, Massachusetts, and studied philosophy and psychology first at Amherst College, and later at Harvard University: James was his teacher as Münsterberg had returned to Freiburg at that time. In 1899 he received his doctorate in psychology from Columbia University under James McKeen Cattell (1860–1944), and returned to teach there after conducting physiological research with Sherrington at Liverpool. He was an enthusiastic member of the American Psychological Association, missing few of its annual meetings, and he was elected president in 1914.

The muscle sense and its control were among the first issues that Woodworth examined experimentally. He is portrayed in diagram representing a dynamic act—striking a surface with the hand. The graph (which has been rotated) represents a simultaneous record of the extent of a hand movement and the corresponding force of a blow when the subject was trying to produce blows of equal force.

Portrait after a photograph in: Murchison, C., ed. 1926. *Psychologies of 1925.* Worcester, Mass.: Clark University Press.

Goal Seeker

William McDougall (1871–1938) like Freud and Woodworth, emphasized the role of motivation in behavior, but he focused on its instinctive basis. Instincts were the driving force of behavior, directing it toward the goal of their satisfaction. For this reason he called his psychology purposive, and later, hormic. "The hormic psychology imperatively requires recognition not only of instinctive action but of instincts. . . . Hormic activity is an energy manifestation; but hormic theory does not presume to say just what form or forms of energy or transformations of energy are involved. . . . The most essential facts are (*a*) that the energy manifestation is guided into channels such that the organism approaches its goal; (*b*) that this guidance is effected through a cognitive activity, an awareness, however vague, of the present situation and of the goal; (*c*) that the activity, once initiated and set on its path through cognitive activity, tends to continue until the goal is attained; (*d*) that, when the goal is attained, the activity terminates; (*e*) that progress toward and attainment of the goal are pleasurable experiences, and thwarting and failure are painful or disagreeable experiences." He defined psychology as the positive science of conduct, following Janet in using the term "conduct" for what others referred to as "behavior," but his approach to a science of behavior was radically different from Watson's. Indeed, much of his approach to psychology appeared anachronistic: he supported vitalism, utilized introspection as a method, presented long lists of human instincts, and published results of experiments with rats said to favor the inheritance of acquired characteristics. Nonetheless, his books on the behavior of groups—*An Introduction to Social Psychology* (1908) and *The Group Mind* (1920)—did much to encourage social research, although his approach was rooted firmly in his individual psychology: "The department of psychology that is of primary importance for the social sciences is that which deals with the springs of human action."

McDougall was born in Oldham, Lancashire, and studied science at Manchester University followed by medicine at Cambridge. After graduation he joined an anthropological expedition to the Torres Straits and Borneo. His main influence was James's *Principles* and he pursued his psychological interests at Göttingen with G. E. Müller. He first taught at University College, London, initiating experiments on visual perception, the area that he later referred to as "his favorite field of experiment." His readership at Oxford University did not provide access to any laboratory facilities, but he did continue with his experimental work. After World War I he was appointed to fill Münsterberg's post at Harvard, after which he spent the last eleven years of his life at Duke University. Like Münsterberg and Titchener, McDougall was not at ease in the United States; in part this was a consequence of his unpopular views and in part because of his seeming arrogance. His portrait is made up of goal-directed arrows reflecting the many instinctive forces he considered shape our conduct.

Portrait after a photograph in: Schultz, D. P., and S. E. Schultz. 1987. *A History of Modern Psychology*, ed. 4. San Diego: Harcourt Brace Jovanovich.

Motif after a drawing of Amoeba in: Washburn, M. F. 1917. *The Animal Mind. A Text-book of Comparative Psychology*, ed. 2. New York: Macmillan.

Simple Minds

Margaret Floy Washburn (1871–1939) wrote a textbook on comparative psychology that applied an anthropomorphic interpretation to the experimental literature. In *The Animal Mind* (1908) she wrote, "we are obliged to acknowledge that all *psychic interpretation of animal behavior must be on the analogy of human experience.*" This reflected her belief that all animals down to *Amoeba* exhibited consciousness, and therefore mind, and the task of the comparative psychologist was "to discover *wherein the simplest type of mind, supposing it to be that belonging to the simplest type of animal, necessarily differs from our own.*" The growing concentration on animal behavior was a reflection of the Zeitgeist, both in popular and scientific circles. The horse, Clever Hans, was confounding all but the most astute observers with his ability to count, while Thorndike's cats were displaying their skills at escapology. Although Washburn's introspective analysis was diametrically opposed to that of the emerging behaviorists, *The Animal Mind* did provide a compendium of experimental studies that were open to alternative interpretations. Her earlier work had been in the German tradition, concerned with the psychophysics of touch and with visual perception. She did not accept introspection uncritically, and contrasted the differences in the methods applied by Wundt and her mentor, Titchener. Later she integrated aspects of structuralism and behaviorism in proposing a motor theory of mental imagery. In *Movement and Mental Imagery* (1916) she proposed that thinking is accompanied by tentative movements. This position was extended further in her system of motor psychology which shared many, but not all, features of competing schools: it rejected "the materialism of the behaviorists, on the one hand, and the interactionism of the functional psychologists and vitalists, on the other hand. It will not have recourse to any mysterious agents or indwelling purposes which by hypothesis cannot belong in a mechanistic system. Thus it is as much opposed to McDougall as to Watson."

Washburn was born in New York City. She studied at Vassar and was to return there later. Her interests in psychology originated from independent reading of Wundt and they were encouraged by Cattell at Columbia, with whom she took courses. Unable to obtain a degree from Columbia she continued her research at the more liberal Cornell University, where she became the first graduate student of Titchener, who had just arrived there. She taught at Wells College for six years (where her professorial salary was half that of her male colleagues), at Cornell, and from 1903 at Vassar, where she built up a thriving psychology department. She was elected president of the American Psychological Association in 1921, and to the National Academy of Sciences in 1931.

Washburn's portrait is integrated with a diagram of *Amoeba,* the mind of which she sought to examine.

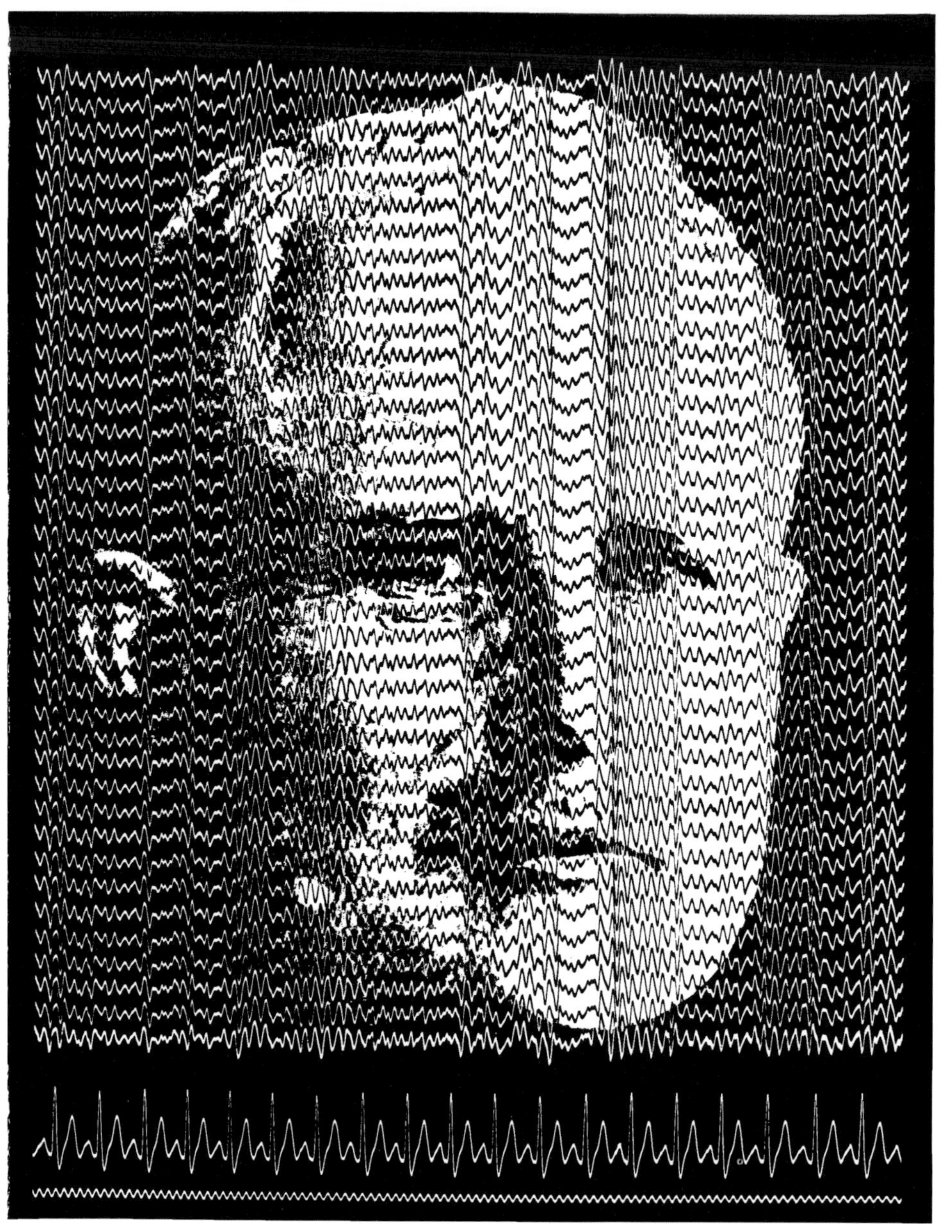

Portrait after a photograph in: *Five Pioneers in the Study of the Electrical Activity of the Brain.* Presented at the 11th International Congress of Electroencephalography and Clinical Neurophysiology, London, August 25–30, 1985.

Motif after an EEG pattern in: Berger, H. 1930. Über das Elektrenkephalogramm des Menschen. Zweite Mitteilung. *Journal für Psychologie und Neurologie 40*:160–179.

Alpha Rhythm

Hans Berger (1873–1941) recorded electrical potentials on the surface of the human scalp and plotted the electroencephalogram (EEG). His lifelong search was for an objective index of subjective experience. He initially measured variations in brain circulation and temperature in an attempt to capture the essence of psychic energy, but he abandoned that approach. Small cortical potentials had been recorded from the exposed brains of rabbits, cats, and monkeys as early as 1875 by the Liverpool surgeon Richard Caton (1842–1926), but no success had been achieved with recordings from humans. After many vain attempts on his patients, Berger achieved some success with recordings from his teenage son and from himself, and he was able to report in 1929: "I believe I have indeed discovered the electroencephalogram in man"; thirteen more papers on the human EEG followed. They are examples of experimental rigor and cautious interpretation. Berger found that "in many experimental subjects opening of the eyes, while recording the curve from the skull surface, caused an immediate change in the E.E.G. and that during mental tasks, *e.g.* when solving a problem in arithmetic, the mere naming of the task sometimes caused the same change of the the E.E.G." After demonstrating the characteristics of the EEG in normal subjects he applied the technique to pathological cases.

Berger was born in Neuses, near Coburg, and studied medicine at the universities of Würzburg, Berlin, Munich, and Jena. After obtaining his medical degree he specialized in psychiatry, joined the clinic at Jena as assistant in 1900, and was appointed its director in 1919. He conducted his research on brain physiology in isolation, and the publication of his first papers on the EEG were either ignored or ridiculed, partly because they appeared in journals of psychiatry rather than of physiology. The significance of EEG recordings was only appreciated after other neurophysiologists replicated what was called the "Berger rhythm" in 1934.

Berger is shown together with the first tracing of the alpha rhythm published, in his second report of 1930. The record of the alpha rhythm has been multiplied and is above those for the heart rate and time base: "At the top one sees the electroencephalogram recorded with the double-coil galvanometer; in the middle the electrocardiogram, and at the bottom, time is indicated in tenths of a second. . . . One sees very clearly how in the electroencephalogram the larger waves, the waves of first order, appear besides the smaller ones, the waves of second order. . . . For the sake of brevity I shall subsequently designate the waves of the first order as alpha waves =α-w, the waves of the second order as beta waves =β-w, just as I shall use 'E.E.G.' as the abbreviation for electroencephalogram and 'E.C.G.' for the electrocardiogram."

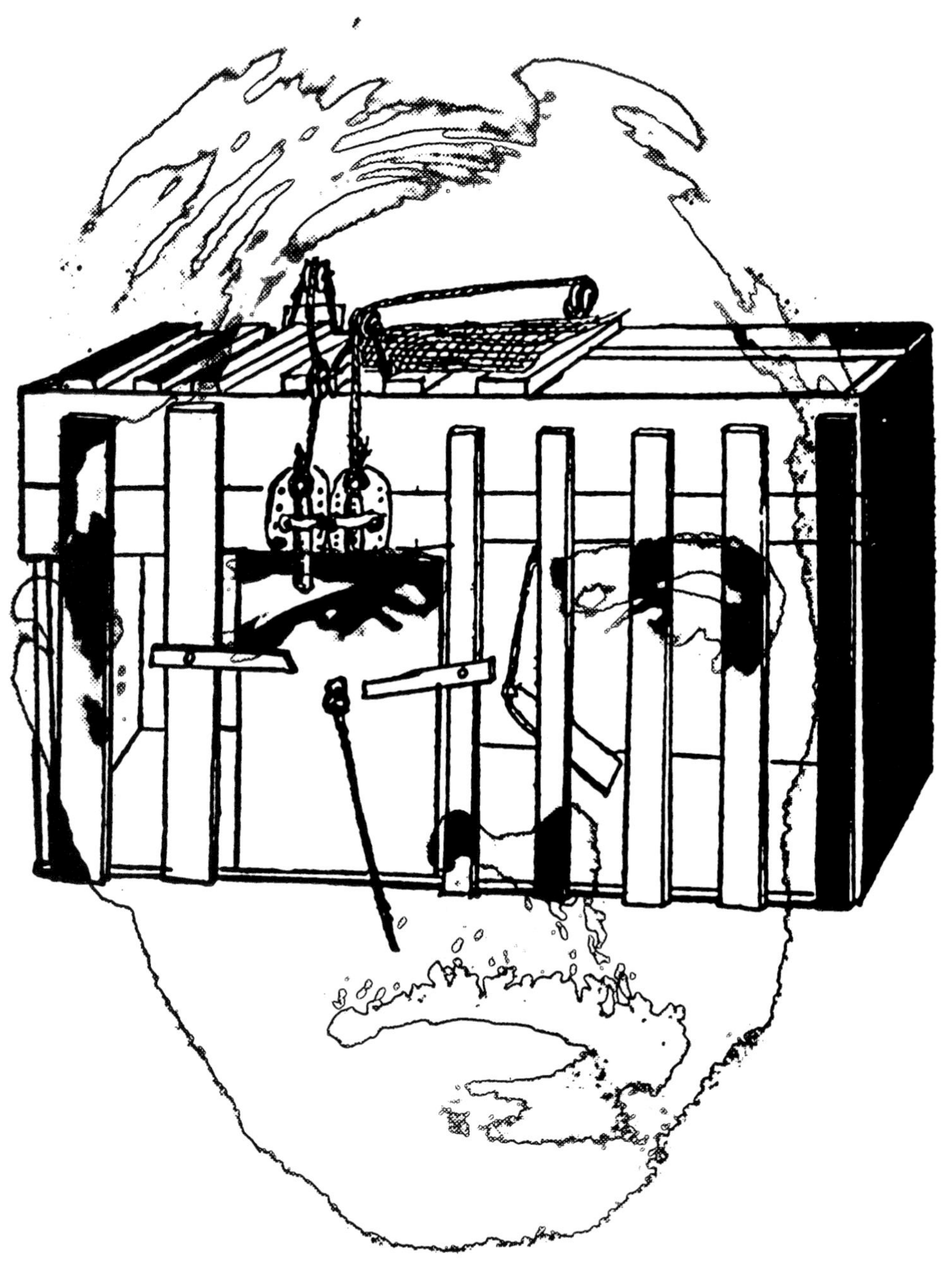

Portrait after a frontispiece photograph in: Thorndike, E. L. 1949. *Selected Writings from a Connectionist's Psychology.* New York: Appleton-Century-Crofts.

Motif after a figure in: Thorndike, E. L. 1898. Animal intelligence. An experimental study of the associate processes in animals. *Psychological Review. Monograph Supplement 2.* No. 4 (Whole No. 8).

Puzzle Box

Edward Lee Thorndike (1874–1949) applied Lloyd Morgan's canon to laboratory studies of animal learning. He started his animal experiments while at Harvard and, lacking a laboratory, James made space available in the basement of the house in which he boarded. His monograph *Animal Intelligence* (1898) was his doctoral thesis. In it he derided the fact that "most of the books do not give us a psychology, but rather a *eulogy,* of animals. They have all been about animal *intelligence,* never about animal *stupidity.*" In order to make good this want, "experiment must be substituted for observation and the collection of anecdotes. . . . After considerable preliminary observation of animals' behavior under various conditions, I chose for my general method one which . . . put animals when hungry in enclosures from which they could escape by some simple act, such as pulling at a loop of a cord, pressing a lever, or stepping on a platform." His subjects were cats and they initially displayed random behavior, making the appropriate response for release by chance. Thorndike measured how long it took for them to escape on each trial and plotted their learning curves. On the basis of this work he formulated several general principles of learning. The law of effect stated that responses followed by satisfaction to the animal are likely to recur, whereas those followed by discomfort are less likely; the strength of connections (associations) depended on the degree of satisfaction or discomfort. The law of exercise asserted that repeated responses strengthen associations. Thorndike revised or renounced these laws in 1929, arguing that discomfort (punishment) did not weaken associations and that associations were not strengthened by practice alone. Nonetheless, most subsequent learning theories have built upon his laws, and he is generally seen as a bridge between the functionalists and the behaviorists.

Thorndike was quick to put his principles to practice in an educational setting. With Woodworth in 1901, he demonstrated that training in formal subjects, like Latin, did not transfer to other subjects. His subsequent research was directed mainly toward human learning and he wrote many books on educational psychology. He took intelligence to be inherited, as Galton had argued, and his interpretations of it were at variance with those of Spearman; Thorndike considered that it was made up of a set of specific aptitudes. He also shared with Galton a penchant for measurement. He carried out a count of the frequency of words in written English that proved a boon to later research on verbal learning.

Thorndike was born in Williamsburg, Massachusetts and received degrees from Wesleyan College, Harvard, and Columbia. Almost all his academic career was spent at Columbia Teachers College. He was president of the American Psychological Association in 1912. He is shown partially enclosed in the puzzle box he designed.

Portrait after a photograph in: Runes, D. G. 1959. *Pictorial History of Philosophy.* New York: Philosophical Library.

Yin-Jung

Carl Gustav Jung (1875–1961) established an analytic psychology that emphasized the self—the achievement of harmony among the various strands of personality. He displayed an early ambivalence in his approach to psychology: on the one hand, he developed a method of determining emotionality from associative reaction times to words (as had Wertheimer earlier); on the other, he studied occult phenomena and alchemy. Jung was closely associated with Freud between 1907 and 1912, but thereafter Jung developed his analytic psychology, concentrating upon individual differences in personality and cross-cultural comparisons. His system became increasingly complex and amorphous, in contrast to Freud's more constrained model of personality. Jung's approach to individual differences focused on the resolution of contrasting attributes, like extroversion and introversion (terms he introduced). Personality was taken to be comprised of the persona (the socialized self), the anima or animus (characteristics of the opposite sex of which the individual is unaware), and the shadow (the instincts). The integration of these components defines the self, which undergoes changes throughout life, particularly in middle age. Reality for Jung was psychical and the unconscious involved personal and collective components. Dreams provided an avenue into both aspects of the unconscious, either through underdeveloped features of the shadow or through the archetypal themes expressed. "The symbols of the process of individuation that appear in dreams are images of an archetypal nature which depict the centralizing process or the production of a new centre of personality." It was the emphasis on the collective unconscious, archetypes, and synchronicity that placed Jung more firmly in the Romantic tradition than Freud.

Jung was born in Thurgovia, Switzerland, and spent his life in his native land. He studied medicine at the University of Basel, and subsequently practiced psychiatry at the Burghölzli hospital in Zurich under Bleuler. He worked with Janet before becoming a colleague of Freud; he was seen by the latter as his successor, and they visited America together in 1909. Jung was the first president of the International Psychoanalytic Association. The collaboration ceased in 1914, when their disparate views on the importance of psychosexuality led to a bitter split. Following the schism Jung entered a depression and sought to express his feelings in paintings. Initially they were representational but became increasingly abstract—often in the form of circular, quartered designs. He was later struck by the similarity of his paintings to the symbols and myths used in all human cultures. In particular, the mandala was treated as a symbol of total unity. Even his graphical model of mind consisted of concentric circles, with sensations in the outermost annulus, progressing centripetally through thinking, feeling, intuition, and memory to the central core of the personal unconscious.

Jung studied comparative religion and the occult throughout his life, and he placed particular significance on visual symbols, like the mandala, used in different cultures. These included yin-yang—representing the union of opposites—and Jung is shown within a variant of this symbol made up of concentric circles.

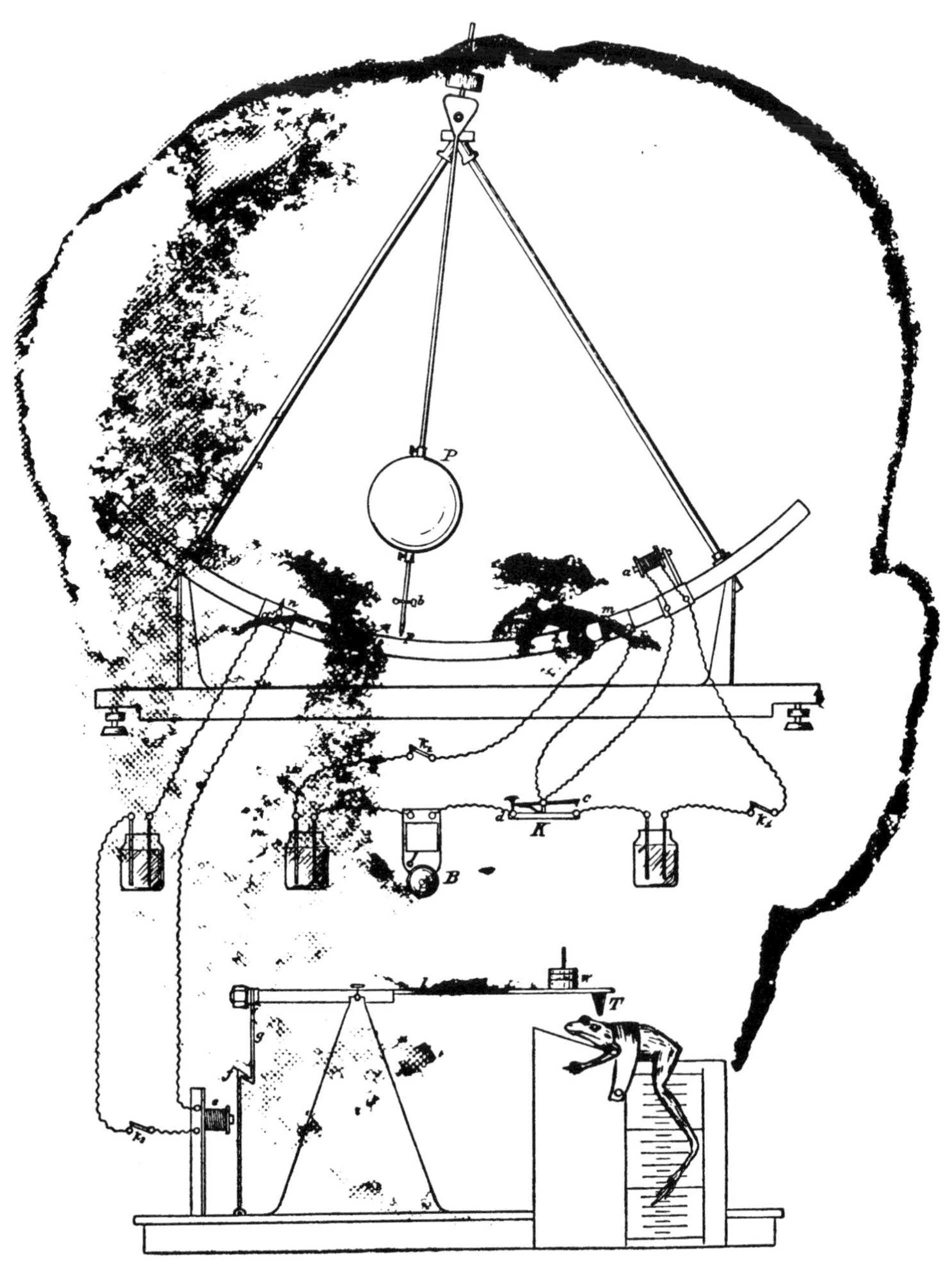

Portrait after a photograph in: Murchison, C., ed. 1932. *A History of Psychology in Autobiography,* Vol. 2. Worcester, Mass.: Clark University Press.

Motif after a figure in: Yerkes, R. M. 1906. The mutual relations of stimuli in the frog *Rana clamata* Daudin. In *Harvard Psychological Studies,* Vol. 2. H. Münsterberg, ed. Boston: Houghton Mifflin, pp. 545-574.

Psychobiologist

Robert Mearns Yerkes (1876–1956) studied learning in a wide variety of animals, from earthworm to ape, and he established the first primate laboratory. His interest in animal behavior was stimulated by Darwin's studies of learning in the earthworm. Although his experimental research was concerned with comparative psychology he preferred to be called a psychobiologist: "Always my research has been more nearly physiological then psychological, for I have dealt with problems of behavior, not with experience." Despite this assertion he never accepted Watson's behaviorism, remaining more closely tied to Titchener's structuralism. Yerkes displayed great ingenuity in the design of apparatus. He wrote that his work was: "characterized rather by ingenuity and originality than by technical skill and mechanical gift. Theoretically, method conditions progress." He constructed multiple-choice apparatus for studying discrimination in chimpanzees, and much of his later research was concerned with primate behavior. His early work on the influence of motivation on learning resulted in the Yerkes-Dodson law, which states that high levels of motivation assist performance on simple tasks but retard performance on difficult tasks. This relationship has continued to be used widely in studying the effects of arousal on performance.

Yerkes was born in Breadysville, Pennsylvania and obtained a doctorate in psychology from Harvard University under Münsterberg. Yerkes remained at Harvard until 1917, during which time he was friendly with Thorndike and collaborated with Watson. He was president of the American Psychological Association in 1917 and joined the army in that year to assist the war effort. He was involved in developing intelligence tests for recruits—the *Army Alpha* and *Army Beta,* for literate and illiterate soldiers, respectively. They were administered to almost two million recruits by the end of World War I, but they were not of much utility in selection. Yerkes did propose new methods of scoring intelligence tests, and, on the basis of results from the army tests, he was a keen advocate of eugenics. In 1924 he resumed an academic career at Yale University, and founded and directed primate laboratories, initially at New Haven, and later at Orange Park, Florida.

Yerkes is portrayed in the context of apparatus he designed for auditory-tactual reinforcement of the frog. The pendulum closed first one switch, which resulted in the delivery of an auditory stimulus, and then a second switch, which delivered a tactile stimulus. Although he conducted experiments with many species, he did not derive any general relationship linking learning to level in the phylogenetic scale. However, by the first decade of the twentieth century the pendulum of psychology had swung toward America. The introspective method was proving to be unreliable and the subject matter of psychology was shifting toward animal learning rather than human consciousness.

Portrait after a photograph in: Schultz, D. P., and S. E. Schultz. 1987. *A History of Modern Psychology,* ed. 4. San Diego: Harcourt Brace Jovanovich.

Behaviorist

John Broadus Watson (1878–1958) redefined psychology as the study of behavior, and he turned his back on its short history as the study of conscious experience. Watson avoided working with human subjects because he considered that introspection was unreliable and an unsuitable method on which to base any science, and so established the rat and the maze as the subjects for psychology. His ideas nurtured into a *Psychological Review* article (1913) in which he set out the behaviorist manifesto: "Psychology as the behaviorist views it is a purely objective experimental branch of natural science. Its theoretical goal is the prediction and control of behavior. Introspection forms no essential part of its methods, nor is the scientific value of its data dependent upon the readiness with which they lend themselves to interpretation in terms of consciousness." In the following year Watson learned about Pavlov's research on conditioning, and made it one of the cornerstones of behaviorist learning theory. Psychology was reduced to measuring stimuli (S) and predicting the responses (R) that they elicited. This position is stated with stark clarity in Watson's *Behaviorism* (1924): throughout the book there are simple S . . . R diagrams for interpreting tasks like the link between applying electric shock and hand withdrawal, as well as their elaboration to situations like Prohibition as S with R too complicated to predict, or truthfulness as R with S unknown! His views were both radical and initially unpopular, but they were propagated with a religious fervor. He was disparaging of his critics and was treated in like manner. In 1924 McDougall and Watson engaged in a public debate on their opposing views of psychology; McDougall's acerbic tongue and arrogant tone won the battle but lost the war. He said that behaviorism attracted those who liked whatever was bizarre and outrageous and that Watson marketed it like a brand of cigarettes.

Watson was born in Greenville, South Carolina. He received his doctorate in psychology for research on animal education from the University of Chicago, and he remained there until 1908. He was appointed professor of psychology at Johns Hopkins at the age of 30, and conducted his most significant research there. He was elected president of the American Psychological Association in 1914. He was forced to resign from Johns Hopkins in 1920 over a scandal surrounding his divorce. He then embarked on a successful career in advertising, but continued writing and reporting on psychological issues to a popular audience.

Watson's radical behaviorism sought to predict all behavior in terms of S . . . R bonds. In rejecting introspection as the legacy of Wundt, he did retain the associative theory with which structuralism was bound. While his theory was not lasting, the methodological behaviorism on which it was based has permeated the whole of psychology. Watson is represented in the context of sequences of S . . . R bonds, produced with the mechanical precision of a typewriter.

Portrait after a photograph in: Runes, D. G. 1959. *Pictorial History of Philosophy.* New York: Philosophical Library.

Good Gestalt I

Max Wertheimer (1880–1943) redefined psychology as the study of configurations or *Gestalten.* Like Watson and at about the same time, he rejected Wundt's psychology, but for different reasons: he opposed Wundt's atomism, considering that complex percepts could not be reduced to simple sensory elements. Gestalt psychology had its origins in perception but its ambit encompassed the whole of psychology. Its precursors were to be found in Kant's innate categories of space and time, in Mach's emphasis on the analysis of experience, and in Brentano's holistic mental acts. Earlier, Ehrenfels had shown that the perception of a musical tune was not dependent on the precise notes played as long as the Gestalt qualities—the relations between the parts—were retained. Wertheimer extended this approach with a series of experiments on apparent movement (the phi phenomenon), initially using Plateau's phenakistoscope, and later a tachistoscope. It was the inability to distinguish between real and apparent motion that was taken as damning of any approach that explained perception in terms of its sensations. Perception was holistic rather than atomistic. "There are wholes, the behavior of which is not determined by that of their individual elements, but where the part-processes are themselves determined by the intrinsic nature of the whole. It is the hope of Gestalt theory to determine the nature of such wholes." Not only was it said that the whole is more than its parts, but the perception of the whole is prior to that of its parts. Publication of the work on the phi phenomenon, in 1912, is taken as the origin of a new movement called Gestalt psychology. It was in the mainstream of continental philosophy and used the methods of phenomenology as adumbrated by Goethe, Purkinje, and Hering. Gestalt psychology was principally concerned with perception, and a range of robust demonstrations was devised to support its holistic nature. Wertheimer described many principles of perceptual organization, of which proximity, similarity, symmetry, and good continuation were the principal ones. These were illustrated with sets of figures consisting of filled and open dots arranged in patterns which demonstrated the grouping principles. Much of the attraction of Gestalt psychology lay in the power of its perceptual demonstrations. Later Wertheimer applied a similar approach to the study of creativity in his *Productive Thinking* (1945).

Wertheimer was born in Prague. He studied philosophy at the University of Prague, and psychology at the University of Berlin, where he met Koffka and Köhler. He obtained his doctorate from the University of Würzburg for his thesis on lie detection by means of word association. After returning to Berlin, he was called to the chair of psychology at the University of Frankfurt, but left for America in 1933 and took a position at the New School for Social Research.

Some of the grouping principles are in operation in the pattern of filled and open dots here, which portrays Wertheimer. It could be said that the holes are different from some of the parts!

Portrait after a photograph in: Hilgard, E. R. 1987. *Psychology in America. A Historical Survey.* San Diego: Harcourt Brace Jovanovich.

Motif after action photographs in: Gesell, A. 1925. *The Mental Growth of the Pre-school Child. A Psychological Outline of Normal Development from Birth to the Sixth Year, Including a System of Developmental Diagnosis.* New York: Macmillan.

Child Psychologist

Arnold Lucius Gesell (1880–1961) observed and recorded the growth and development of normal preschool children. "Development is conditioned in a basic and almost curious manner by the factor of time. Only in mythology does a fully formed, fully fledged creature spring from the forehead of a god. In nature time is necessary for the production of an organism. Little as we know about the phenomenon of development, it appears that the relation between time units, developmental life cycles, and periodicities is of a lawful character." He sought to determine these laws and he published many age norms of child development. Among his many books were *The Mental Growth of the Pre-school Child* (1925), *An Atlas of Infant Behavior* (1934), and *The First Five Years of Life* (1940). Gesell listed the different procedures employed to study development: observational and biographical methods, questionnaires, experiments, and psychometrics. He adopted the first and his observations were under controlled laboratory conditions as well as in less constrained clinical settings. In the laboratory he utilized motion pictures, which could subsequently be analyzed frame by frame. Indeed, he made an analogy of human development with the frames of a film: both can be stopped at a particular instant in order to describe what is happening. Gesell carried out some twin studies that were taken to support the natural course of growth over that of learning. When one twin was taught a task before the other, both later achieved the same level of performance. He viewed maturation as the most powerful force operating on children, and one that is principally influenced by their constitution rather than their environment. Thus, his was a passive approach to change in contrast to the more adaptable outlook of Watson with the latter's emphasis on learning and environmental determinism. Gesell suggested that there were parallels between physical and mental growth: "Mental development is dynamic and elusive but it is essentially no more elusive than physical development and, just as the science of embryology is clarifying the phenomena of physical growth through countless sectional studies, so may genetic psychology attain an insight into the obscure developmental mechanics of the growth of behavior."

Gesell was born in Alma, Wisconsin, and attended the University of Wisconsin. He studied for his doctorate in psychology under Hall at Clark University, where his interests in maturation were fostered, and went on to obtain qualifications in medicine from Yale. He established and directed the Yale Psychological Clinic in 1911.

Gesell's portrait is combined with a series of photographs of a one-month-old child who is (in successive frames) yawning, sleeping, awake, finger fanning, toe fanning, and engaging in reflex holding. As was his wont, Gesell intruded minimally on the behavior he observed.

Portraits after a photograph in: *The National Cyclopedia of American Biography*, Vol. 44. New York: White, 1962.

Motifs after figures in: Ittelson, W. H. 1952. *The Ames Demonstrations in Perception. A Guide to Their Construction and Use*. Princeton, N.J.: Princeton University Press.

Ames' Ruminations

Adelbert Ames (1880–1955) devised some intriguing perceptual demonstrations that pitted assumptions about the world against the pattern of stimulation. For example, the Ames room consists of a non-rectangular (trapezoidal) space; the floor and ceiling are inclined to the horizontal and the facing wall is higher and farther away at one side than the other, but it is constructed in such a way that it appears rectangular when viewed with one eye through a peephole. Perceptual problems arise when people stand in the corners of the room or look through the windows. He also produced dynamic demonstrations, like the trapezoidal window: rotation of the window results in its apparent oscillation, and any object attached to it appears to rotate "through" the window frame. Ames's approach was called transactional functionalism: perception was treated as a transaction between the individual's assumptions about the world, based on past experience, and the stimulation at the eye. Essentially, the static demonstrations are inversions of the issues addressed by painters in perspective: observation of the environment with one eye from a fixed station point is multiply ambiguous. The painters captured this ambiguity in two dimensions, whereas Ames achieved it in three dimensions. That is, he arranged for the optical projection from one three-dimensional object to be equivalent to another. Ames's theory is a modern version of empiricism and the demonstrations work best with one eye. He did make some discoveries about binocular vision and the condition of aniseikonia was first described by him: it refers to the magnification of the image in one eye with respect to the other along a single axis. Wearing aniseikonic lenses results in specific distortions of space, particularly when no monocular cues for depth are available, as in his leaf room.

Ames was born in Lowell, Massachusetts. He graduated from Harvard Law School in 1906, but his interests were in art rather than advocacy. He moved to Paris with the intention of becoming a neo-Impressionist painter, and in the process realized that a thorough understanding of visual optics was a necessary prerequisite. He "undertook to determine scientifically the characteristics of the images of those objects upon which the eye is not focused in the belief that an intellectual conception of the characteristics of such images would help in the visual recognition and analysis of them, and thus be an aid in the technique of art." On his return to America he studied physiological optics at Clark University. His research focused initially on optical aberrations, and broadened into a study of visual distortions. He constructed a variety of demonstrations at the Dartmouth Eye Institute.

Ames is shown at different sizes in a rectangular representation of his trapezoidal room; the smaller portrait on the left corresponds to the more distant distorted window. He is also portrayed passing through a trapezoidal window.

Portrait after a photograph in: Trahair, R.S. 1984. *The Humanist Temper: The Life and Work of Elton Mayo.* New Brunswick, N.J.: Transaction Books.

Motif after a photograph in: Blum, M. L., and J. C. Naylor. 1968. *Industrial Psychology. Its Theoretical and Social Foundations.* New York: Harper & Row.

The Hawthorne Effect

Elton George Mayo (1880–1949) found that the productivity of industrial workers was dependent upon the social rather than the physical conditions prevailing. Despite Münsterberg's optimistic outlook for industrial psychology, most work practices in the 1920s were determined by considerations of human movement efficiency, like the time-study approach introduced by Frederick Winslow Taylor (1856–1915), and by an analysis of the worker as an isolated unit. The adequacy of these considerations were put to the test in the Hawthorne plant of the Western Electric Company, near Chicago. The first studies were concerned with the effects of illumination on inspecting and assembling relays. Increasing the light levels increased productivity in an experimental group, but the output of the control group increased, too! The experimental group continued performing better with decreases in illumination almost to the level of moonlight. The essence of the Hawthorne effect, which applies generally to experimental procedures, is that any intervention can influence behavior. Directing attention to people during experiments in social settings can itself result in changing their behavior. This effect lies at the heart of using placebo controls in medical research, which generally result in improvements in patients' health. It is a necessary control in social psychological experiments in order to avoid reaching spurious conclusions.

The second phase of the Hawthorne study, which lasted for five years, monitored productivity with changes in hours worked per week, and with the introduction of rest pauses of varying duration. The workers were observed throughout, were informed about the changes, and were encouraged to comment on the procedures. Productivity improved with most of the schemes; however, returning to the original conditions increased productivity to its highest level ever. On the basis of these results and interviews Mayo proposed a social rather than engineering interpretation. He argued that assigning workers to a specially designed test room enhanced their identity as a group, and that work was a social activity that depended on the formation of such informal groups. Mayo contrasted the "rabble hypothesis," which was rather like Hobbes's analysis of human nature, with his own theory of work in which "the workers have—whether aware of it or not—formed themselves into a group with appropriate customs, duties, routines, even rituals."

Mayo was born in Adelaide, Australia. He studied psychology at the universities of Queensland and South Australia before moving to the United States in 1922. He became professor of industrial research at the Harvard Business School. The Hawthorne studies were initiated before Mayo was involved, but he provided the voice for the interpretation of the results with his book *The Human Problems of an Industrial Civilization* (1933). Mayo is depicted observing workers in the relay assembly test room which was specially constructed for the Hawthorne studies.

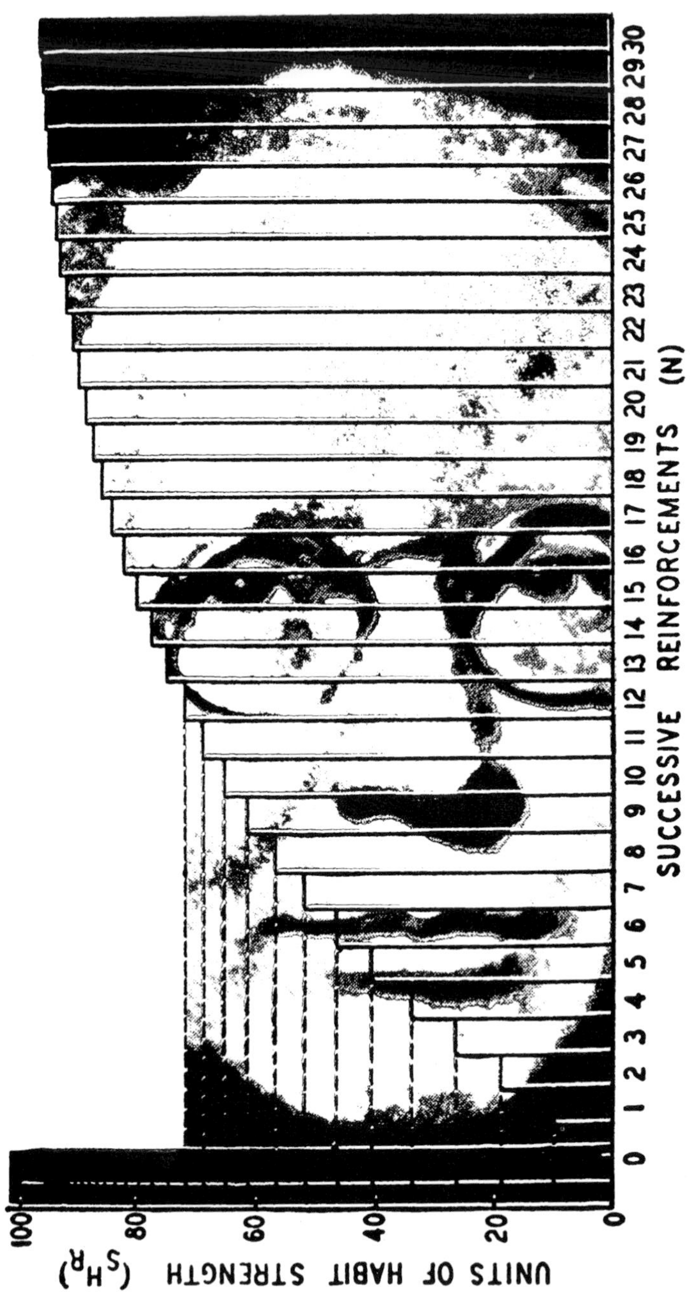

Portrait after a frontispiece photograph in: Boring, E. G., H. Werner, H. S. Langfeld, and R. M. Yerkes, eds. 1952. *A History of Psychology in Autobiography,* Vol. 4. New York: Russell & Russell.

Motif after a learning curve in: Hull, C. L. 1943. *Principles of Behavior. An Introduction to Behavior Theory.* New York: Appleton-Century.

Habit Strength

Clark Leonard Hull (1884–1952) was a neobehaviorist who proposed "a behaviorism mainly concerned with the determination of quantitative laws of behavior and their deductive systematization." Learning was conceived as dependent on drive reduction: biological needs, like hunger, increased in tension according to the state of deprivation (which could be measured in terms of the hours since last eating). The strength of habits was increased by their association with drive reduction. The learning curve showed how habit strength increased with successive reinforcements. In his terms, the likelihood that a stimulus trace would evoke an associated response increased as a positive growth function of the number of trials.

Hull's learning experiments were systematic and followed the hypothetico-deductive method: formulating experimentally testable hypotheses and testing them rigorously. He applied Tolman's concept of intervening variables between stimulus and response, and these were linked operationally to objective measures; the system was formulated as a set of postulates and theorems. The emphasis on drive reduction stated in *Principles of Behavior* (1943) was moderated in favor of secondary reinforcement in *A Behavior System* (1952). Hull saw this analysis of learning extending to more complex, even social, behavior: "It seems incredible that nature would create one set of primary sensory-motor laws for the mediation of individual behavior and another set for the mediation of group behavior. Presumably, then, the laws which are derived for social behavior will be based for the most part on the same postulates as those which form the basis of individual behavior."

Hull was born near Akron, New York, and moved to Michigan in his infancy. He developed an early interest in applied psychology, perhaps as a consequence of his initial training as an engineer. He received his doctorate in psychology from the University of Wisconsin, and remained there for a decade before moving to Harvard and then to Yale. He was president of the American Psychological Association in 1936. It was at Yale that his interests changed from hypnotism and suggestibility to learning, and he became a theorist in the tradition of Watson. He turned toward behaviorism in part as a reaction to Koffka's advocacy of Gestalt theory and partly by being impressed with reading the translation of Pavlov's experiments. He commenced with his own studies on human learning before adopting the white rat as his subject.

Hull's reductionist theory was so constrained by definitional precision that it was difficult to derive any general principles from it. The glossaries of symbols employed in his system extended from *A* = amplitude or intensity of a reaction to *Z* = absolute zero of reaction potential, through reactive inhibition and stimulus-intensity dynamism. Hence, his portrayal sealed within the hermeneutic world of his learning curve.

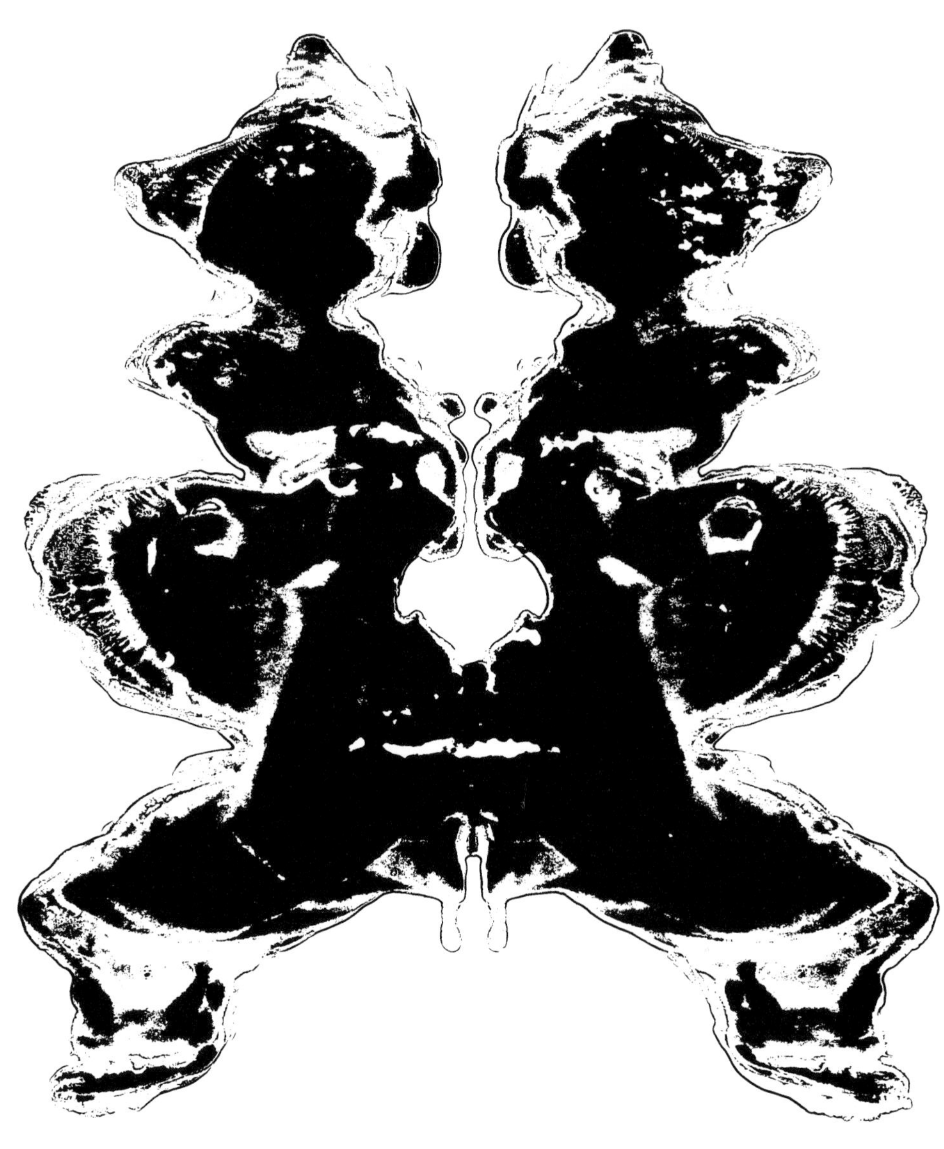

Portrait after a photograph in: Cohen, J. 1969. *Personality Assessment.* Chicago: Rand McNally.

Inkblots

Hermann Rorschach (1884–1922) used inkblots to gain indirect access to personality types. Rather than associating freely as in psychoanalysis, the associations were focused by nonspecific or accidental forms: "The production of such accidental forms is very simple: a few large ink blots are thrown on a piece of paper, the paper folded, and the ink spread between the two halves of the sheet." The Rorschach test, published in 1921 as *Psychodiagnostik,* consists of ten inkblots, half of which are colored. The use of inkblots was by no means new. They were employed by the physician Justinus Kerner (1786–1862) to provide inspiration for his poetry; he appreciated the difficulty of avoiding projecting meaning into the inkblots, but he did not pursue the individual differences of such projections. Binet did suggest that inkblots could be used to assess personality, but it was left to Rorschach to develop an inkblot test for psychodiagnostic purposes. The stimuli are presented to subjects in a set order and their descriptions are noted. Scoring is in terms of how the various parts of the patterns are described rather than imaginative projections—to the form of the responses rather than their content. Particular emphasis is placed on responses to color and to movement, to the number of associations, and to descriptions relating to the whole inkblot and parts of it. The vagaries of scoring the tests exercised those who used it considerably, and complicated schemes were devised that required extensive training by those who administered the test.

The Rorschach test was but one of a variety of projective tests that were phenomenally popular in the middle decades of the century. Another, the Thematic Apperception Test (TAT), introduced in 1935, utilized twenty drawings concerning which subjects told a story. Such tests were a reaction to the self-report inventories, of the type developed by Woodworth, and that led to the Minnesota Multiphasic Personality Inventory (MMPI). The inventories might not have had lofty aims as projective tests, but they were more amenable to scoring and analysis. The popularity of projective tests waned from the 1960s, in part because of the difficulties of validating them, and in part because they did not place sufficient emphasis on the social determinants of the responses.

Rorschach was born in Zurich. He studied medicine at the universities of Berlin and Bonn, and graduated from the University of Zurich. He worked with Bleuler, and was influenced by Freud's psychoanalytic theory and by Jung's typology: personality was described in terms of introversive and extratensive types, and the aim of development was to reach some state of "ambiequality." Rorschach commenced his investigations of inkblots in 1911; initially he compared word associations in children to responses to inkblots. His psychodiagnostic stimuli reflect the symmetry of the human face, hence this specially constructed inkblot reflects the symmetry of Rorschach's portrait, although it will require a degree of projection on behalf of the observer to see him.

Portrait after a photograph in: Murchison, C., ed. 1926. *Psychologies of 1925.* Worcester, Mass.: Clark University Press.

Good Gestalt II

Kurt Koffka (1886–1941) was the second member of the Gestalt triumvirate. He served as a subject in Wertheimer's experiments on the phi phenomenon, which were conducted in Frankfurt in 1910. After being apprised of their significance Koffka became the leading advocate of the Gestalt approach. He used Gestalt concepts in studies of development and thinking, and in 1922 his *Psychological Bulletin* paper entitled "Perception: An Introduction to Gestalt-theorie" made American psychologists aware of the new movement and he made several visits to the United States to lecture on Gestalt psychology. The article gave the impression that Gestalt psychology was concerned only with perception, and in this area he did pose the fundamental question, "Why do things look as they do?" He also emphasized that visual perception is three-dimensional and that it is in terms of the object properties (the distal stimulus) rather than those at the receptor surface (the proximal stimulus).

Koffka's *The Growth of Mind* (1924) broadened the scope of Gestalt psychology and made it accessible to educators. In it he attacked atomistic approaches to development: "Is it not possible that phenomena, such as 'friendliness' and 'unfriendliness' are very primitive—even more so than the visual impression of a 'blue spot'? However absurd this possibility may seem to a psychologist who regards all consciousness as being ultimately made up of elements, it ceases to be absurd if we bear in mind that all psychological phenomena stand in closest relation to objective behavior." Koffka's *Principles of Gestalt Psychology* (1935) was the most general statement of its aims: "Science will find gestalten of different rank in different realms, but we claim that every gestalt has order and meaning, of however low or high degree, and that for a gestalt quantity and quality are the same." He saw the growing fragmentation of psychology in America and tried to halt it with his broadly based *Principles,* but its impact turned out to be rather limited. He was also one of the founders of the *Psychologische Forschung,* in 1921, which became the organ of Gestalt psychology. While Koffka was the most prolific writer of the Gestalt school, he was not as ardent a nativist as his colleagues. His studies of development as well as of perception led him to an interactionist position in which innate and environmental factors converged on one another.

Koffka was born and educated in Berlin. He studied psychology under Carl Stumpf (1848–1936) and had earlier studied philosophy at Edinburgh University. He worked with Wertheimer and Köhler in Frankfurt before obtaining a teaching post at the University of Giessen. He moved to America in 1924 and became professor of psychology at Smith College in 1927.

Koffka's wistful features are represented in a configuration made up of two sets of overlapping open dots. The extraction of his portrait from this field of dots addresses an issue with which he was much concerned, namely, the problem of shape.

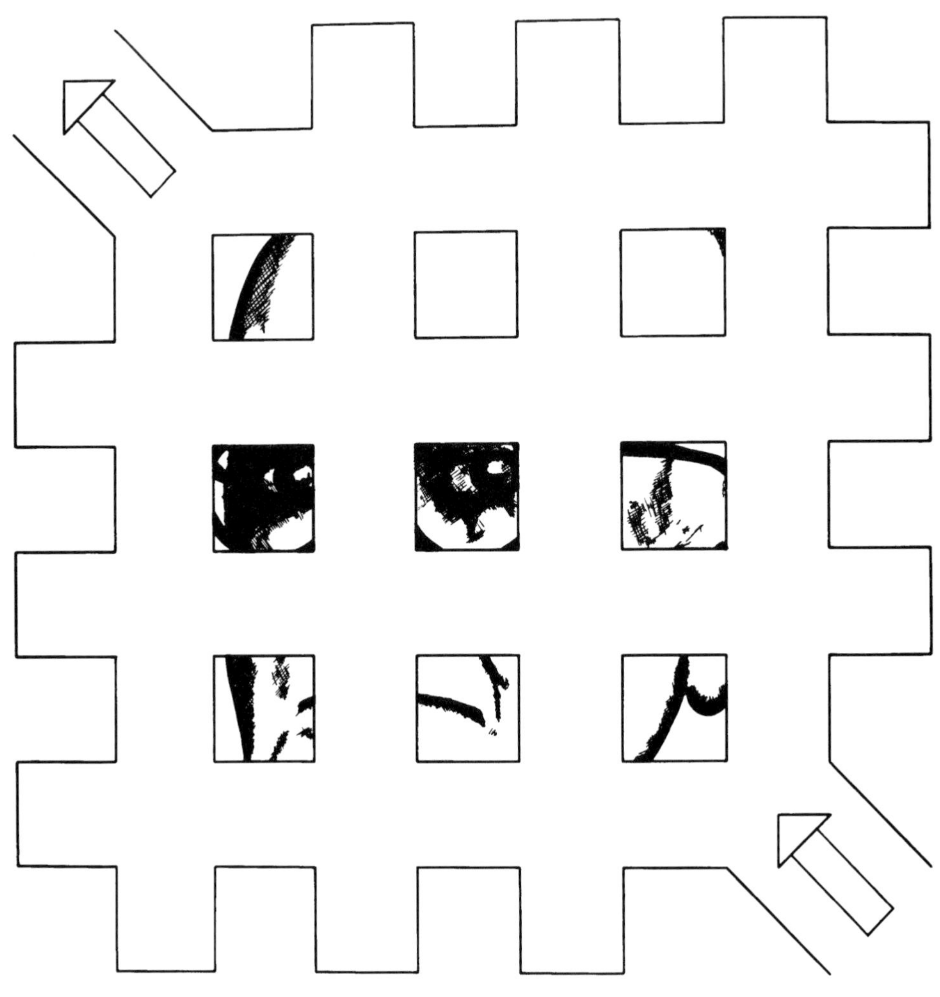

Portrait after a frontispiece photograph in: Boring, E. G., H. Werner, H. S. Langfeld, and R. M. Yerkes, eds. 1952. *A History of Psychology in Autobiography,* Vol. 4. New York: Russell & Russell.

Motif after a maze diagram in: Tolman, E. C. 1949. *Purposive Behavior in Animals and Men.* Berkeley: University of California Press.

Cognitive Mapper

Edward Chace Tolman (1886–1959) introduced cognitive concepts into learning theory. He was attracted to Watson's behaviorism, but rejected the molecular stimulus-response approach to learning; he also rejected Thorndike's law of effect. "Behavior, as such, is a molar phenomenon as contrasted with the molecular phenomena which constitute its underlying physiology. And, as a molar phenomenon, behavior's immediate descriptive properties appear to be those of: getting to or from goal-objects by selecting certain means-objects-routes as against others and by exhibiting specific patterns of commerces with these selected means-objects. . . . Such purposes and cognitions, such docility, are, obviously, functions of the organism as a whole." Thus, he fused more molar Gestalt concepts with the behaviorists' methodological rigor, to fashion a theory of *Purposive Behavior in Animals and Men* (1932). His theory bore many similarities to McDougall's purposive psychology, but he criticized McDougall for being mentalistic. Tolman introduced the concept of intervening variables between experience and behavior, and he tried to define them operationally, but his own theorizing took on an increasingly mentalistic flavor. His system "conceives mental processes as functional variables intervening between stimuli, initiating physiological states, and the general heredity and past training of the organism, on the one hand, and the final resulting responses, on the other." He distinguished between learning and performance on the basis of experiments concerned with latent learning. The white rat could learn features of a maze without any reinforcement, and latent learning "manifests itself as having taken place, the moment a real differential reward is introduced." For Tolman, learning involved sign Gestalten, patterns of which formed a cognitive map, and not sequences of stimulus-response bonds. The idea of a cognitive map derived in large part from experiments on maze learning. A maze of the type shown here offers a wide variety of routes of equal length to the goal: direct access to the exit is blocked by the square obstructions. Rats did not learn a particular route through the maze, but took different routes to reach the goal, thus exhibiting (in Tolman's words) means-end-expectations. He believed that almost everything of importance in psychology could be investigated by experiment and analysis of maze learning in rats.

Tolman was born in West Newton, Massachusetts. He trained as a chemist at Massachusetts Institute of Technology before studying psychology at Harvard and Giessen universities. His early influences were Yerkes and Koffka. Most of his academic life was spent at the University of California, Berkeley, although he was very shoddily treated by that institution because of his support of academic freedom during the 1950s, when McCarthyism was rampant.

Parts of Tolman's portrait are drawn in the square blocks of a maze so that a spatial reconstruction is required in order to recognize the face.

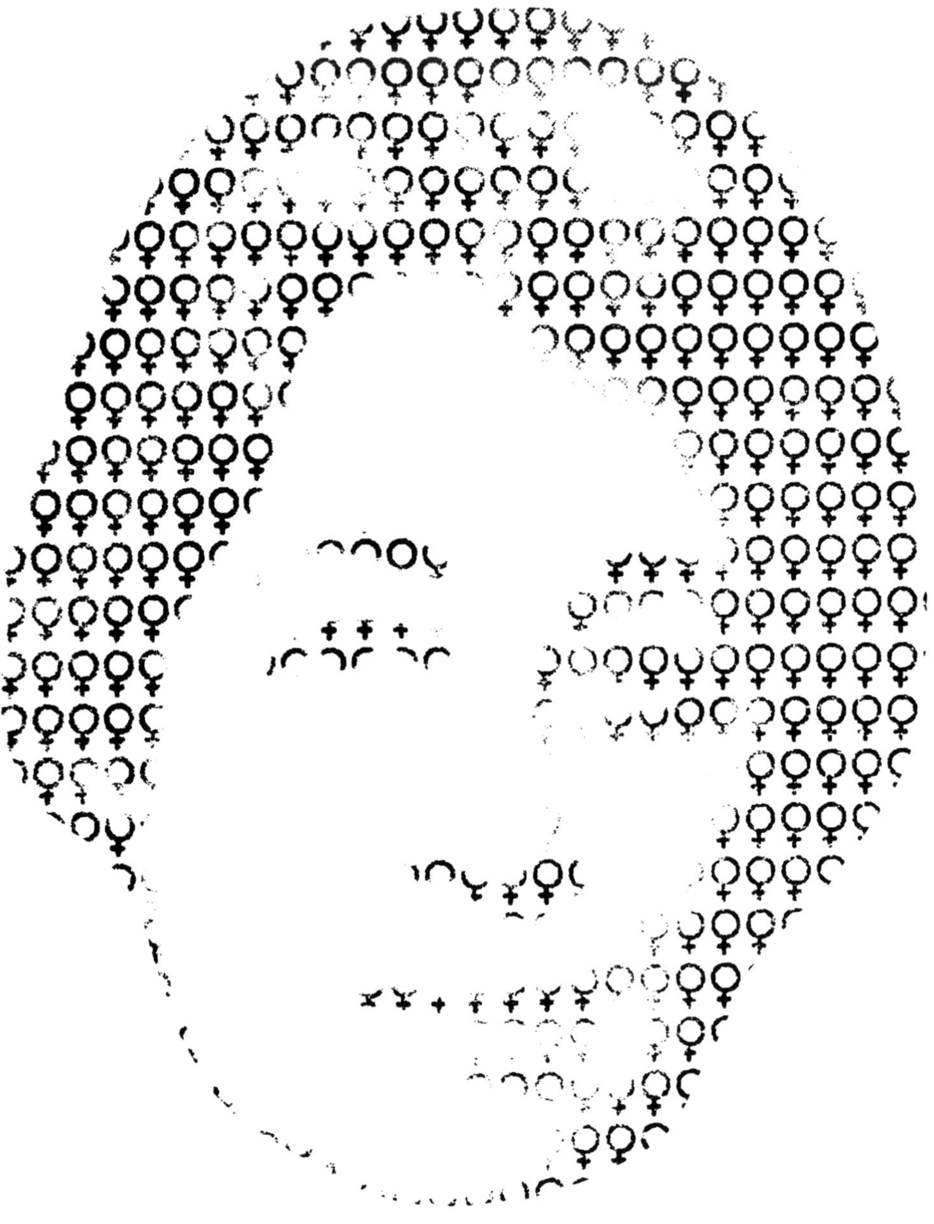

Portrait after a photograph in: Schultz, D. P., and S. E. Schultz. 1987. *A History of Modern Psychology,* ed. 4. San Diego: Harcourt Brace Jovanovich.

New Woman

Leta Stetter Hollingworth (1886–1939) destroyed the shibboleths surrounding sex differences in intellectual performance. At the beginning of the century differences in achievement or eminence between men and women were attributed to the underlying biological variations present in the two sexes. Individual differences between males were thought to be greater than those between females, with evolutionary pressures on males favoring progression and change, whereas those operating on females were taken to favor physical and mental conservatism. The evidence for this derived from the greater proportion of males found in institutions for the insane as well as for the learned. Population distributions for the sex differences were readily drawn in the absence of evidence to support them. Hollingworth conducted experiments to test the hypothesis and found it wanting: test performance for boys was not different from that for girls. She accounted for the differences in achievement in social rather than biological terms, since the tasks performed by the majority of women were not ranked for eminence. "No one knows who is the best housekeeper in America. Eminent housekeepers do not and cannot exist. If we discuss at all the matter of sex differences in achievement, we should consider first the most obvious conditioning factors. Otherwise our discussion is futile scientifically." More recently a superiority of girls on measures of verbal intelligence has been found. Hollingworth also had demonstrated the falseness of another widely held myth, that of "functional periodicity." Psychological performance of women was considered to be impaired during menstruation, but her studies failed to find any such dependence.

Hollingworth developed her interests in individual differences by studying both subnormal and gifted children, and she campaigned for special provisions to be made available for the gifted as they had been for the subnormal. "So far from being irritated by the idiosyncracies of our fellows, we ought to cherish their variety as a thing that makes life worth living. Instead of striving to force all children to learn the same things, at the same time, in the same way, because that would be cheap and convenient, we ought to foster individuality in its socially valuable aspects, so that the charm of human contact may be increased." Her longitudinal studies of gifted children pointed to the problems they encounter, and how they can be ameliorated. Her text on *The Psychology of Adolescence* (1928) replaced Hall's as a standard.

Hollingworth was born near Chadron, Nebraska, and received her doctorate in psychology from Columbia Teachers College, under Thorndike, who supported her research but was uncomfortable with its conclusions. Most of her career was spent at Columbia. She did realize that she was breaking new ground in supporting the cause of women, and she was not blind to the problems: "The essential fact about the New Women is that they differ among themselves, as men do, in work, in play, in virtues, in aspirations and in rewards achieved. They are women, not woman." Hollingworth is portrayed in a symbol of her sex.

'schema'. It is at once too definite and too sketchy. The word is already widely used in controversial psychological writing to refer generally to any rather vaguely outlined theory. It suggests some persistent, but fragmentary, 'form of arrangement', and it does not indicate what is very essential to the whole notion, that the organised mass results of past changes of position and posture are actively *doing* something all the time; are, so to speak, carried along with us, complete, though developing, from moment to moment. Yet it is certainly very difficult to think of any better single descriptive word to cover the facts involved. It would probably be best to speak of 'active, developing patterns'; but the word 'pattern', too, being now very widely and variously employed, has its own difficulties; and it, like 'schema', suggests a greater articulation of detail than is normally found. I think probably the term 'organised setting' approximates most closely and clearly to the notion required. I shall, however, continue to use the term 'schema' when it seems best to do so, but I will attempt to define its application more narrowly.

'Schema' refers to an active organisation of past reactions, or of past experiences, which must always be supposed to be operating in any well-adapted organic response. That is, whenever there is any order or regularity of behaviour, a particular response is possible only because it is related to other similar responses which have been serially organised, yet which operate, not simply as individual members coming one after another, but as a unitary mass. Determination by schemata is the most fundamental of all the ways in which we can be influenced by reactions and experiences which occurred some time in the past. All incoming impulses of a certain kind, or mode, go together to build up an active, organised setting: visual, auditory, various types of cutaneous impulses and the like, at a relatively low level; all the experiences connected by a common interest: in sport, in literature, history, art, science, philosophy and so on, on a higher level. There is not the slightest reason, however, to suppose that each set of incoming impulses, each new group of experiences persists as an isolated member of some passive patchwork. They have to be regarded as constituents of living, momentary settings belonging to the organism, or to whatever parts of the organism are concerned in making a response of a given kind, and not as a number of individual events somehow strung together and stored within the organism.

Portrait after a photograph in: Zangwill, O. L. 1970. Sir Frederic Bartlett (1886–1969). *Quarterly Journal of Experimental Psychology* 22:77–81.

Motif after text in: Bartlett, F. 1932. *Remembering: A Study in Experimental and Social Psychology.* Cambridge, England: Cambridge University Press.

Schema

Frederic Charles Bartlett (1886–1969) approached memory from a cognitive viewpoint. He rejected the use of Ebbinghaus's nonsense syllables and employed meaningful stories or pictures in order to discover how they were remembered and recalled. He developed the method of serial reproduction in which subjects were presented with stories and then recalled them at intervals. He found that unfamiliar material was selectively recalled according to the past experiences of the subject. He referred to this as an "effort after meaning" and used the concept of schema to reflect the organization of memory, as is shown in the text bearing his portrait. His research on memory was presented in *Remembering: A Study in Experimental and Social Psychology* (1932), and he concluded that "Remembering is not the re-excitation of innumerable fixed, lifeless, and fragmentary traces. It is an imaginative reconstruction, or construction, built out of the relation of our attitude toward a whole active mass of past experience." The neurologist Henry Head (1861–1940) had introduced the concept of schema in the context of his research with aphasic patients; it referred to a labile internal representation of past experiences. Bartlett rejected associationist models of memory and his cognitive theory provided a middle road between the molecular behaviorists and molar Gestaltists. He can be seen as ushering in the cognitive revolution that was eventually to replace behaviorism, although his work was neglected in America until the 1950s. Bartlett analyzed perception and thought as skilled activities, and he related most cognitive functions to tasks in the real world, seeing little distinction between experimental and applied psychology. "The essential requirement of any performance that can be called skilled becomes much more plain if we look at a few actual instances. The player in a quick ball game; the operator, engaged at his work bench, directing his machine, and using his tools; the surgeon conducting an operation; the physician arriving at a clinical decision—in all these instances and in innumerable others that could just as well be used, there is a continuing flow from signals occurring outside the performer and interpreted by him to actions carried out. . . . From beginning to end the signals and their related actions form a series, not simply a succession."

Bartlett was born in Stow-on-the-Wold, Gloucestershire. He obtained degrees from the universities of London and then Cambridge, where he became the first professor of experimental psychology in 1931. His main influences were the psychological philosopher James Ward (1843–1925) and the anthropologist William Halse Rivers (1864–1922), who together founded the *British Journal of Psychology* in 1904; Bartlett was the editor from 1924 to 1948. Bartlett's influence on British psychology was enormous, not only in terms of providing it with a cognitive orientation but also in training those who were to direct it, for psychology departments came late to the conservative academic institutions of Britain.

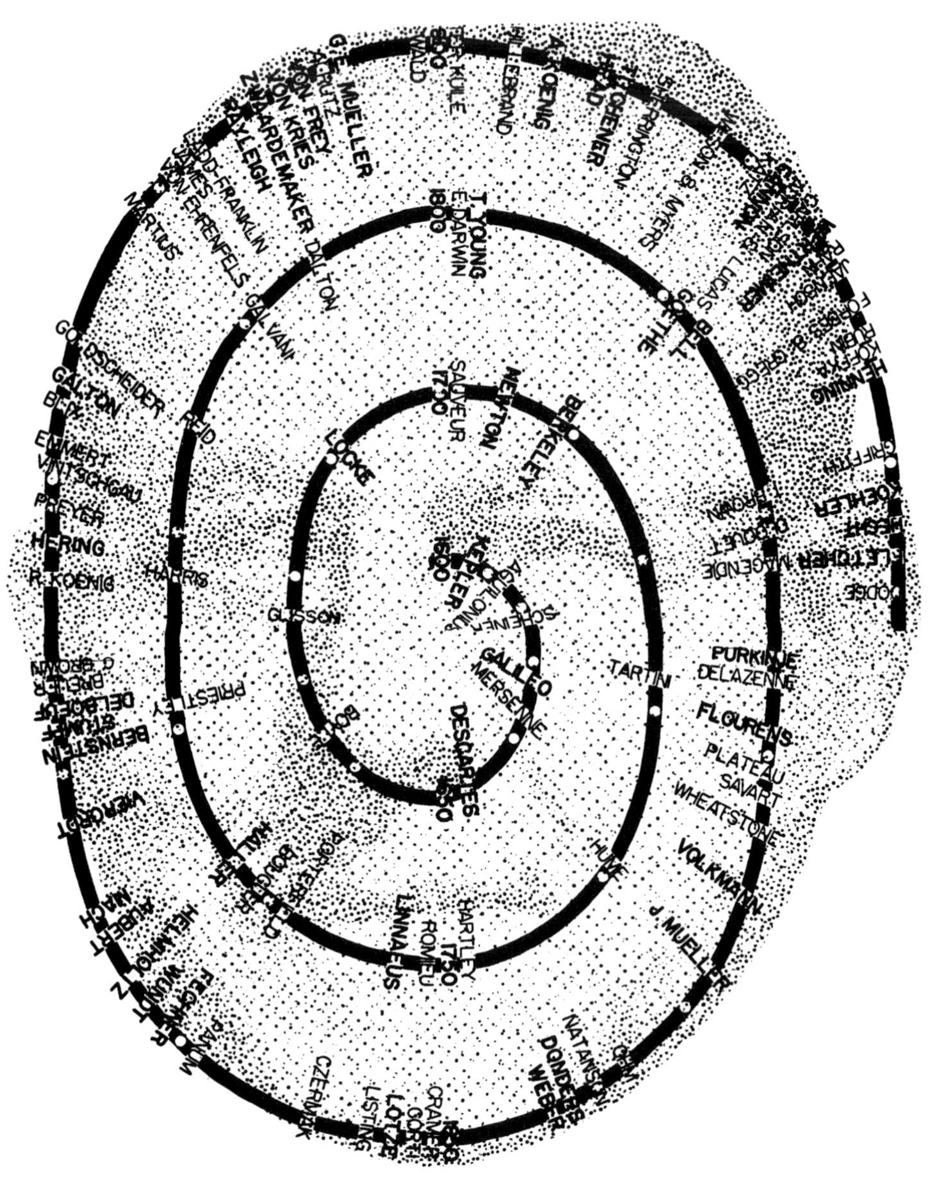

Portrait after a photograph in: Boring, E. G., H. Werner, H. S. Langfeld, and R. M. Yerkes, eds. 1952. *A History of Psychology in Autobiography,* Vol. 4. New York: Russell & Russell.

Motif after a figure in: Boring, E. G. 1942. *Sensation and Perception in the History of Experimental Psychology.* New York: Appleton-Century.

Historian of Psychology

Edwin Garrigues Boring (1886–1968) charted the history of psychology in general and of perception in particular. He gained an interest in history from Titchener to whom his *History of Experimental Psychology* (1929) is dedicated. "The experimental psychologist, so it has always seemed to me, needs historical sophistication within his own sphere of expertness. Without such knowledge he sees the present in distorted perspective, he mistakes old views for new, and he remains unable to evaluate the significance of new movements and methods. In this matter I can hardly state my faith too strongly." These sentiments echoed Titchener's belief that a sense of history distinguished the scholar from the experimenter. He also pursued Titchener's contention that psychology was not concerned with applied or abnormal behavior, and so these topics were neglected. Boring's *History* was revised in 1950, and he made his orientation to it explicit: "I wanted to get more into the dynamics of history, to say something about why, as well as how, science emerged, to speak of the rôle of the *Zeitgeist* and of the great man in determining progress in science, and to show that these two views of the development and emergence of thought are not mutually exclusive but obverse and reverse of every historical process." Boring's other major text, *Sensation and Perception in the History of Experimental Psychology* (1942), was dedicated to Helmholtz, and it reflected the area in which Boring had been most active experimentally. He examined the nature of the psychophysical law; auditory, cutaneous, and visceral sensitivities; the moon illusion; and size constancy. However, it was his historical, theoretical, and editorial writing that commanded most attention.

Boring was born in Philadelphia, and was trained as an engineer and as a psychologist at Cornell University, where he came under Titchener's spell. During World War I he worked with Yerkes in the army, and they collaborated on writing the final report on mental testing of army conscripts. The experience stimulated his involvement with statistics and probability theory. After the war he taught first at Clark University. In 1922 he was appointed professor of psychology at Harvard, where he remained for the rest of his career. He was president of the American Psychological Association in 1928, and edited the *American Journal of Psychology* for forty-eight years. The journal of book reviews *Contemporary Psychology* was founded by him in 1956, and he edited it for the first five years.

Boring is represented in the spiral of history, with its significant figures, displayed in the endpaper diagrams that sandwiched his *Sensation and Perception.* As with all good historians, he barely intrudes on the history he presents, but his presence is evident throughout.

Portrait after a photograph in: Schultz, D. P., and S. E. Schultz. 1987. *A History of Modern Psychology,* ed. 4. San Diego: Harcourt Brace Jovanovich.

Good Gestalt III

Wolfgang Köhler (1887–1967) introduced the concept of field forces operating in both perception and in its underlying neurophysiology. "It is now almost generally acknowledged that psychological facts have 'correlates' in the biological realm. These correlates, the so-called psycho-physical processes, are events in the central nervous system. A given visual field, for instance, is biologically represented by a certain distribution of processes in the occipital lobes." Moreover, the brain processes were considered to be isomorphic (having the same form) with the percept, so that principles of brain function could be inferred from perceptual phenomena. He went on to develop a speculative neurophysiology based mainly on the principles of perceptual grouping and on his experiments with figural aftereffects. It could be said that these speculations did more to hasten the demise of Gestalt theory than any other factor: neurophysiologists failed to find any evidence for such fields of electrical activity in the brain, and so tended to dismiss Gestalt theory in general rather than Köhler's unsuccessful attempt at neuroreductionism in particular. The robust visual phenomena at the heart of Gestalt psychology remained an enigma.

Köhler was born in Revel, Estonia. He was a student at the universities of Tübingen and Bonn before obtaining a doctorate in psychology (under Stumpf) at Berlin, where he met Koffka. He arrived in Frankfurt in 1910, shortly before Wertheimer conducted his experiments on the phi phenomenon there, and participated in them with Koffka. Between 1913 and 1920 he studied the behavior of chicks and chimpanzees while interned on the island of Tenerife; he applied Gestalt concepts to problem solving and wrote his influential book, *The Mentality of Apes*. He argued that animals learn the relations between events rather than between stimuli and responses, and that they applied insight to the solution of problems. Evidence for the latter derived from observations of chimpanzees stacking crates and constructing tools to obtain food otherwise out of reach: "The most striking phenomenon in these tests is still the sudden occurrence of perfectly clear and definite solutions." Köhler returned to the study of perception following his enforced sojourn on Tenerife, and sought to link it more firmly with physical field processes, like those of soap bubbles and magnetism. His book on physical Gestalten was instrumental in his appointment in 1922 to the chair of psychology in Berlin. He left Berlin for Swarthmore College in 1935, and continued editing the *Psychologische Forschung* from there, as well as conducting many fruitful experiments in perception, particularly on figural aftereffects. Köhler was the youngest member of the Gestalt trio, and he adapted most successfully to life in the United States. He was president of the American Psychological Association in 1959.

Köhler can be seen here composed of the same motif as his erstwhile colleagues, but in this case he is defined by fields of open circles.

	16	17	18	19	20	21	22	23	24	25	26	27	28	29	30
1...	117	-039	-155	-121	-050	-099	-135	-245	-071	151	-005	-030	-073	136	-043
2...	-112	-047	-201	-121	-043	-018	-176	-153	-031	159	084	010	026	067	024
3...	-138	002	[illegible]	-072	-124	-022	-078	-201	037	156	024	-117	-131	224	-082
4...	-069	-050	[illegible]	-084	-158	016	021	013	-103	070	026	-083	081	083	-146
5...	-060	-025	[illegible]	-015	005	-031	002	-032	088	023	058	-101	-087	032	013
6...	-035	-054	-063	-044	027	-103	-015	-043	-028	-029	112	046	142	040	098
7...	-184	097	-120	-091	-136	-144	-066	-182	036	212	-006	-103	032	083	-073
8...	-047	-104	-017	078	-109	078	047	-083	-092	053	108	-130	079	021	019
9...	003	035	051	-033	-087	088	-096	-107	009	153	-142	094	-051	061	-099
10...	-074	003	-025	002	019	117	-028	-126	-037	139	072	-067	088	090	-097
11...	-272	003	020	011	003	159	-040	-062	119	029	096	073	-132	094	-005
12...	178	-025	119	-010	027	-060	-015	070	-060	001	033	031	012	-107	-094
13...	013	069	-195	-002	-114	-097	009	-065	-022	212	035	-130	096	150	-104
14...	106	-018	-077	007	-018	-117	008	-072	-066	195	100	-084	046	108	-010
15...	205	-081	146	-094	-088	-048	053	-055	-013	-050	-061	040	129	140	-102
16...		-318	-015	-068	177	-131	-012	008	-170	-114	-060	045	-009	000	086
17...	-318		-018	174	005	043	115	-116	061	-003	217	-046	-006	007	-118
18...	-015	-018		407	-058	125	-014	062	031	-102	037	049	056	-045	038
19...	-068	174	407		051	082	032	002	195	-083	190	-005	-039	057	040
20...	177	005	-058	051		-048	026	[illegible]	[illegible]	-145	005	-091	-088	-062	090
21...	-131	043	125	082	-048		[illegible]	098	[illegible]	-009	023	-041	-087	072	-018
22...	-012	115	-014	032	016	[illegible]		[illegible]	[illegible]	[illegible]	183	047	-084	044	030
23...	008	-116	062	000	-076	098	[illegible]		[illegible]	-197	-042	071	-134	-159	153
24...	-170	061	031	195	108	091	166	-041		[illegible]	060	-028	013	-053	050
25...	-114	-003	-102	-083	-145	009	043	-197	019		-096	-126	-075	066	-068
26...	-060	217	037	190	005	023	183	-042	060	-096		-147	015	169	-144
27...	045	-046	049	-005	-091	-041	047	071	-028	-126	-147		-122	-304	314
28...	-009	-006	056	-039	-088	-087	-084	-134	013	-075	015	-122		124	-187
29...	000	007	-045	057	-062	072	044	-159	-053	066	169	-304	124		-353
30...	-086	-118	038	040	090	-018	030	153	050	-068	-144	314	-187	-353	
31...	-135	003	-087	-047	-036	056	-103	035	-020	001	-067	211	-130	-123	139
32...	-115	-006	174	049	-071	080	185	063	016	-031	022	114	-129	-082	150
33...	-084	-119	040	-032	075	045	-077	056	-146	022	-091	148	-069	067	144
34...	-013	-011	086	-099	106	-037	131	068	121	[illegible]	-044	096	-005	[illegible]	-087
35...	077	-071	-110	-072	-050	-046	-029	015	-070	[illegible]	-040	069	023	[illegible]	061
36...	-025	010	005	032	-015	-071	[illegible]	-060	-187	025	-010	032	-036	[illegible]	083
37...	091	-084	152	-024	239	061	[illegible]	[illegible]	[illegible]	-103	-248	200	-010	[illegible]	184
38...	135	-095	098	-045	134	010	142	217	[illegible]	[illegible]	227	351	-179	-221	[illegible]
39...	-062	019	074	[illegible]	053	029	144	131	050	-101	114	071	[illegible]	-028	[illegible]
40...	-067	162	-037	022	-080	002	252	-020	133	-059	273	099	[illegible]	[illegible]	115
41...	100	-071	-037	-164	031	-008	-164	-164	-099	135	-011	-067	[illegible]	-012	131
42...	018	-120	039	-003	013	098	059	271	104	-060	-192	[illegible]	[illegible]	[illegible]	[illegible]
43...	-077	-036	068	-034	-139	106	-186	161	-085	037	-062	009	[illegible]	[illegible]	[illegible]
44...	-046	-123	-055	-095	-275	006	-103	033	-027	000	-103	-013	109	[illegible]	[illegible]
45...	006	164	002	135	-047	[illegible]	-087	-150	-099	201	181	-120	001	[illegible]	[illegible]
46...	-036	035	-049	040	-175	-026	[illegible]	[illegible]	-022	183	197	-186	051	097	[illegible]
47...	-252	217	117	038	043	[illegible]	[illegible]	071	082	075	040	091	-112	-050	018
48...	-124	169	-019	-036	-021	[illegible]	084	-028	-091	-028	-040	106	-011	073	060
49...	-025	063	030	072	025	132	-156	-150	-086	115	011	-139	139	010	053
50...	-178	267	112	037	076	-004	014	-135	-041	065	128	-034	-044	052	047
51...	-086	245	009	038	-021	061	-041	-077	-094	109	022	120	-025	063	-006
52...	-049	-003	047	[illegible]	[illegible]	017	171	282	182	-195	-118	069	-100	-045	172
53...	-020	104	091	[illegible]	[illegible]	157	-030	072	075	011	006	033	-129	044	-074
54...	-044	053	-064	[illegible]	[illegible]	114	-094	-005	182	-051	-062	-028	006	070	056
55...	-046	125	024	[illegible]	[illegible]	112	-098	052	094	063	-063	-007	-125	025	-002
56...	122	014	-064	[illegible]	[illegible]	-007	028	049	125	-111	-013	-056	027	-005	048
57...	-094	061	[illegible]	-011	[illegible]	-112	000	018	-042	-024	-036	064	-200	-212	030
58...	043	-062	[illegible]	126	029	-013	052	171	069	-151	-065	-064	[illegible]	066	105
59...	-212	[illegible]	[illegible]	072	[illegible]	054	-037	000	069	016	039	146	-087	-055	172
60...	174	-025	[illegible]	-089	171	-097	-152	-204	-136	144	135	-134	146	192	-143

Portrait after a photograph in: Boring, E. G., H. Werner, H. S. Langfeld, and R. M. Yerkes, eds. 1952. *A History of Psychology in Autobiography,* Vol. 4. New York: Russell & Russell.

Motif after a table in: Thurstone, L. L. 1944. *A Factorial Study of Perception.* Chicago: University of Chicago Press.

Psychometrician

Louis Leon Thurstone (1887–1955) measured subjective states ranging from intelligence to attitudes, and he developed a method of multiple factor analysis. His starting point was psychophysics, and he adapted the methods to test a wide variety of psychological phenomena: "I shall suppose that every psychophysical judgement is mainly conditioned by four factors, namely, the two stimulus magnitudes or the separation between them, the dispersion or variability of the process which identifies the standard stimulus, and the dispersion or variability of the process which identifies the variable stimulus." On this basis he constructed the first attitude scales which fostered a new era of quantitative studies in social psychology. The methods involved deriving a scale from ratings made by judges; individuals' attitude could then be determined from the median ratings of the statements they agreed with. His book *The Measurement of Attitudes* appeared in 1929. A similar approach was taken to the measurement of values: "Human values are essentially subjective. They can certainly not be adequately represented by physical objects. Their intensities or magnitudes cannot be represented by physical measurement. At the very start we are faced with the problem of establishing a subjective metric. This is the central theme in modern psychophysics in its many applications to the measurement of social values, moral values, and aesthetic values. Exactly the same problem reappears in the measurement of utility in economics. In order to establish a subjective metric, we must have a subjective unit of measurement. . . . One of the main requirements of a truly subjective metric is that it shall be entirely independent of all physical measurement." In the area of intelligence he devised new methods of factor analysis in an attempt to resolve the conflict between Spearman's general factor and Thorndike's multiple special abilities. Thurstone proposed that mental abilities could be factored into primary mental functions of verbal comprehension, word fluency, number faculty, memory, visualizing or space thinking, perceptual speed, induction, and speed of judgment. While this appeared to support Thorndike's position, the factors were still intercorrelated as predicted by Spearman, and so Thurstone's position was a compromise between the two extremes.

Thurstone was born in Chicago, and studied engineering at Cornell before obtaining a doctorate in psychology from the University of Chicago. He subsequently conducted research on applied psychology at the Carnegie Institute of Technology and on educational psychology for the government before returning to Chicago, where he established a psychometric laboratory. He moved the laboratory to the University of North Carolina in 1952. He was among the founders of the journal *Psychometrika* and was the first president of the Psychometric Society. He was elected president of the American Psychological Association in 1932.

Thurstone is almost hidden within a correlation matrix derived from a battery of perceptual tests.

Portrait after a photograph in: Mead, M. 1959. *An Anthropologist at Work. Writings of Ruth Benedict.* London: Secker & Warburg.

The Chrysanthemum and the Sword

Ruth Fulton Benedict (1887–1948) envisaged culture as personality writ large. She proposed that cultures select certain aspects of individual personality at the expense of others, with the consequence that characteristics of normal or abnormal behavior could be expressed in more extreme form in cultures than in individuals. Cultural anthropology sought to place human behavior in the context of society (with every attempt to reduce the emphasis of the culture from which the anthropologists themselves were drawn). It provided a counterweight to the analysis of individuals in isolation, as well as to the preoccupation with the concerns of one's own culture. "The inner workings of our own brains we feel to be uniquely worthy of investigation, but custom, we have a way of thinking, is behaviour at its most commonplace. As a matter of fact, it is the other way round. Traditional custom, taken the world over, is a mass of detailed behaviour more astonishing than what any one person can ever evolve in individual actions no matter how aberrant." Initially she studied the concept of the guardian spirit in North American Indians, and she became an authority on American folklore. Her configurational thesis of society was expressed in *Patterns of Culture* (1935): "The vast proportion of all individuals who are born into any society always and whatever the idiosyncracies of its institutions, assume . . . the behaviour dictated by that society. This fact is always interpreted by carriers of that culture as being due to the fact that their particular institutions reflect an ultimate and universal sanity. The actual reason is quite different. Most people are shaped to the form of the culture because of the enormous malleability of their original endowment. They are plastic to the moulding force of the society into which they are born." While Benedict investigated the many distinguishing features of particular groups, she was acutely aware of the division separating an appreciation of differences to one of deploring them. In her book *Race and Racism* (1942) she clarified the relationship between differentiation and discrimination in the context of social groups: "To recognize Race does not mean to recognize Racism. Race is a matter for careful scientific study; Racism is an unproven assumption of the biological and perpetual superiority of one human group over another."

Benedict was born in New York City. She studied literature at Vassar and came to anthropology late; she obtained a doctorate from Columbia University under the functional anthropologist Franz Boas (1858–1942) in 1923. One of her later developments was the study of cultures from afar, by examining their products, like literature and the performing and visual arts. This was applied to Japanese society after World War II and it resulted in *The Chrysanthemum and the Sword* (1946). Benedict is represented in a design that could be read as a chrysanthemum and a sword. The chrysanthemum motif also reflects the radiations of the emblematic rising sun.

Portrait after frontispiece photograph in: Bennett, J. H., ed. 1974. *Collected Papers of R. A. Fisher,* Vol. 5. *1948–62.* Adelaide, Australia: University of Adelaide Press.

Significant Figure

Ronald Aylmer Fisher (1890–1962) developed a number of statistical procedures that have become indispensable tools for the experimental psychologist. Many of the common terms in statistics, like degrees of freedom, Latin square, randomization, and the null hypothesis, were introduced by him. Fisher argued that experiments should be designed to incorporate simultaneous variation of factors so that interactions between them could be detected, using his method of analysis of variance. "A type of data, which is of very common occurrence, may be treated by methods closely analogous to that of the correlation table, while at the same time it may be more usefully and accurately treated by the analysis of variance, that is by the separation of the variance ascribable to one group of causes from the variance ascribable to other groups." This procedure opened up new areas of experimental inquiry because experiments could be designed and analyzed in ways that had not previously been possible. Like Pearson, with whom he engaged in vitriolic disputes, he was concerned with applying statistical procedures to the Darwinian theory of evolution. Unlike Pearson, he applied statistical methods to demonstrate the compatibility of Mendelian genetics and Darwinian natural selection, establishing a neo-Darwinian theory of evolution. In so doing he distinguished between sample statistics and population parameters, and provided means for estimating the latter from the former. Pearson's biometrical background resulted in distrust of small-sample statistics, and his antipathy to Fisher was exacerbated by Fisher's elegant elaboration of problems in the use of chi-square and of the sampling distribution of r. Fisher conducted breeding experiments to demonstrate the operation of dominant and recessive genes and concluded: "The rate of increase in fitness of any organism at any time is equal to its genetic variance in fitness at that time."

Fisher was born in London and was trained in mathematics and physics at Cambridge University. After working for an investment company and as a teacher he was appointed as the sole statistician at Rothamstead Experimental Station in 1919. There he carried out experiments in agriculture involving split plots that led to the development of analysis of variance. His innovations in the application of statistical procedures were internationally acknowledged and in 1929 he was elected a Fellow of the Royal Society. In 1933 Fisher succeeded Pearson as Galton Professor of Eugenics at University College, London. Ten years later he was appointed professor of genetics at Cambridge.

Fisher is depicted by the letter F, which signifies the value derived from the analysis of variance and which is so denoted in recognition of him. Like the other statistician (Pearson) presented earlier, Fisher is depicted using a single letter. The antipathy displayed between Pearson and Fisher is hinted at by the contrasting ways in which the letters have been assembled to define them: Pearson's face is formed from r whereas Fisher is visible against a sea of F's.

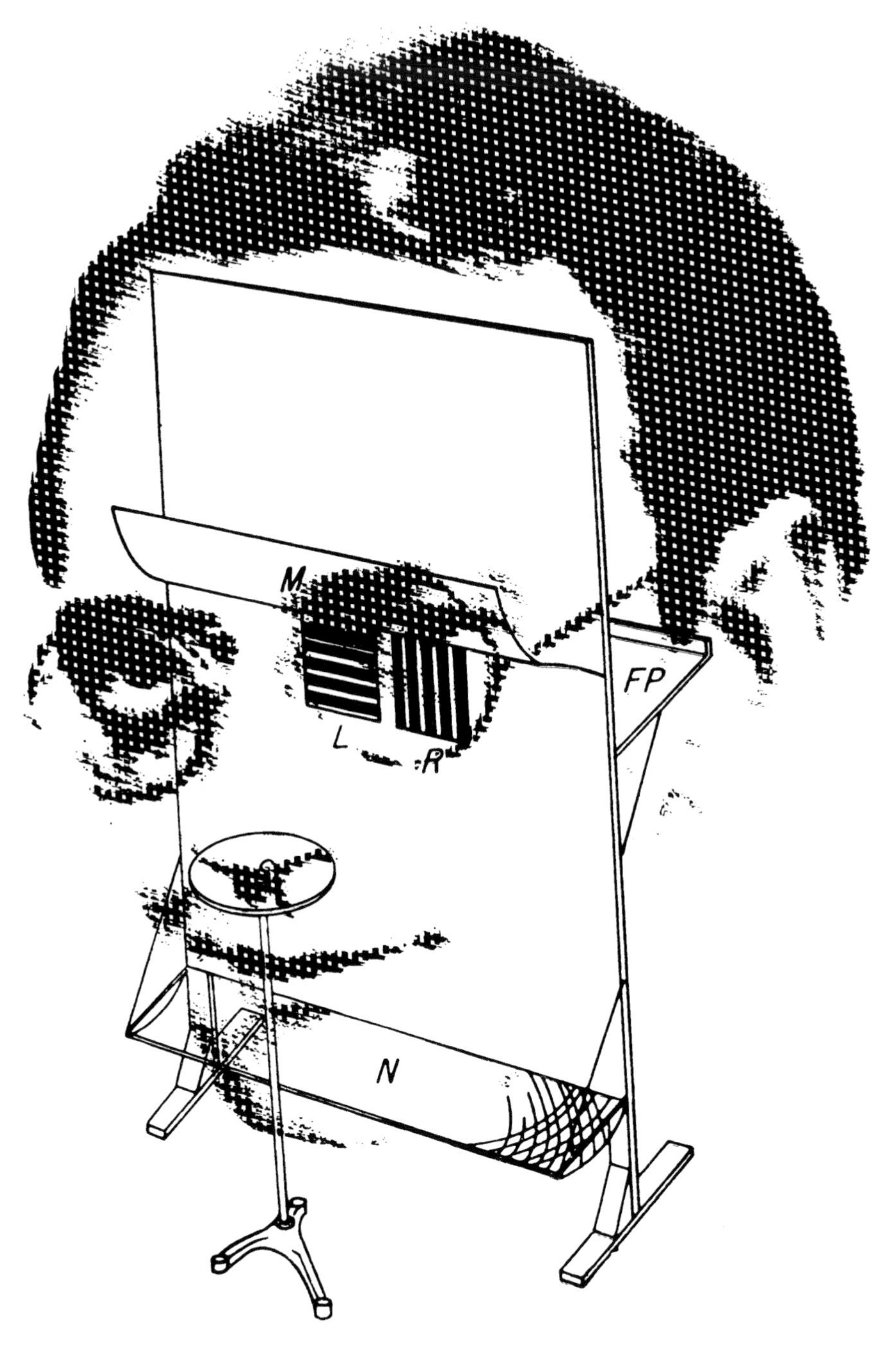

Portrait after a photograph in: Kimble, G. A., and K. Schlesinger, eds. 1985. *Topics in the History of Psychology,* Vol. 1. Hillsdale, N.J.: Erlbaum.

Motif after a diagram of a jumping stand in: Lashley, K. S. 1930. The mechanism of vision. I. A method of rapid analysis of pattern-vision in the rat. *Journal of Genetic Psychology* 37:453–460.

Lashley's Jumping Stand

Karl Spencer Lashley (1890–1958) searched in vain for the traces left by memory—the engram. "Innumerable studies have defined conditions under which learning is facilitated or retarded, but, in spite of such progress, we seem little nearer to an understanding of the nature of the memory trace than was Descartes. I sometimes feel, in reviewing the evidence on the localization of the memory trace, that the necessary conclusion is that learning just is not possible." He used behavioral measures to examine the effects of ablating parts of the brain in rats. Contrary to the expectations from theories of cortical localization, Lashley found that the deficits in learning depended on the amount of brain removed and not on the region from which it was taken. His law of mass action stated that the reduction in the rate and accuracy of learning was proportional to the amount of brain tissue removed. He revived Flourens's concept of the brain as an organ with the capacity to carry out functions that are lost following the destruction of other parts (equipotentiality): "For learning of the mazes no part of the cortex is more important than any other." This turned out to be so for maze learning because it can be performed using a plethora of cues for all modalities; more specific learning tasks do show localized deficits with ablation.

Lashley was born in Davis, West Virginia. He studied biology at the University of Pittsburgh and received a doctorate in genetics from Johns Hopkins University, where he remained to work with Watson. They collaborated on ethological research of homing in terns, and on salivary conditioning in humans. The latter led to Lashley's lifelong interest in learning and its neural correlates. He held academic positions at the universities of Minnesota, Chicago, and Harvard, and was director of the Yerkes Laboratories of Primate Biology from 1942 to 1956. His presidential address to the American Psychological Association, in 1929, describing his ablation experiments was taken as support for Gestalt field processes in the cortex. His address to the Hixon Symposium in 1948 "On the problem of serial order in behavior" galvanized psychologists to question the adequacy of stimulus-response approaches in accounting for complex processes like speech. Planning and hierarchical organization were considered necessary for initiating and controlling such sequences of actions.

Lashley is seen with the jumping stand he devised for studying visual discrimination in rats. This apparatus was widely adopted as it provided a much more rapid method of studying discrimination learning than the variety of maze tasks that were generally employed. The contours defining Lashley's portrait correspond in orientation to those involved in the visual discrimination task set for the rat.

Portrait after a photograph in: Hearst, E., ed. 1979. *The First Century of Experimental Psychology.* Hillsdale, N.J.: Erlbaum.

Motif of personal space after a diagram in: Lewin, K. 1936. *Principles of Topological Psychology.* F. and G. M. Heider, trans. New York: McGraw-Hill.

Good Gestalt IV

Kurt Lewin (1890–1947) extended Gestalt theory into the social field. He applied Gestalt concepts initially to motivation, then to personality, and finally to group dynamics. Behavior (*B*) was considered to result from an interaction between individuals and their environment, which defined their life space. "In psychology one can begin to describe the whole situation by roughly distinguishing the person (*P*) and his environment (*E*). Every psychological event depends on the state of the person and at the same time the state of the environment, although their relative importance is different in different cases. Thus we can state our formula.. for every psychological event as $B = f(PE)$. . . . In the following we shall use the term psychological life space to indicate the totality of facts which determine the behavior of an individual at a certain moment." The psychological facts in the life space could have positive or negative valences, so that a dynamic field of conflicting attractions and repulsions was in operation. The analysis of conflict situations in terms of interacting positive and negative valences mapped onto those examining learning in terms of approach and avoidance conflicts. Lewin chose to use topology to describe mathematically and represent pictorially life space, which was typically shown as an ellipse divided into areas of various sizes. Koffka had earlier used a similar elliptical representation of an individual interacting with the environment, but he had not described it mathematically. The essential characteristics of life-space topology were the boundaries between the spaces and the vectors operating at them. While the mathematics of topology were tractable, reflecting the psychological variables in the life space numerically posed serious problems, and it was the emphasis on interactions between individual and environment that was fruitful rather than its vague mathematical formulation. The latter was important for Lewin because he described three epochs of psychology—the speculative (Aristotelian), descriptive, and constructive (Galilean)—and contrasted them in terms of their ability to predict individual cases from laws. His was a "constructive system based on a group of interrelated concepts."

Lewin was born in Mogilno, then a part of Prussia, and moved to Berlin in his teens. Like Koffka and Köhler, he received his doctorate in psychology at the University of Berlin under Stumpf's supervision. After serving with valor in World War I he worked with Wertheimer and Köhler in Berlin until his move to America in 1933. He held posts at Cornell and Iowa universities before becoming director of the Research Center for Group Dynamics at Massachusetts Institute of Technology.

Lewin is represented in a similar motif to the other Gestalt psychologists, but in his case the circles denote the interacting fields which in turn enclose the topology of the person.

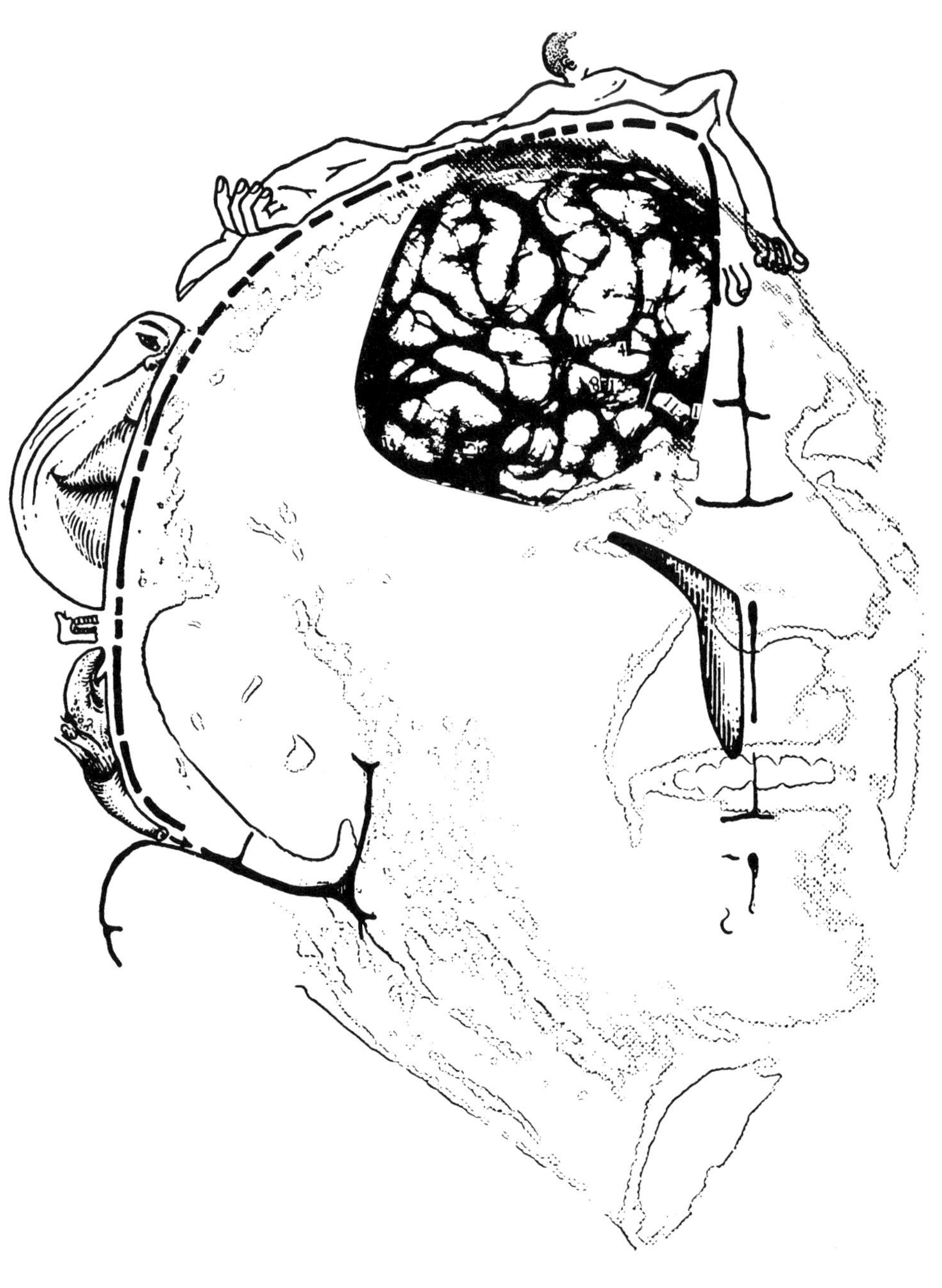

Portrait after a photograph in: Blakemore, C. 1988. *The Mind Machine.* London: BBC Books.

Motif of the exposed brain after a photograph in: Penfield, W. 1958. *The Excitable Cortex in Conscious Man.* Liverpool: Liverpool University Press.

Motif of the sensory homunculus after a diagram in: Penfield, W., and T. Rasmussen. 1950. *The Cerebral Cortex of Man. A Clinical Study of Localization of Function.* New York: Macmillan.

Cortical Cartographer

Wilder Graves Penfield (1891–1976) electrically stimulated the brains of conscious humans and mapped the sensory and motor areas of the cortex. He extended Ferrier's techniques by stimulating the exposed cerebral cortices of patients who were undergoing surgery to alleviate epileptic seizures. He presented a summary of his research in the Ferrier Lecture to the Royal Society of London in 1947. The operations were carried out under local anesthetic because brain tissue itself is not sensitive to pain. Penfield was able to confirm and refine Ferrier's localized regions of motor control: stimulation of a particular part of the precentral gyrus resulted in muscle twitches on the opposite side of the body. Moreover, he was able to draw a precise map of the motor regions of the brain, and a similar sensory map could be plotted along the surface of the postcentral gyrus. Those body parts that had the greatest articulation or sensitivity (like the fingers and mouth) were represented over larger cortical areas than other parts. The technique yielded some unexpected results. When the surface of the temporal lobe was stimulated Penfield claimed it elicited surprisingly vivid descriptions of past events. "Apparently the *memory* that is stored or 'filed' in the temporal cortex, whether visual picture, musical piece, or significant experience, must have come to the patient's attention before being filed there. The thousands of visual impulses that reach the occipital cortex and serve to guide a man in his daily task but which he does not 'notice' do not seem to find any lasting repository in the temporal cortex." His conclusions about cortical localization were diametrically opposed to those of Lashley. However, it was difficult to confirm the validity of elicited recollections, and it is uncertain to what extent the patients' histories of epilepsy influenced the responses to electrical stimulation. A further factor was that the stimulation of the cortical surface would have spread to other cortical as well as subcortical sites (like the limbic system), and so the force of the arguments for localization was tempered.

Penfield was born in Spokane, Washington. He studied at Princeton University and then at Oxford, before qualifying in medicine from Johns Hopkins University. He returned to Britain to work with Sherrington, whom he had met in Oxford, and specialized in neurosurgery thereafter. He held posts in New York and Baltimore, and he was the first director of the Montreal Neurological Institute, where most of his brain stimulation research was conducted.

Penfield is portrayed in the context of his two major discoveries: the illustration of the exposed brain, with the numbers indicating the locus of stimulation, and the mapping of the somatosensory cortex.

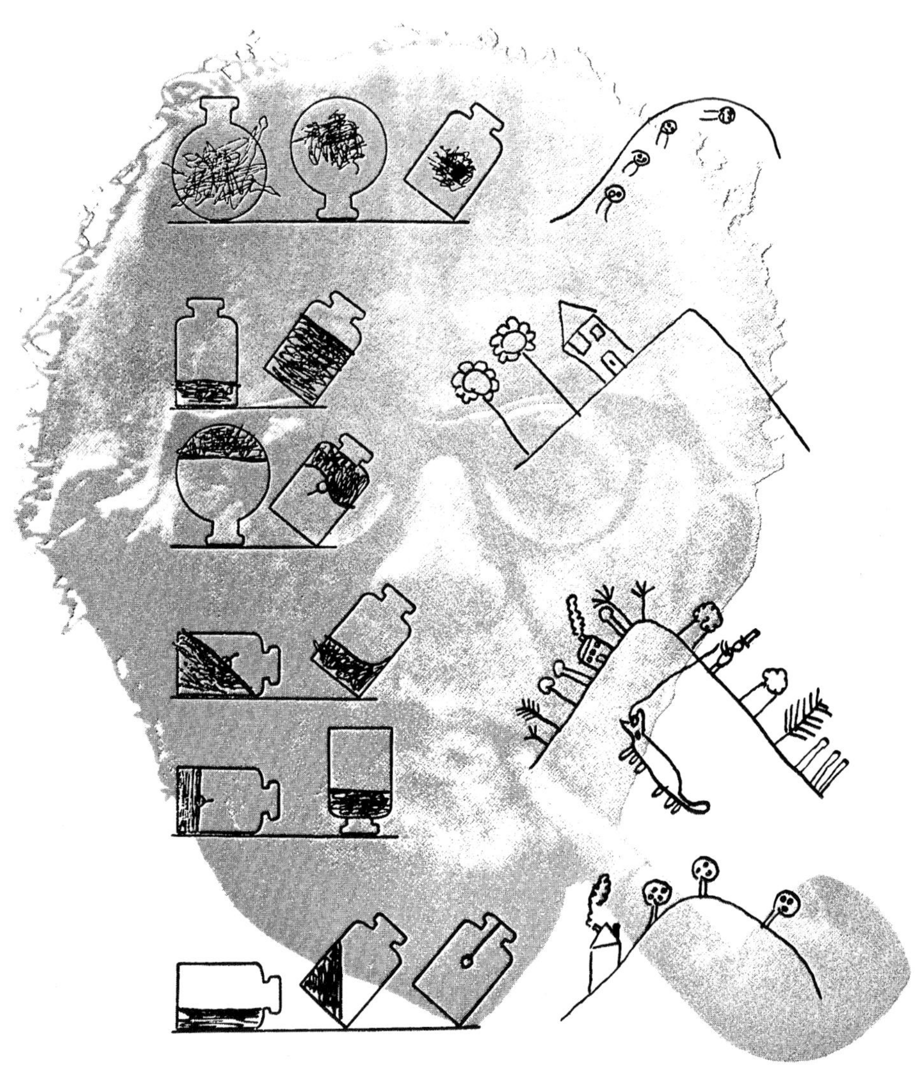

Portrait after a photograph in: Baldwin, A. L. 1967. *Theories of Child Development*. New York: Wiley.

Motif after children's drawings in: Piaget, J., and B. Inhelder. 1948. *La représentation de l'espace chez l'enfant*. Paris: Presses Universitaires de France.

Genetic Epistemologist

Jean Piaget (1896–1980) isolated specific stages of cognitive development through which children pass and which could be assessed by particular tasks. That is, he argued that intelligence progresses in discrete steps, which he called the sensori-motor and preoperational stages, followed by the stages of concrete and formal operations. This was contrary to Binet's view that intelligence increased steadily with age. The sensori-motor stage applies from birth to about two years of age and is mainly concerned with relating motor responses to patterns of stimulation. Cognitive concepts emerge in the preoperational stage (from two to around seven years), but there remain tasks, like conservation, that are not solved until the concrete operational stage (from about seven to eleven years). "Until about 11, to think is to speak—either with the mouth or with the little voice situated in the head—and speaking consists in acting on things themselves by means of words, the words sharing the nature of the things named as well as of the voice producing them." Abstract reasoning develops in the formal operational stage, beyond eleven years of age. Throughout the stages of cognitive development processes of assimilation and accommodation interact. Recognizable features of the world are assimilated into the cognitive framework, whereas novel ones require learning to accommodate them.

Piaget was born in Neuchâtel. He developed an early interest in natural history and received his doctorate in that subject from his home university. His introduction to child psychology was under the guidance of Simon in Paris, where he investigated reasoning tests in children. Piaget did not simply note whether children performed the test items correctly or not, he asked them why they gave the answers they did. One outcome was the appreciation that tasks involving parts and wholes were particularly difficult for children under twelve. "First of all it became clear to me that the theory of the relations between the whole and the part can be studied experimentally through the analysis of the psychological processes underlying logical operations." He then decided that the progress of the developing intellect could best be charted by means of careful observation and inference, as had proved successful in following embryological development, and he termed this approach *genetic epistemology*. This program of research was actively pursued at the Rousseau Institute in Geneva when he became its director in 1921 and where he remained until his death. Piaget's writing almost matched Wundt's in volume. As was the case with Bartlett, his cognitive approach did not initially resonate with the behaviorism dominant in America, but his influence became widespread in the second half of the century.

Piaget is represented, with his much loved pipe, in the context of children's drawings of fluid in a container and of objects on a hill, made between about four and eight years of age.

Portrait after a frontispiece photograph in: Vygotsky, L. S. 1978. *Mind in Society. The Development of Higher Psychological Processes.* M. Cole, V. John-Steiner, S. Scribner, and E. Souberman, eds. Cambridge, Mass.: Harvard University Press.

Motif after an arrangement of Vygotsky's blocks.

Vygotsky's Blocks

Lev Semionovich Vygotsky (1896–1934) argued that language integrated the cognitive and social development of the child. "The most significant moment in the course of intellectual development, which gives birth to the purely human forms of practical and abstract intelligence, occurs when speech and practical activity, two previously completely independent lines of development, converge." His concern with the activity of the child was shared with Piaget, but he placed more emphasis on speech and on the social dimension. Speech was considered to be intimately involved in children mastering their behavior and in applying some degree of control over the surroundings: the more complex the behavior the more dependent it was on language. The meanings attached to words passed through emotional and concrete stages before becoming abstract. "Thought and language, which reflect reality in a way different from that of perception, are the key to the nature of human consciousness. Words play a central part not only in the development of thought but in the historical growth of consciousness as a whole." Vygotsky frequently referred to Köhler's work on learning in chimpanzees, and contrasted it with that in children; whereas chimpanzees were dominated by what they could perceive, children attained a conceptual independence from their surroundings. He saw tool and sign use as the defining characteristics of humans, but they fostered social rather than biological evolution.

Vygotsky was born in Orsha, near Minsk, and studied literature at the University of Moscow. After teaching for several years he returned to Moscow to work at the Institute of Psychology, and he later founded the Institute of Defectology. Although he died young, his research was exceedingly influential within the Soviet Union, particularly through his student and collaborator, Luria. He brought consiousness back into materialistic psychology by stressing its importance to the historical development of society. It is ironic that Vygotsky, who emphasized the social dimension of speech, should have his own works banned by the society in which he lived. His work remained essentially unknown in the West until the translation of *Thought and Language* (originally published in 1934) in 1962. Since then his ideas have received an enthusiastic reception and his attempts to find a middle road between the overtness of physiological and the covertness of descriptive psychologies correspond to contemporary cognitive concerns.

Vygotsky also worked on problems in psychopathology. He devised a test for investigating thought disorders in schizophrenia which was modified to examine concept formation in children. It involves twenty-two wooden blocks varying in shape, volume, height, and color. The task of the child is to sort the blocks into four groups so that the blocks in any one group share some feature in common, but this feature is not present in the other groups. Vygotsky's portrait is shown composed of the blocks forming his test.

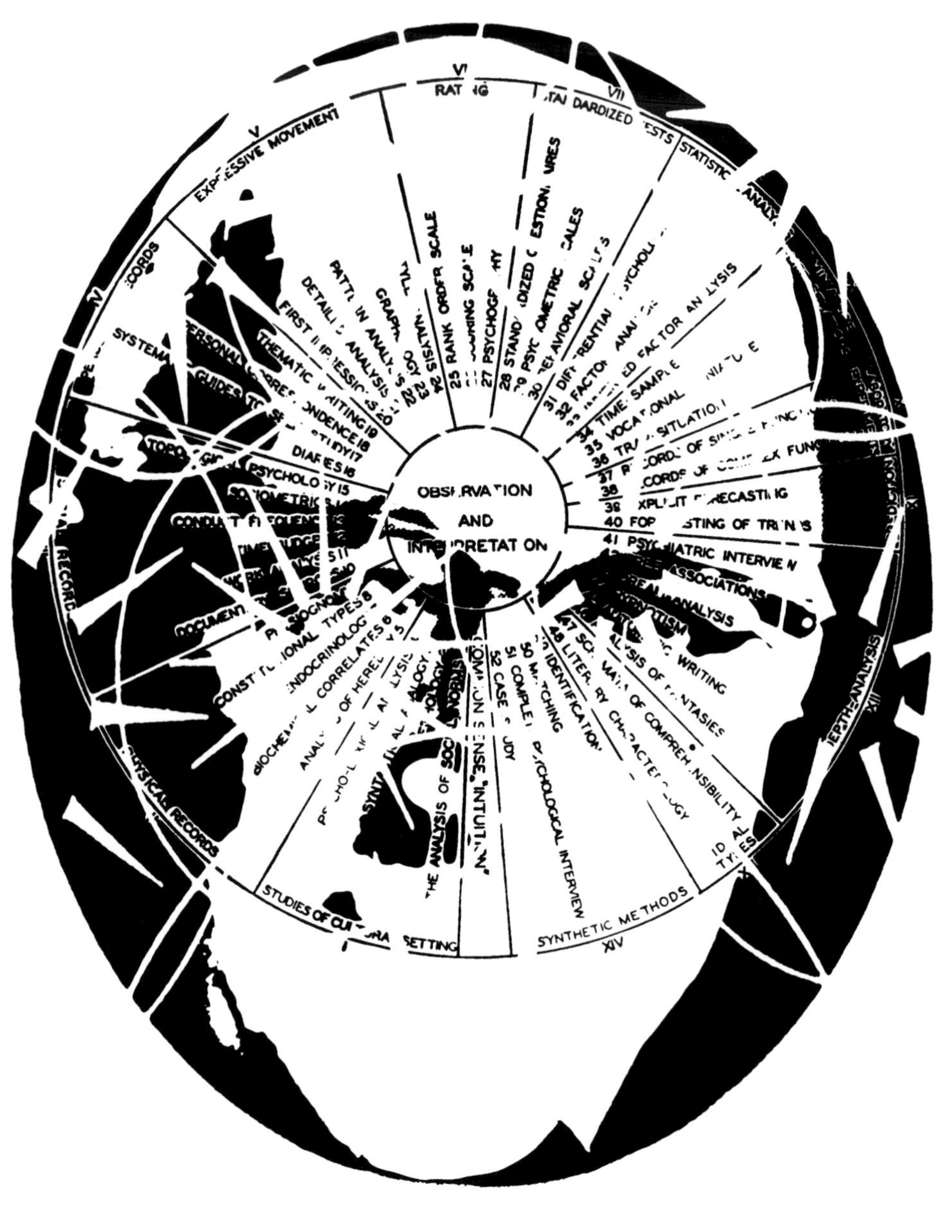

Portrait after a photograph in: Boring, E. G., and G. Lindzey, eds. 1967. *A History of Psychology in Autobiography,* Vol. 5. New York: Appleton-Century-Crofts.

Motifs after diagrams in: Allport, G. W. 1937. *Personality. A Psychological Interpretation.* New York: Holt.

Por-trait

Gordon Willard Allport (1897–1967) advocated an approach to personality in terms of traits rather than types. "Psychology has never been able to do without some conception of determining tendency (implying a readiness for response). Without such a conception it could never pretend to account for the manifest stability and consistency of behavior and experience. . . . To accept traits requires no radical revision of the psychologist's creed, for traits are biophysical in the same sense that determining tendencies, attitudes, or other dynamic influences have always been considered by psychology as biophysical." Traits were considered to be hierarchically organized, descending from cardinal to central to secondary traits. A cardinal trait could dominate most activities of an individual, whereas there are several central and a multitude of secondary traits. Allport's research covered a wider range of topics than personality. He examined the nature of prejudice, the study of values, the psychology of rumor, and the formation of attitudes. Throughout his research he adopted an idiographic rather than a nomothetic approach. That is, he studied individual cases in preference to groups because he considered that psychology, unlike the exact sciences, was not able to establish general laws. This situation is difficult to sustain, as is evident in Allport's discussion of functional autonomy (a term he introduced): "The principle of functional autonomy is a declaration of independence for the psychology of personality. Though in itself a general law, at the same time it helps to account, not for the abstract motivation of an impersonal and purely hypothetical mind-in-general as do other dynamic principles, but for the concrete, viable motives of any mind-in-particular."

Allport was born in Montezuma, Indiana. He was an undergraduate and later a postgraduate student at Harvard University, and returned there in 1930 to a professorship. Following his doctorate he traveled in Europe for two years, where he met many of the leading psychologists in Germany including Stumpf, Wertheimer, Köhler, and Stern; he also worked with Bartlett at Cambridge. It was his exposure to European psychology, and most particularly to Stern's personalistic theory, that set Allport apart from most of his contemporaries in America. In 1946 he was a cofounder of the Department of Social Relations at Harvard, and he can be seen as a forerunner of third force or humanistic psychology that was to gain momentum later.

Allport's portrait is presented in "a graphic tabulation of the major methods employed in psychological investigations of personality. At the centre lie the indispensable operations of observation and interpretation shared by science and common sense." Enclosing both the portrait and the tabulation is a representation of Allport's trait-conception which sees "a single personality as a system of focal but interdependent sub-structures, the units being essentially different in every personality"; this model was contrasted with the factorial conceptions which consisted of independent elements.

Portrait after a photograph in: Blakemore, C. 1977. *Mechanics of the Mind.* Cambridge, England: Cambridge University Press.

Motif after a diagram in: Luria, A. R. 1970. *Traumatic Aphasia. Its Syndromes, Psychology and Treatment.* The Hague: Mouton.

Neuropsychologist

Alexander Romanovich Luria (1902–1977) is best know today as a neuropsychologist. He defined neuropsychology as the exploration of the functional organization of the brain. He summarized his approach by saying "that the higher psychological processes represent complex functional systems, social in their genesis, mediated in their structure, and carried out by whole complexes of jointly working zones of the brain." He was initially concerned with reconciling the objective methods of psychology with the richness of real-life mental processes. Under Vygotsky's guidance he investigated cognitive development in regions of the Soviet Union undergoing rapid and imposed transition from preliterate to industrial cultures, and concluded that cognitive functioning can be modified by social change. During and after World War II he worked with soldiers who had received head wounds. He examined brain injury without slavish adherence to either the equipotentialists or the localizers, and in the process developed many new tests for detecting subtle deficits in perception, thought, and language. In his later work Luria examined the perceptual and cognitive problems associated with injury to the right cerebral hemisphere. By demonstrating spatial and perceptual deficits he provided a balance to the emphasis placed on left hemisphere function dating from Hughlings Jackson's description of it as the leading hemisphere. He also pointed to the importance of subcortical structures in laying down memory traces: "The deep zones of the brain, neighbouring on the reticular formation of the upper part of the brain stem, and including the limbic structure, are directly concerned not only with the maintenance of optimal cortical tone, but also with the creation of the necessary conditions for retention of traces of direct experience." However, he is perhaps most popularly known for an account he made of a man (referred to as *S*) with a remarkable memory—*The Mind of a Mnemonist* (1968). Luria examined *S* over a period of 30 years, and recorded his amazing feats of memory. *S* was able to recall lists of numbers and nonsense syllables presented years earlier. Luria discovered that *S* formed visual images of the items to be learned and placed them in familiar visual scenes, such as by a fence or in a tree.

Luria was born in Kazan and graduated in humanities from its university. He worked at the Moscow Institute of Psychology and later in his life he studied medicine at Moscow University. His research career took many turns as a consequence of turbulent political upheavals in Russia. At one stage he was dismissed from his post at the Institute of Neuropsychology in Moscow because of his less than enthusiastic support of Pavlovian principles.

The outline skull shown here indicates the paths of bullets through the brain and the overlapping parietal lesions in the left hemisphere of ten patients; all suffered semantic aphasia as a consequence. This is symbolized in the illustration by the coincidence of these regions with Luria's mouth.

Portrait after a photograph in: Boring, E. G., and G. Lindzey, eds. 1967. *A History of Psychology in Autobiography,* Vol. 5. New York: Appleton-Century-Crofts.

Nondirective Therapist

Carl Ransom Rogers (1902–1987) developed what was first called nondirective therapy and a related personality theory as an alternative to psychoanalysis. "It is about both the client and me as we regard with wonder the potent and orderly forces which are evident in this whole experience, forces which seem deeply rooted in the universe as a whole." This reflects Rousseau's optimistic belief in the inherent goodness of humans and their potential for growth. Nondirective therapists neither diagnose problems nor suggest solutions; they avoid offering advice so that the onus is shifted onto patients to resolve their own difficulties. Rogers found that the absence of any direction in the therapeutic process was unrealistic and some focus was required. This was reflected in the changes of its name to client-centered and then person-centered therapy. Patients were called clients in order to redress the power balance between them and therapists, and the clients defined the goals of the treatment. The therapy is based on two central ideas: "(1) the individual has within him the capacity, at least latent, to understand the factors in his life that cause him unhappiness and pain, and to reorganize himself in such a way as to overcome those factors; (2) these powers will become effective if the therapist can establish with the client a relationship sufficiently warm, accepting and understanding." Worthy as these sentiments are, they are difficult to encompass within a theoretical framework, although Rogers did attempt to achieve this in his *Client-Centered Therapy* (1951). The concepts employed, like positive self-regard, unconditional positive regard, and conditions of worth, were equally amorphous. The goal of the individual is to become a fully functioning person: a "characteristic of the person who is living the process of the good life appears to be an increasing trust in his organism as a means of arriving at the most satisfying behavior in each existential situation." The appeal of the approach owed more to a disenchantment with psychoanalysis than to a more clearly defined theory. Rogers did apply quantitative procedures to try to understand what happened during therapy, and to assess the relative merits of psychoanalytic and client-centered therapies. In so doing he removed much of the mystique associated with the former. Toward the end of his life he broadened his approach to include education and politics and encounter groups and sensitivity training.

Rogers was born in Chicago. He obtained his doctorate in psychology at Columbia Teachers College, where Leta Hollingworth was among his teachers, and he specialized in child psychology. His experiences in child guidance at Rochester over a twelve-year period sowed the seeds of dissatisfaction with psychoanalytic therapy. He returned to academic life with posts at Ohio State, Chicago, and Wisconsin universities. In 1963 he moved to La Jolla, California, where he later founded the Center for the Studies of the Person.

Rogers is portrayed in a nondirective manner—it is difficult to determine the orientation of the faces in the composite picture.

Portrait after frontispiece photograph in: Hammond, K. R., ed. 1966. *The Psychology of Egon Brunswik.* New York: Holt, Rinehart & Winston.

Motif after a schematic face in: Brunswik, E. 1956. *Perception and the Representative Design of Psychological Experiments.* Berkeley: University of California Press.

Schematic Face

Egon Brunswik (1903–1955) introduced probabilistic functionalism into psychology. His was a functionalist theory because it emphasized the adaptive nature of behavior with respect to objects in the environment; it was probabilistic because behavior in an unpredictable environment must be based on the statistical regularities that occur within it. He was influenced by the Vienna circle of logical positivist philosophers and believed that the probabilistic methods applied to the physical sciences were appropriate to psychology, too. He applied probabilistic functionalism principally in the area of perception: "Not only is the psychology of perception older than that of such other fields as learning or motivation, but it also has served as a pacemaker in the way of decisive changes in basic outlook. Perception thus may be best suited as a paradigm not only for the past but also for things likely to come." He was concerned with how we derive veridical information about objects; how the distal stimulus is perceived as constant despite wide variations in the proximal stimulus. Accordingly he examined perceptual constancy and devised a formula for assessing it, now known as the Brunswik ratio. Veridical perception was based on the use of a family of cues that differ in their ecological validity—the correlation between proximal cues and distal stimulus. By experience, greater statistical weight was placed on the cues with high ecological validity. "Any fairly consistent rapport, be it intuitively perceptual or explicitly rational, with distal layers of the environment presupposes the existence of proximal sensory cues of some degree of ecological validity to serve as mediators of the relationship." In order to investigate the probabilistic nature of behavior Brunswik proposed that not only should subjects be representative but stimuli should be also: "only by such 'representative design' of experiments can ecological generalizability of functional regularities of behavior and adaptation be ascertained."

Brunswik was born in Budapest but was educated in Vienna. After studying engineering he turned to psychology and obtained his doctorate from the University of Vienna. He became acquainted with Tolman during the latter's visit to Europe in 1933, and Brunswik accepted a post at the University of California, Berkeley, in 1937, where he remained for the rest of his life.

Brunswik conducted a series of studies on the perception of schematic faces. The same oval outline contained four simple structures—single lines for the nose and mouth, together with elliptical eyes. The separation of the eyes, the length of the nose, and the height of the mouth were varied systematically to yield 189 faces. Observers were requested to rank the faces according to characteristics like narrow-minded, joyful, embittered, sad, and sarcastic, and there was reasonable agreement over which faces had these attributes. Brunswik is portrayed with a schematic face that reflects his own soft, sad, and intellectual features.

Portrait after a photograph in: E. G. Boring and G. Lindzey, eds. 1967. *A History of Psychology in Autobiography,* Vol. 5. New York: Appleton-Century-Crofts.

Skinner Boxed

Burrhus Frederic Skinner (1904–1990) was a radical behaviorist in the mold of Watson. Rather than building learning theory on classical conditioning, as Watson had done, Skinner based his on operant conditioning. Respondent behavior (as in classical conditioning) is elicited, whereas operant behavior is emitted, and it could readily be studied in a box device he developed. The Skinner box consisted of a lever, which the animal (usually a rat) could press, and dispensers of reinforcement (food and water). Depression of the lever provided reinforcement and it was recorded automatically, providing a cumulative record of lever presses on an event recorder. "A natural datum in a science of behavior is the probability that a given bit of behavior will occur at a given time. An experimental analysis deals with that probability in terms of frequency or rate of responding. Like probability, rate of responding would be a meaningless concept if it were not possible to specify topography of response in such a way that separate instances of an operant can be counted. The specification is usually made with the help of a part of the apparatus—the 'operandum'—which senses occurrences of a response." Working with this device one weekend Skinner had only a small supply of food pellets so he made reinforcement contingent upon a number of lever presses rather than just one. To his surprise he found that the rats performed at a much higher rate. This serendipitous discovery was exploited by Skinner who then studied a variety of schedules of reinforcement to find which elicited the highest performance and greatest resistance to extinction. His atheoretical approach was Baconian and positivist and he was highly critical of Hull's and Tolman's theories which interposed hypothetical constructs between stimuli and responses. "Research designed with respect to theory is also likely to be wasteful. That a theory generates research does not prove its value unless the research is valuable." He extended his operant approach to learning into the realms of programmed instruction, language aquisition, behavior modification, and social behavior. He retained a distaste for all aspects of cognitive psychology to the end of his life.

Skinner was born in Susquehanna, Pennsylvania. He studied literature and embarked on a disastrous career as a writer before discovering psychology. He received his doctorate from Harvard University in 1931 and returned there in 1947, after posts at Minnesota and Indiana universities. His operant conditioning research initially met with indifference, but appreciation of the generality of its application resulted in Skinner becoming one of the most widely known psychologists of his day.

Skinner was reluctant to be linked eponymously with his box rather than with his ideas, but so it has remained. He is shown here made up of and contained within metaphorical boxes. Regular geometrical black and white patterns of this type can induce subjective colors—pastel shimmering color appearances between the white shapes. Skinner studied this phenomenon during his first period at Harvard.

Portrait after a photograph in: Boring, E. G., and G. Lindzey, eds. 1967. *A History of Psychology in Autobiography,* Vol. 5. New York: Appleton-Century-Crofts.

Texture Gradients

James Jerome Gibson (1904–1979) was a student of perception who defined a novel approach to it which he called ecological optics; for him it was a new solution to the ancient puzzle of how organisms perceive. "The ecological approach to visual perception . . . begins with the flowing array of the observer who walks from one vista to another, moves around an object of interest, and can approach it for scrutiny, thus extracting the invariants that underlie the changing perspective structure and seeing the connections between hidden and unhidden surfaces." It was this integration of time (motion) with space that provided the richness of stimulation for an active observer. Gibson referred to himself as a direct realist and he followed in the tradition of Reid. Gibson modified Koffka's basic question, "Why do things look as they do?" to his own, "Why do things look as they are?" Like Brunswik, Gibson was concerned with ecological validity, but his theory was much more radical. He bypassed the traditional problems associated with internal representation by denying their existence: "The simple formula proposed—perception is a function of stimulation and stimulation is a function of the environment; hence perception is a function of the environment—is a radical departure from classical theories of perception." Accordingly, like Skinner, he had little interest in the physiological underpinnings of behavior. His experiences as a psychologist in the Air Force training pilots during World War II made him suspicious of the value of laboratory studies on vision. They were considered to rely too much on simplified stimuli observed with an unmoving eye and head. In their place he argued that objects in space should be examined and not patches of light on a screen, or pictures of objects. The perception of objects was said to be direct, involving an equivalence between the higher-order variables of stimulation and perception; that is, there are invariant features of the optic flow that the observer picks up. He sought to study such higher-order variables like texture gradients in the static optic array and their transformations (the optic flow) due to observer movements.

Gibson was born in Muskingum Valley, Ohio. He received his doctorate in psychology from Princeton University, and his first teaching post was at Smith College. There he met Koffka, who was to guide his initial analysis of perception. In *The Perception of the Visual World* (1950) Gibson provided illustrations of shaded figures that appeared as hollows in one orientation and as humps when inverted. A play on this theme is evident in Gibson's portrayal: the features of his face and the backgound are both provided by the same texture gradient of dots, but its polarity is reversed vertically. Superimposed on both patterns is a further, ecologically sound, texture gradient—the planks of a pier receding into waters near those lapping Cornell University, where he worked for more than thirty years.

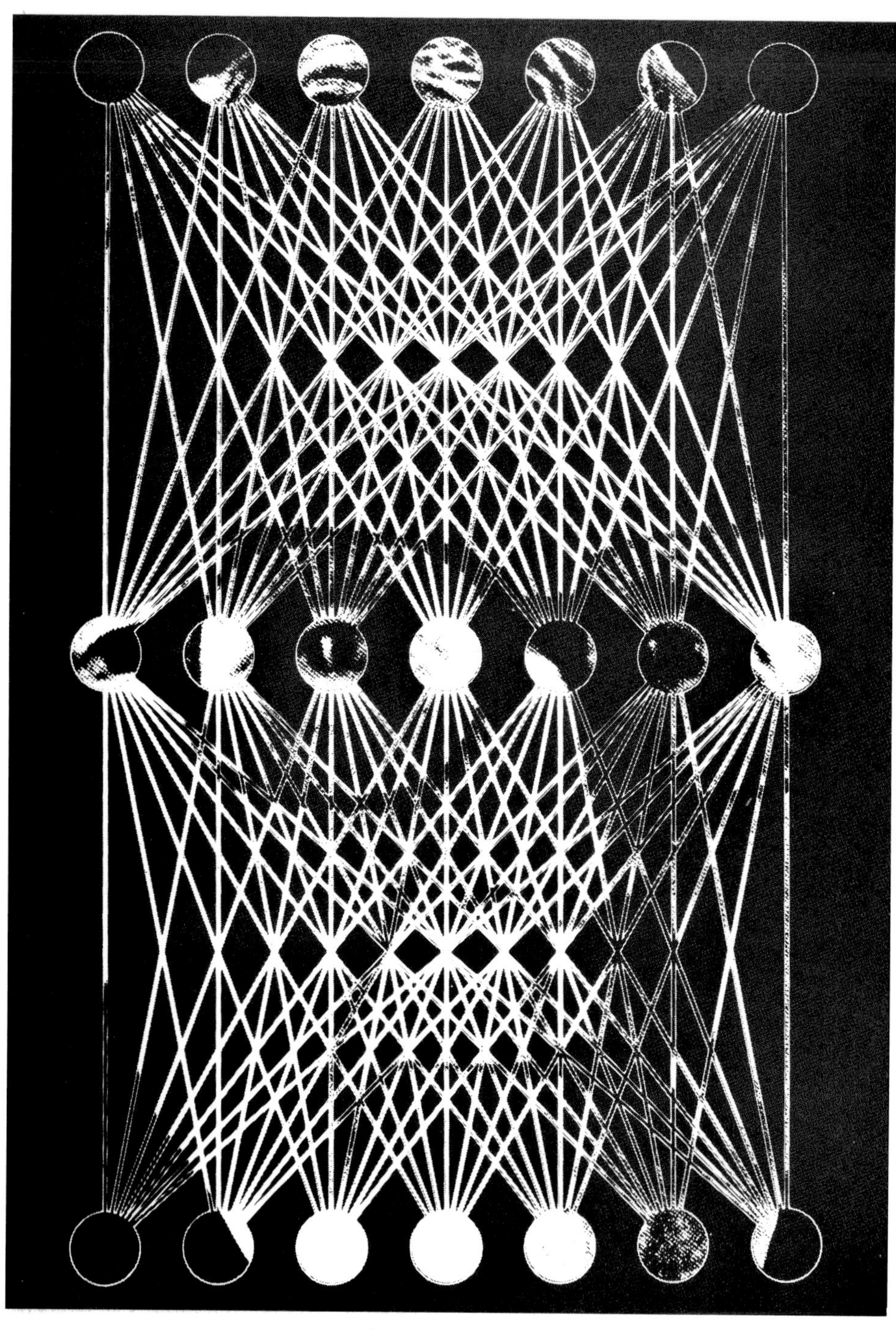

Portrait after a photograph in: Lindzey, G., ed. 1980. *A History of Psychology in Autobiography,* Vol. 7. San Francisco: Freeman.

Face Sequences

Donald Olding Hebb (1904–1985) suggested that much of the activity in the brain proceeds independently of the messages received via the senses, and that the latter merely amplify some of the former. This established a pattern that was to be pursued by him more widely, namely the relationship between experience and brain processes. Lashley's search for the engram, the memory trace, in the brains of rats had proved fruitless, and Hebb proposed an attractive alternative—that memory is stored in the activity of circuits of nerve cells which he called cell assemblies. These ideas were expressed in *The Organization of Behavior* (1949), in which he made speculative neurophysiological interpretations of perception, attention, learning, intelligence, and motivation. He proposed that perceptual learning takes place when assemblies of cells fire together; their reverberating activity resulted in synaptic changes which further increased the probability of the nerves firing together. He made an assumption very much like Bain's cited earlier (similarly trying to reconcile principles of association with adaptability of behavior) but Hebb had the advantage of greater neurophysiological knowledge: "When an axon of cell A is near enough to excite cell B and repeatedly or persistently takes part in firing it, some growth process or metabolic change takes place in one or both cells such that A's efficiency, as one of the cells firing B, is increased." The activities of different cell assemblies acting at the same time could be linked into more complex units called phase sequences: "The *phase sequence* is a temporally integrated series of assembly activities. . . . Each assembly activity in the series might be aroused (1) sensorily, (2) by excitation of other assemblies, or (3) in both ways. It is assumed that the last, (3), is what usually happens in an organized flow of behavior." Hebb's ideas were among the first to be subjected to computer simulation. The initial results were not too successful, but the concepts at the heart of Hebb's theory enjoy renewed life in the context of neural networks and parallel distributed processing.

Hebb was born in Chester, Nova Scotia. He commenced his studies at Dalhousie and McGill universities and was slow in deciding on psychology. He completed his doctorate under Lashley at Harvard and continued his research with Penfield at the Montreal Neurological Institute. He derived his interests in perception and learning from Lashley, and in arousal from Penfield. Hebb worked at Queen's University, Kingston, Ontario, before his appointment as director of the Yerkes Laboratories of Primate Biology in 1942. He returned to McGill in 1947, where he remained for the rest of his career.

Hebb's face can be seen in the middle layer of a three level network: each cell in the middle layer is connected to every other one in the levels above and below it. More complex neural networks, involving more levels, have hidden layers the activity of which cannot be determined from either the input or the output layer.

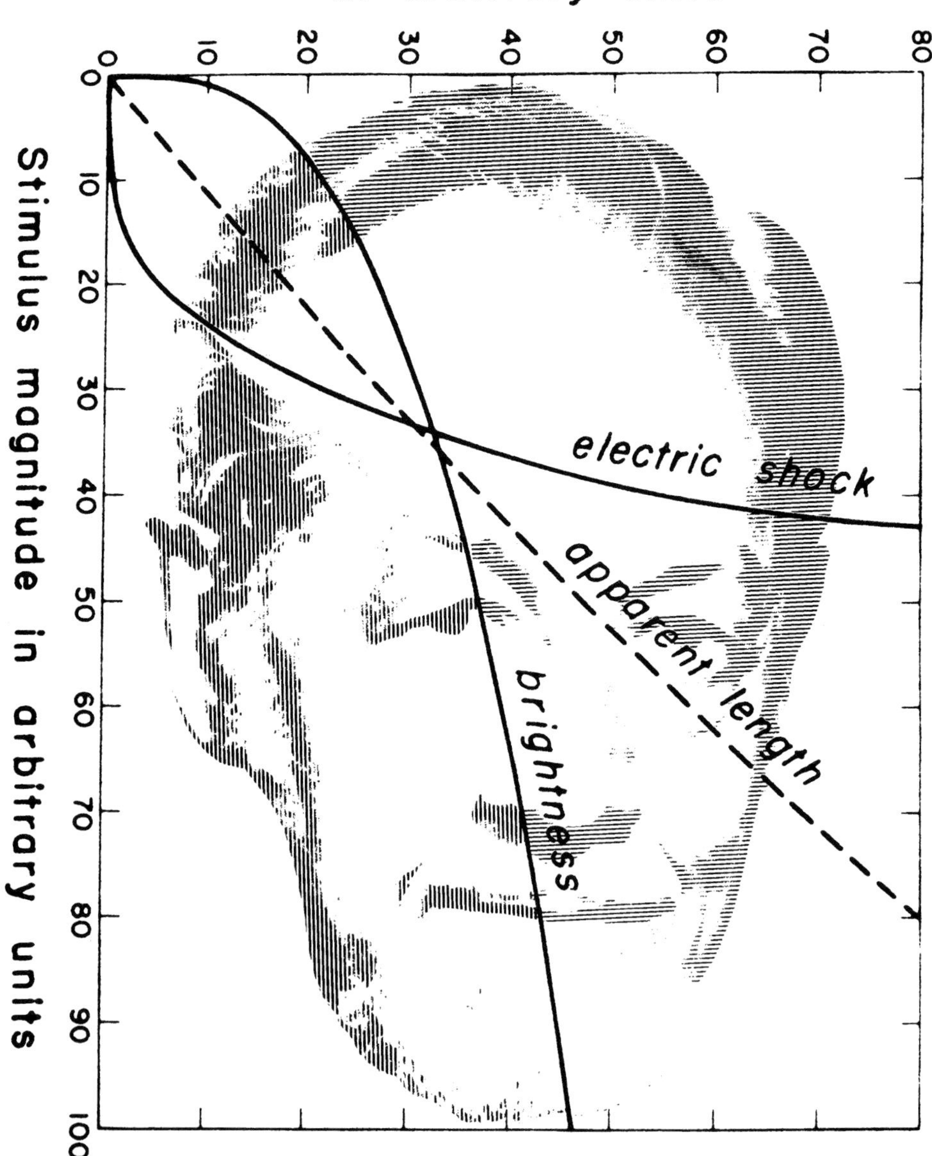

Portrait after a photograph in: Lindzey, G. ed. 1974. *A History of Psychology in Autobiography,* Vol. 6. Englewood Cliffs, N.J.: Prentice-Hall.

Motif after a graph in: Stevens, S. S. 1975. *Psychophysics.* New York: Wiley.

Power Functions

Stanley Smith Stevens (1906–1973) marked the centenary of *Elements of Psychophysics* by honoring Fechner and repealing his law. "Perhaps the most insistent question on this 100th anniversary of Fechner's monumental opus is how its author could have known so much and have made such a wrong guess. (He believed that, unlike errors in general, errors in perception are independent of the perceived magnitude.)" Stevens was dissatisfied with the indirect category methods Fechner had used for scaling sensory magnitude, preferring the direct ratio techniques pioneered by Plateau. He was also influenced by Brentano's suggestion that Weber's law could be applied symmetrically to sensation differences and to stimulus differences. Stevens developed a range of methods for estimating magnitudes of sensation directly: by assigning numbers to stimuli varying in intensity, by providing a modulus relative to which other intensities could be judged, or by matching the intensities of stimuli in different modalities. When these methods were applied to a variety of stimulus dimensions the resulting curves did not conform to Fechner's logarithmic law and Stevens proposed an alternative power law which could describe the functions. The essential difference between the laws was the assumptions on which each was based: for Fechner, equal stimulus differences produced equal sensory differences, whereas for Stevens, equal stimulus ratios led to equal ratios of sensory magnitude. "The power function shows us that there exists a beautifully simple relation between stimulus and sensory response. We can sum it up in seven words. Equal stimulus ratios produce equal subjective ratios. That statement about ratios captures the essence of the psychophysical law." He argued that the power function was a general feature of both perception and its underlying neural substrate. That is, the neural signals increased as a power function of increased stimulus intensity rather than logarithmically. Stevens had an intense interest in the philosophy of science; he was instrumental in bringing the physicists' application of operationism to the attention of psychologists.

Stevens was born in Ogden, Utah. His youthful desire to be a writer and artist was unfulfilled, and he sampled many courses at Utah and Stanford universities before obtaining his doctorate in psychology from Harvard under Boring's guidance; he stayed there for almost all his academic life. He was a founder of the journal *Perception and Psychophysics* in 1966.

Stevens is shown within the dimensions beloved of psychophysicists—psychological and physical magnitudes—with the former measured by magnitude estimation. The three functions are plotted on linear-linear axes and only one of them (brightness) would conform to Fechner's logarithmic law. Plotting the curves on log-log axes yields straight lines, the gradients of which are the exponents in Stevens' power law. The brightness curve separates vertical and horizontal lines in the portrait of Stevens, one set being slightly brighter than the other. The lines are also of different apparent (and physical) lengths.

Portrait after a photograph in: Schultz, D. P., and S. E. Schultz. 1987. *A History of Modern Psychology,* ed. 4. San Diego: Harcourt Brace Jovanovich.

Humanistic Psychologist

Abraham Harold Maslow (1908–1970) was the principal protagonist of third-force or humanistic psychology. In 1968 he wrote: "Humanistic Psychology—that's what it is being called most frequently—is now quite solidly established as a viable third alternative to objectivistic, behavioristic (mechanomorphic) psychology and to orthodox Freudianism." Thus, the whole of experimental psychology was cast in the mold of the natural sciences and all analytic treatments that were based upon mental pathology were labeled as Freudianism. Humanistic psychology sought a middle road by emphasizing the potential for human growth and the study of self, personality, and motivation. Although most of the movement's ideas were derived from European thought, it never attracted popular support in Europe as it did in America, possibly because the extreme positions to which it reacted were not as widely pursued in Europe. Humanistic psychology was based on Brentano's intentionality, Husserl's phenomenology, Gestalt holism, and Jungian self-actualization. Clearly, Allport's concern with idiographic studies of personality, and Rogers's emphasis on the power of individuals to heal themselves were contributory currents. "For the writers of various groups . . . growth, individuation, autonomy, self-actualization, self-development, productiveness, self-realization, are all crudely synonymous, designating a vaguely perceived area rather than a sharply defined concept. In my opinion, it is *not* possible to define this area sharply at the present time. Nor is it desirable either, since a definition which does not emerge easily and naturally from well-known facts is apt to be inhibiting and distorting rather than helpful."

Maslow believed that more could be learned about human personality from studies of those who had become self-actualized than from those who required psychological assistance. Accordingly, he gathered biographical information on the likes of Lincoln and Einstein in order to discover their commonalities. Maslow's research was mainly in the area of personality and motivation. He proposed that human needs are hierarchically organized, from the most basically biological to those of self-actualization, which "refers to man's desire for self-fulfillment, namely, to the tendency for him to become actualized in what he is potentially. This tendency might be phrased as the desire to become more and more what one is, to become everything one is capable of becoming." At the bottom of the hierarchy there are D-needs based on some physiological deficiency that requires satisfaction, and at the top are the B-needs that are based on being, belonging, and love. Maslow is portrayed in a graphical representation of his hierarchy of needs.

Maslow was born in Brooklyn. He studied psychology at the University of Wisconsin, and then worked with Thorndike at Columbia Teachers College. He held posts at Brooklyn College and Brandeis University. He was very active in organizing humanistic psychology. He assisted in founding the *Journal of Humanistic Psychology* in 1961, and he saw the establishment of the American Association of Humanistic Psychology. He was president of the American Psychological Association in 1968.

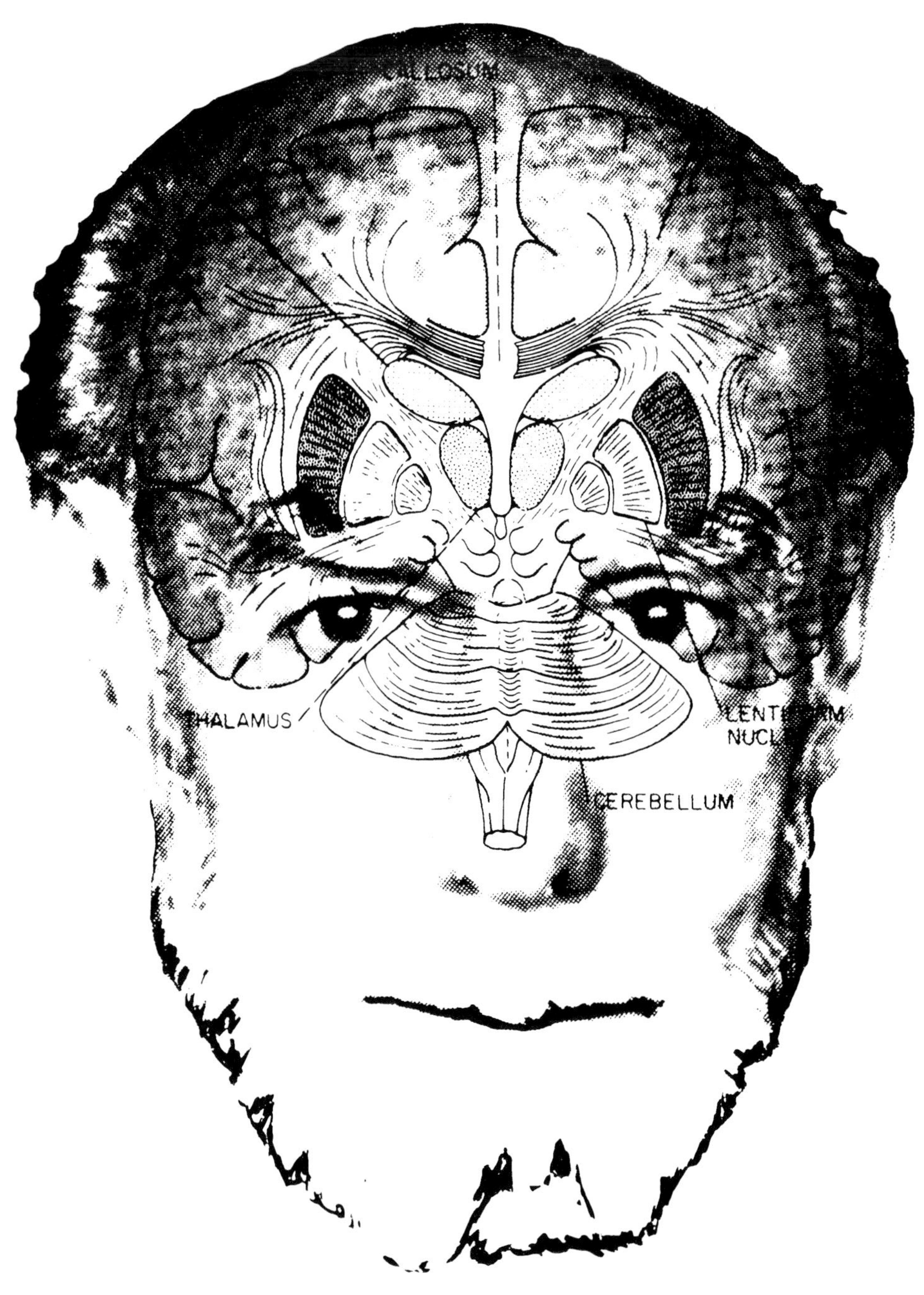

Portrait after a photograph in: Gregory, R. L. 1981. Editorial: the Nobel Prizes. *Perception 10*:243–244.

Motif after a diagram in: Sperry, R. W. 1974. Lateral specialization in the surgically separated hemisphere. In *The Neurosciences: Third Study Program.* F. O. Schmitt and F. G. Worden, eds. Cambridge, Mass.: MIT Press.

Split Brain

Roger Walcott Sperry (1913–1994) severed the nerve pathways that link the two cerebral hemispheres in the course of operating on patients with epilepsy and noted perception and cognition were modified. By presenting visual patterns to one side of a fixation point, thus projecting to one hemisphere alone, it was possible to determine the differences in the functions the hemispheres perform. "The left and right hemispheres of the brain are each found to have their own specialized forms of intellect. The left is highly verbal and mathematical, and performs with analytic, symbolic, computer-like, sequential logic. The right, by contrast, is spatial, mute, and performs with a synthetic, spatioperceptual, and mechanical kind of information processing not yet simulatable in computers." The dominance of the left hemisphere had been noted since Broca's time, but Sperry was able to demonstrate the specialization of the right hemisphere, too. This research provided a tremendous spur to laterality research, although the results were frequently overinterpreted in popular books: the specializations in function were even related to ancient dichotomies such as yin-yang.

Sperry's earlier work was concerned with another basic question for neuroscience: how do nerves make the appropriate connections in the brain? For this research he took advantage of the fact that the nerves of Amphibia regenerate. Severing the optic nerve of a newt resulted in the nerves remaking their original connections. This obtained even when the eye was rotated. "It follows that optic fibers arising from different points of the retina must differ from one another in some way. If the ingrowing optic fibers were indistinguishable from one another, there would be no way in which they could re-establish their different functional connections in an orderly pattern. Each optic fiber must be endowed with some quality, presumably chemical, that marks it as having originated from a particular spot of the retinal field." Similarly, grafting a piece of skin from the thigh onto the shoulder and then stimulating the shoulder produced a scratching response to the thigh.

Sperry was born in Hartford, Connecticut. He studied English, then psychology at Oberlin College, and zoology at the University of Chicago. He held posts at Harvard and Chicago before moving to California Institute of Technology in 1954. He received the Nobel Prize for medicine and physiology in 1981. In the last decades of his life he addressed the philosophical questions of ethics and morality from the viewpoint of neuroscience: "In my scheme, values are perceived to be organized in a complex of nested manifolds involving value hierarchies within hierarchies."

Sperry's full-face portrait is matched with a diagram of a transverse section of the brain indicating a lesion of the corpus callosum—the vast structure that contains the nerve fibers connecting symmetrical parts of the cerebral hemispheres.

As remarked above one of the characteristics of memory and perception is the recognition of identity or of similarity. To recognise a thing is surely to react to it, internally or overtly, as the 'same thing' to which we reacted on a previous occasion.

In the above sense mechanical devices can show some degree of recognition. A photocell can respond in the same way to apples having the same colour, a penny-in-the-slot machine to similar coins, and so forth. Men and animals are capable of this, but of much more. The progressive stages of recognition may be classified as:

(1) Those in which all the conditions of stimulation are identical, within the limits of discrimination of the organism;

(2) Those in which there are differences in the peripheral stimulation, but in which these may be 'corrected' by other sensory impulses so as to lead to the production of an identical pattern of central stimulation;

(3) Those in which such correction is inadequate or lacking, so that there are points of difference between the stimulation on two occasions, these points of difference being perceptible by the organism, yet the thing is recognised as the same in certain important aspects; and

(4) Those in which the differences extend to all direct sensory qualities and physical constituents, so that the sameness of the two objects is confined to some abstract characteristic such as triangularity, number, and other spatial or temporal relations or vague qualities such as intellectual difficulty.

Portrait after a photograph in: Bartlett, F. C. 1946. Kenneth J. W. Craik, 1914–1945. *British Journal of Psychology* 36:109–116.

Motif after text in: Craik, K. J. W. 1943. *The Nature of Explanation.* Cambridge, England: Cambridge University Press.

Recognition of Identity

Kenneth John William Craik (1914–1945) drew parallels between the operations performed by minds and machines, and suggested that perception and performance are based on mental models of the environment. "Assuming then the existence of the external world I have outlined a symbolic theory of thought, in which the nervous system is viewed as a calculating machine capable of modelling or paralleling external events, and have suggested that this process of paralleling is the basic feature of thought and explanation. The possessor of a nervous system is thus able to anticipate events instead of making invariable empirical trial." The machine metaphor has proved to be particularly attractive to experimental psychologists. Craik was only able to enlist relatively simple machines, but his insight lies at the heart of the cognitive revolution that was to sweep through psychology. He worked with analogue devices, as the digital computer was still embryonic. Nonetheless, he appreciated the importance of servo systems in adapting to the environment: "The main parts of such a system are the sensory device, the law relating its controlling effect on the counteracting cause which it produces, and the nature of that cause. . . . The essential feature of the sensory device is its ability to translate the change it is to measure . . . into some form of energy which can be amplified and used to drive the restoring cause. . . . The next part is what may be called the computing device and controller, which determines the amount and kind of energy to be released from the effector unit to restore equilibrium. . . . The final part is the power unit or effector (equivalent to the muscles in men and animals) which restores the state of equilibrium." His concern with prediction rather than reaction (shared with Bartlett) reflected his disatisfaction with behaviorism. After his untimely death computing machines increased in speed and complexity so that the tasks that they could simulate became more explicitly cognitive. Concepts from engineering, like information and self-organization, were integrated with a growing knowledge of neurophysiology with the result that the computer became a metaphor for the brain.

Craik was educated in Edinburgh and studied philosophy at its university. He conducted graduate research in psychology under Bartlett at Cambridge University, and became director of the Applied Psychology Research Unit there in 1944. His initial work at Cambridge was on visual adaptation, and he demonstrated that the eye operates like a range-setting device. In one heroic experiment he fixated the sun with his right eye for two minutes and charted the recovery from the scotoma over the next six months. During World War II he applied his ingenuity for mechanical construction in designing aircraft simulators for studying human-machine interaction in complex tasks.

Craik can be recognized in text describing the problems faced by natural and artificial pattern recognizers.

Portrait after frontispiece photograph in: Spillmann, L., and B. Wooten, eds. 1984. *Sensory Experience, Adaptation, and Perception. Festschrift in Honor of Professor Ivo Kohler.* Hillsdale, N.J.: Erlbaum.

Visual Inversion

Ivo Kohler (1915–1985) provided painstaking evidence that the internal models of the environment (of the type proposed by Craik) could be modified by experience. He wore a variety of distorting optical devices for long periods and found that both perception and action adapted to the new spatial relations. In one study he wore a binocular mirror device (which inverted the images on both eyes) continually for almost four months. Initially everything appeared inverted and all actions based on visual input were misguided. After a period of days and weeks his behavior was no longer disrupted by the inverting mirrors: he was able to reach for objects appropriately and even carry out complex skills such as skiing. Throughout the weeks of adaptation he kept detailed protocols and records of his performance on perceptual-motor tasks. When the mirrors were removed, long-lasting aftereffects were reported: the world was transformed once more, but recovery was quicker than adaptation had been. "This experiment, the first of such long duration, was significant. . . . In the first place, the aftereffects obtained were of optimal strength. In the second place, it gave rise to a number of peculiar aftereffects which I have already referred to as 'situational.' Not only curvatures, distortions, deviations, apparent movements, etc., were found to leave traces in the sensorium, but also the variations in intensity of these disturbances." Kohler was extending experiments that had been initiated by Helmholtz who examined the effects of prism distortion on reaching for a visible target—initial errors were corrected with practice and aftereffects occurred in subsequent undistorted vision. Gibson also measured the aftereffects of curvature and tilt following adaptation to prisms. At the end of the nineteenth century George Malcolm Stratton (1865–1957) wore an inverting lens in front of one eye and noted the adaptation over eight days and the aftereffects thereafter. Kohler's experiments reawakened interest in visual adaptation and added many new phenomena to its study, particularly gaze-contingent color aftereffects. His observations led to the study of color-contingent aftereffects generally.

Kohler commenced his studies at the University of Innsbruck in theology, which became transformed first into philosophy and then into psychology. He worked as an assistant at the Institute of Psychology at Innsbruck for ten years before being appointed its director.

Kohler's methods were in the phenomenological tradition of Gestalt psychology, "although my attitude toward this is somewhat ambivalent. I do not deny what is called 'organization' in perception, but I believe we have found a way to change this organization by prolonged exposure to certain kinds of stimulation." This ambiguity is expressed in the portrait of Kohler: while all the parts of the portrait are inverted its organization as a Gestalt is of a normally upright face. It also reflects an unresolved riddle associated with phenomenological reports of vision during inversion—whether the visual world appears normal after perceptual-motor adaptation.

Portrait after a photograph kindly provided by John Robson.

Contrast Sensitivity

Fergus William Campbell (1924–1993) provided a new stimulus for vision. Drawing an analogy with sound, where the simplest stimulus is a tone of a given temporal frequency, he suggested that patterns with a single spatial frequency were the ideal visual stimulus. "The simplest sound signal is a pure sine wave. In vision the equivalent is a grating pattern whose brightness varies in a simple sinusoidal manner." Hebb had considered that spots of light were the simplest stimuli, and this received support from initial discoveries of the neurophysiology of vision. Microelectrode recordings from single cells in the optic nerve of cat indicated that the receptive fields were circular and concentric. However, cells in the visual cortex were later found to have linear receptive fields—they could be excited most strongly by features of patterns like lines or edges in particular orientations. Campbell proposed an alternative to these feature-analytic approaches: complex patterns were processed by channels selective to specific spatial frequencies. According to this view, a single line was a complex stimulus made up of a family of analyzers varying in spatial frequency, contrast, and phase. "A fundamental insight of sensory physiology is that there are many parallel pathways within a sensory system, each specialized to carry information about a different type of stimulus element." The channel hypothesis was eagerly adopted by visual scientists and it proved to be empirically fertile. At one and the same time it provided a definition of the stimulus (in terms of spatial frequencies) and a theory of its processing (in terms of spatially selective channels). The visual system was examined in the way physicists assessed the optical quality of lenses by determining their modulation transfer function, to which the mathematics of Fourier analysis could be applied. For vision this was called the contrast sensitivity function. Moreover, evidence was provided to suggest that the channels operated independently of one another, could be selectively adapted, produced specific visual evoked potentials, and could be recorded electrophysiologically.

Campbell was born in Glasgow and received his education there. He studied medicine and then ophthalmology at its university before residing briefly at Oxford University and then settling at Cambridge, where he was appointed professor of neurosensory physiology. His early research was concerned with physiological optics, and he devised an improved version of Young's optometer in order to measure the quality of the retinal image. He was elected a Fellow of the Royal Society in 1978.

Campbell is portrayed in the stimulus he championed—a sine-wave grating. His method of measuring contrast sensitivity was to determine the threshold contrast (the luminance difference between the lightest and darkest parts of the grating) at different spatial frequencies. The portrait is carried in low spatial frequencies which will be below threshold at normal reading distance. If the illustration is viewed from a greater distance or moved from side to side, so that the spatial frequencies in the portrait are either increased or blurred, then Campbell's smiling face will be visible.

Monitoring of several channels with response to one at a time.—The situation which we will now consider is much closer to real life than those which have gone before. In the present case the listener hears speech from a number of different sources, but ignores any messages which are not for him. He is therefore carrying out a combination of the two simpler tasks: he may listen to two signals simultaneously, but then can ignore one message and deal only with the other. As before, we are interested largely in central processes which may apply to psychology in general rather than to hearing alone. It is more difficult to be sure of the relative roles of sensory and central processes in this case than it was in the simpler ones, but some such distinction can be made by considering the types of score and the effect of instructions. There are comparatively few results from this type of situation on the effect of varying the amount of information presented to the subject. Many data are to be found, however, on the familiar question of the physical methods used to present the messages: and in addition there are results on the effectiveness of certain types of message in securing response.

The spatial arrangement of the sound sources is again important. It will be remembered that spatial separation is highly beneficial when only one message is to be answered, but not when both are to receive a response. In the monitoring situation, which combines both the other tasks, separation is on the whole desirable but not altogether so. Webster and Thompson found that six channels were handled better when fed through six loudspeakers rather than one, and also that provision of 'pull-down' facilities was helpful. Spieth, Curtis and Webster found that three loudspeakers were better than one: This was not because of differences in the quality of the sound produced by different echoes in different places, because separation was still useful when the channels were made artificially different in quality by putting different band-pass filters in the circuits.

Portrait after a photograph in: Lindzey, G., ed. 1980. *A History of Psychology in Autobiography,* Vol. 7. San Francisco: Freeman.

Motifs after text and a figure in: Broadbent, D.E. 1958. *Perception and Communication.* Oxford: Pergamon Press.

Channel Capacity

Donald Eric Broadbent (1926–1993) developed an information processing model of human cognition: "A nervous system acts to some extent as a single communication channel, so that it is meaningful to regard it as having a limited capacity." He adopted Bartlett's approach of examining skilled activity in realistic situations and advanced Craik's machine modeling metaphor. One task selected for early inquiry was that of listening to two messages simultaneously. He appreciated that the problems of selection applied to attention rather than perception, and he suggested that a human operator could be considered in much the same way engineers were analyzing information transmission in radio and telephone communication. In his model, sensory signals were initially stored for very short intervals and filtered according to their probability or importance; the attention mechanism selected which of the filtered signals was to be processed further by the limited capacity channel. The information-flow model and the empirical evidence supporting it were published in *Perception and Communication* (1958). The model had the virtue of combining evidence from experiments on perception, performance, memory, learning, vigilance, and personality. It was later amplified by Broadbent and extended by many other cognitive scientists. The lure of information-processing models increased with increases in the speed and complexity of computers, and the language of digital computing permeated experimental psychology.

Broadbent was born in Birmingham, England. He studied psychology at Cambridge University, under Bartlett, and then joined the Applied Psychology Unit there, becoming its director in 1958. He moved to Oxford in 1974, and was elected a Fellow of the Royal Society in 1968. A constant theme in his research was the effect of environmental stress on cognitive performance. His interests were influenced by his experiences as a pilot, when he became acutely aware of the decision errors made under conditions of stress or monotony. He argued that the major insights in psychology derived from applied research, and he adapted his experimental work to the burgeoning technology of everyday life, particularly to human-computer interaction. His defense of empirical psychology was robust at a time when it was under attack: "We can tell nothing of our fellow men except by seeing what they do or say in particular circumstances. If one dispenses with this procedure, and so claims to be treating other people as persons rather than machines, one is exposed to the danger of assuming that everybody should be the kind of person one is oneself."

Broadbent is shown in the context of a task he examined in great detail: several messages are presented simultaneously, but here in vision rather than hearing; two are of text describing the problem and a third is his information-processing model. The channel capacity of the observer is exceeded by these signals so that processing has to be limited to one at a time.

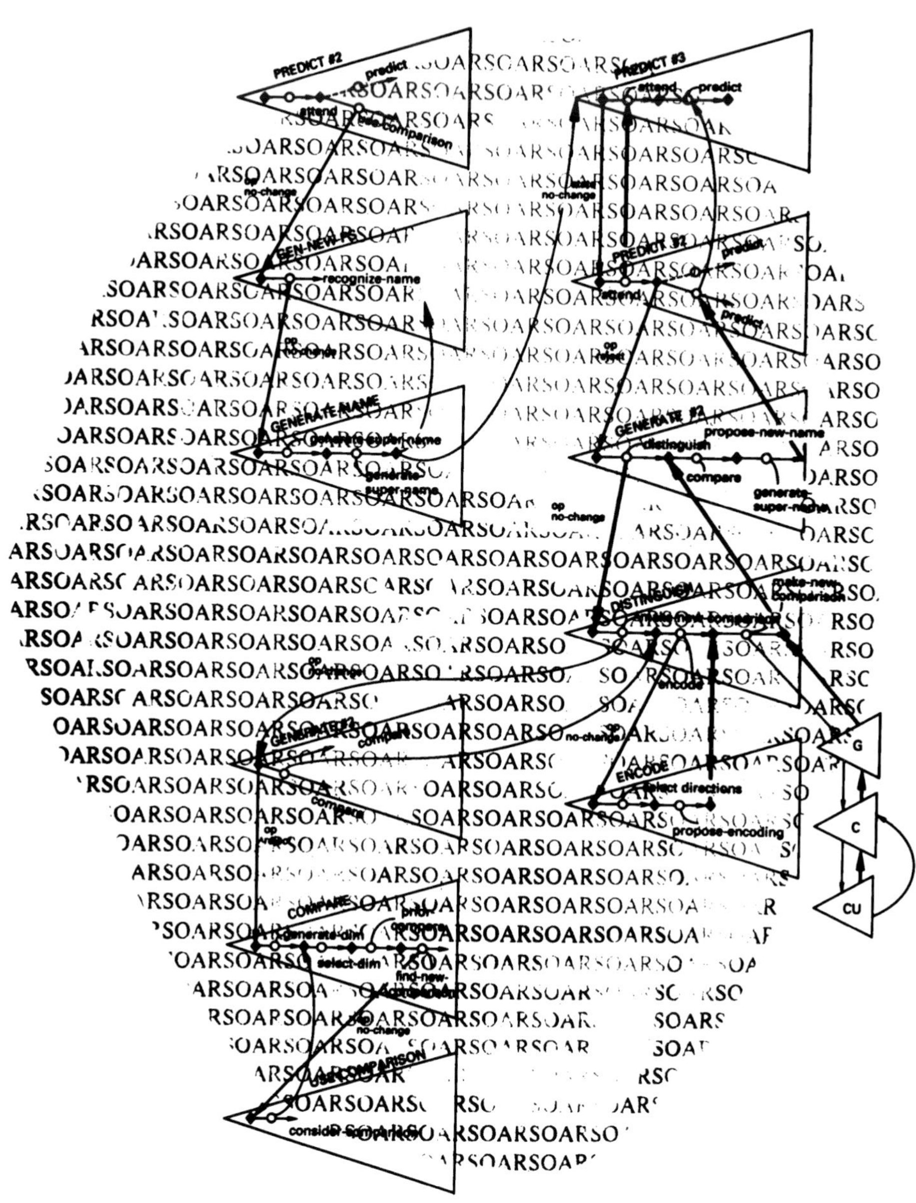

Portrait after a photograph in: *American Psychologist* 4:347, 1986.

Motif after a figure in: Newell, A. 1990. *Unified Theories of Cognition.* Cambridge, Mass.: Harvard University Press.

Artificer of Intelligence

Allen Newell (1927–1992) was one of the first to simulate cognitive functions using a computer. Descartes had marveled at the machines that could mimic the mechanical actions of the human body. Newell, in collaboration with Herbert Simon (born 1916), implemented programs on computers that performed tasks that would be referred to as intelligent in humans: they mimicked the mind. Artificial intelligence was one of the cornerstones of cognitive science that transformed psychology in the 1960s; others were Broadbent's information processing model, Piaget's analysis of cognitive development, experiments on the organization of memory, psycholinguistics, the logic and mathematics of computation, cybernetics, and the simulation of neural networks. The digital computer provided the medium that linked many of these approaches. Its principal constituents are input devices, encoder, central processor, decoder, and output devices. The human brain could be described in similar terms. Both were seen as manipulators of symbols. The fact that the signals were electronic in one case and neural in the other was not considered of importance, and Newell did not attempt to make an equation at this level. The tasks Newell and Simon started with were those of symbolic logic, and in 1956 their program, the Logic Theorist, discovered proofs of theorems using selective search strategies. In order to achieve this they developed high level list processing languages for programming. "The heart of the approach is describing the behavior of a system by a well specified program, defined in terms of elementary information processes. In this approach, a specific program plays the role that is played in classical systems of applied mathematics by a specific system of differential equations." With the development of faster computers a wider range of tasks was tackled—their General Problem Solver played chess and a variety of other logical games. Moreover, the protocols of humans performing the same tasks bore many similarities to those produced by the computer, lending support to the contention that both were performing the tasks in similar symbolic ways. In 1990 Newell produced a grand synthesis with *Unified Theories of Cognition,* in which SOAR was the vehicle for his theory of cognition. "Soar already has the major mechanisms of a cognitive system. . . . It has a symbol system and a goal hierarchy. It uses a production system as a foundation of the architecture, thus being a kind of recognize-act system. It uses problem spaces everywhere to do all of its business, that is, to formulate all its tasks. It has a chunking mechanism as part of its architecture, and it learns by chunking on everything it does."

Newell was born in San Francisco. He studied mathematics at Stanford and Princeton, and took a research post at the Rand Corporation in Santa Monica, California, working on human information processing. He undertook graduate research at Carnegie Tech and remained at Carnegie Mellon University for the rest of his career. He is represented in terms of his SOARing achievement.

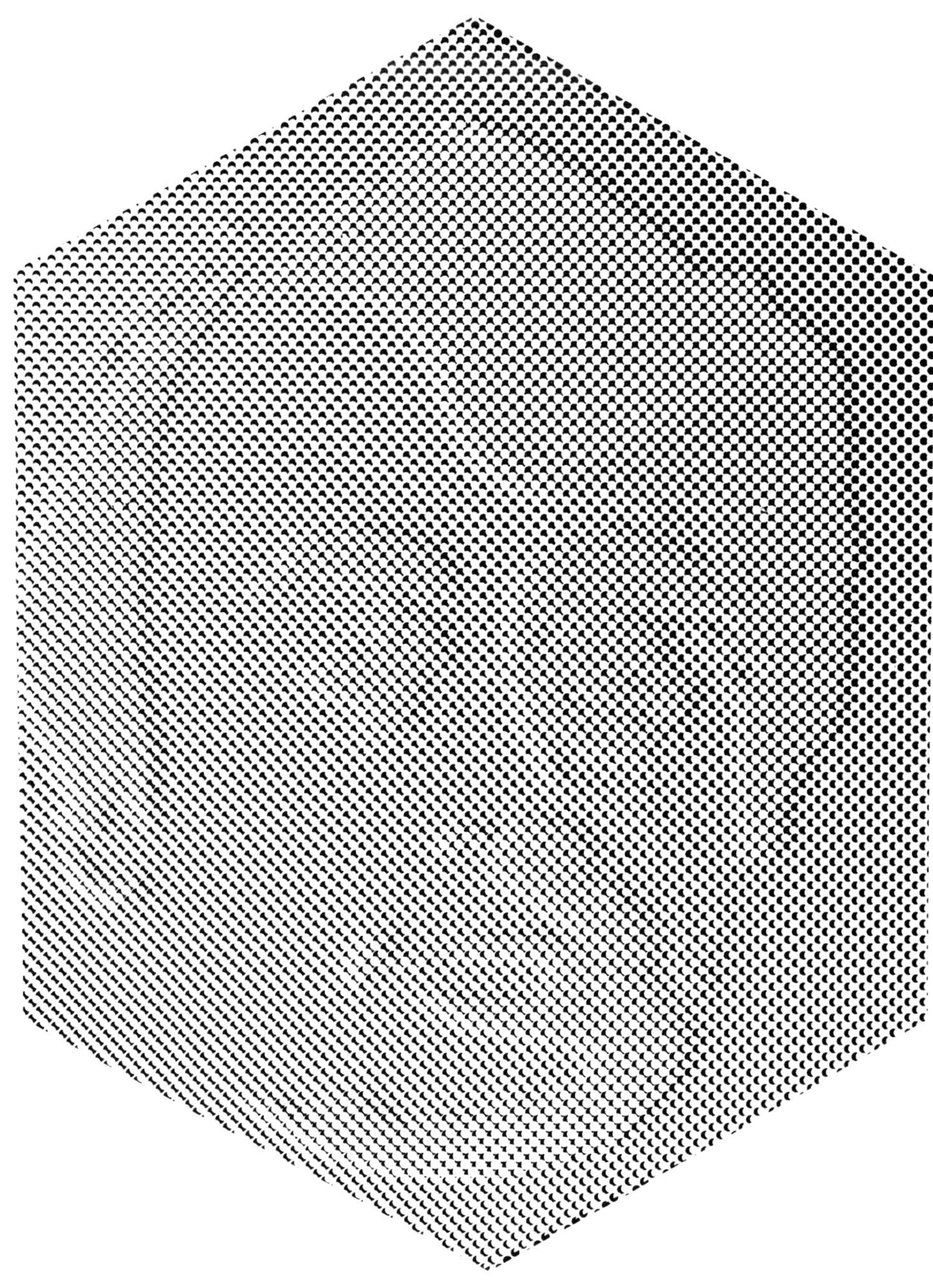

Portrait after a photograph kindly supplied by Kent Stevens.

2 1/2-D Sketch

David Courtenay Marr (1945–1980) pioneered a new approach to the computer simulation of vision, by linking concepts from physiology, psychology, and artificial intelligence. While he agreed with Gibson that the purpose of vision is to derive a veridical description of the world, he did not believe that it could be achieved directly. Thus, he proposed that a scene was represented symbolically at several different levels of abstraction. Previous approaches to computer vision had used simplified scenes, like outline blocks or alphanumeric characters. Marr addressed the problem of how an image of a real scene, captured by a camera, can be processed through a sequence of stages to recover a description of the objects in the original scene. The initial stages, referred to as early vision, extracted from the image pattern primitives like edges, line endings, and blobs; these tokens were then grouped to produce a primal sketch. Information from two views (stereo) and from a sequence of frames (motion) enabled a two-and-a-half-dimensional (2 1/2-D) sketch to be formed. This is a description of the surface orientations of the objects with respect to the camera's viewpoint. A cube, for example, would be represented as a 2-D shape with symbols indicating the orientation of the three visible faces with respect to the viewpoint. Up to this stage the processing had been data-driven, without recourse to material stored in memory. In order to derive an object-centered description stored material was drawn upon so that an object could be recognized independently of its viewpoint. Marr's approach to understanding vision consisted of three stages: "At one extreme, the top level, is the abstract computational theory of the device, in which the performance of the device is characterized as a mapping from one kind of information to another, the abstract properties of this mapping are defined precisely, and its appropriateness and adequacy for the task at hand are demonstrated. In the center is the choice of representation for the input and output and the algorithm to be used to transform one into the other. And at the other extreme are the details of how the algorithm and representation are realized physically—the detailed computer architecture, so to speak."

Marr was born in Woodford, Essex, and worked in both Cambridges—in England and Massachusetts. At Cambridge University he developed a mathematical model of cerebellar function. In the course of this he realized the advantages associated with computational approaches, and learned the appropriate skills at the Artificial Intelligence Laboratory at Massachusetts Institute of Technology, where he worked from 1975. While Marr developed algorithms and implemented early stages of representation, it was at the computational level that his impact has been most keenly felt.

Marr is here represented by pattern tokens signifying the contours of his face, and his portrait is embedded in a representation of a cube; there are slight pattern differences to denote the boundaries between the three faces of the cube.

Sources of Quotations

Sources of quotations are listed in the order in which they appear for each subject. The quotations are all from the works of the person under consideration and are taken from original sources, reprinted works, published translations, and translations by the author.

Introduction
  Reid, T. 1821. p. 242

Francis Bacon
  Bacon, F. 1855. p. xxvii
  Bacon, F. 1857. pp. 161–164

Thomas Hobbes
  Hobbes, T. 1651. p. 1, p. 62, p. 63, p. 3

René Descartes
  Hall, T. S. 1972. pp. 77–78

John Locke
  Locke, J. 1695. p. 41

Isaac Newton
  Newton, I. 1704. p. 22

Gottfried Wilhelm von Leibniz
  Diamond, S. 1974. p. 415

George Berkeley
  Berkeley, G. 1709. pp. 1–2, p. 8

Thomas Reid
  Reid, T. 1821. p. 20, p. 203

David Hume
  Hume, D. 1772. p. 24

Jean-Jacques Rousseau
  Roche, K. F. 1974. p. 25, p. 25

Immanuel Kant
  Watson, R. I. 1979. pp. 80–81, p. 85

Franz Anton Mesmer
  Goshen, C. E. 1967. p. 789, p. 794, p. 810

Philippe Pinel
  Zilboorg, G., and G. W. Henry. 1941. p. 322, pp. 323–324
  Goshen, C. E. 1967. p. 257

Johann Wolfgang von Goethe
  Goethe, J. W. 1840. p. 287

Franz Joseph Gall
  Herrnstein, R. J., and E. G. Boring. 1965. pp. 218–219

Thomas Young
  Young, T. 1802. p. 20

Charles Bell
  Gordon-Taylor, G., and E. W. Walls. 1958. p. 226
  Boring, E. G. 1950. p. 87

David Brewster
  Brewster, D. 1844. p. 139

Jan Evangelista Purkinje
  Purkinje, J. 1825. p. 60

Arthur Schopenhauer
Hergenhahn, B. R. 1992. p. 194
Schopenhauer, A. 1896. p. 93

Marie Jean Pierre Flourens
Fancher, R. E. 1990. p. 82
Herrnstein, R. J., and E. G. Boring. 1965. p. 223
Diamond, S. 1974. p. 238

Ernst Heinrich Weber
Ross, H. E., and D. J. Murray. 1978. p. 220, p. 206

Lambert Adolphe Jacques Quetelet
Diamond, S. 1974. p. 683, p. 595

Isadore Auguste Marie François Xavier Comte
Comte, A. 1896. p. 10, p. 3

Gustav Theodor Fechner
Fechner, G. T. 1966. p. 7

Johannes Peter Müller
Boring, E. G. 1950. p. 84

Joseph Antoine Ferdinand Plateau
Plateau, J. 1850. pp. 256–257

Charles Wheatstone
Wheatstone, C. 1838. p. 371

Charles Darwin
Darwin, C. 1900. p. 98

Claude Bernard
Rosenzweig, M. R. 1963. p. 91
Guthrie, D. 1945. p. 281
Grmek, M. D. 1970. p. 27, p. 27

Frans Cornelis Donders
Donders, F. C. 1969 pp. 413–414, p. 418

Alexander Bain
Bain, A. 1855. p. v, pp. v–vi, p. 67
Bain, A. 1873. p. 119

Hermann Ludwig Ferdinand von Helmholtz
Helmholtz, H. 1925. p. 533
Helmholtz, H. 1873. p. 274

Francis Galton
Cowles, M. P. 1989. p. 4
Forrest, D. W. 1974. p. 139

Pierre Paul Broca
Brain, Lord. 1961. p. 32
Young, R. M. 1970. p. 143

Jean Martin Charcot
Macmillan, M. B. 1991. p. 58

Hermann Rudolf Aubert
Duke-Elder, S. 1968. p. 547
Helmholtz, H. 1925. p. 273

Joseph Rémi Leopold Delboeuf
Macmillan, M. B. 1991. p. 82

James Clerk Maxwell
Maxwell, J. C. 1890. p. 122, p. 123
Campbell, L., and W. Garnett. 1882. p. 289

Wilhelm Maximilian Wundt
Diamond, S. 1974. p. 750

Karl Ewald Konstantin Hering
Hering, E. 1942. p. 41

Ernst Mach
Hiebert, E. N. 1973. p. 603
Rand, B. 1912. p. 600, p. 614

Franz Brentano
Brentano, F. 1973. pp. xv–xvi

William James
James, W. 1890. p. vi, p. v, p. 196

Josef Breuer
Macmillan, M. B. 1991. p. 15

David Ferrier
Spillane, J. D. 1981. p. 389
Ferrier, D. 1876. pp. xiv–xv, p. 288

Granville Stanley Hall
Hall, G. S. 1904. p. v

Ivan Petrovich Pavlov
Pavlov, I. P. 1955. p. 394, p. 46
Pavlov, I. P. 1927. p. 318

Hermann Ebbinghaus
Ebbinghaus, H. 1964. p. xiii, p. 22

Conwy Lloyd Morgan
Morgan, C. L. 1894, p. 53
Morgan, C. L. 1932. p. 247
Morgan, C. L. 1900. p. 144
Morgan, C. L. 1894, p. ix

Emil Kraepelin
Kraepelin, E. 1906. pp. 12–13, p. 23

Sigmund Freud
Freud, S. 1953. p. 674

Franz Carl Müller-Lyer
Day, R. H., and Knuth, H. 1981. p. 131, p. 134
Müller-Lyer, F. C. 1931. p. 23

Karl Pearson
Pearson, K. 1900. p. 6, p. 12

Alfred Binet
Binet, A., and T. Simon. 1916. p. 40, p. 182
Macmillan, M. B. 1991. p. 51

Pierre Marie Felix Janet
Goshen, C. E. 1967. p. 887
Macmillan, M. B. 1991. p. 439

Hugo Münsterberg
Münsterberg, H. 1899. p. 3
Münsterberg, H. 1909. pp. 16–17

Mary Whiton Calkins
Herrnstein, R. J., and E. G. Boring. 1965. p. 531
Calkins, M. W. 1930. p. 45

Charles Edward Spearman
Spearman, C. E. 1923. p. 5, p. 5

Edward Bradford Titchener
Watson, R. I. 1979. p. 224, p. 225

Robert Sessions Woodworth
Woodworth, R. S. 1932. p. 375, p. 371
Woodworth, R. S. 1938. p. 1

William McDougall
McDougall, W. 1930. p. 13, p. 14, p. 15

Margaret Floy Washburn
Washburn, M. F. 1908. p. 88
Washburn, M. F. 1917, p. 38
Washburn, M. F. 1930. p. 82

Hans Berger
Diamond, S. 1974. p. 190
Gloor, P. 1969. p. 83, p. 77

Edward Lee Thorndike
Thorndike, E. L. 1898. p. 3, pp. 5–6

Carl Gustav Jung
Jung, C. G. 1953. p. 41

Robert Mearns Yerkes
Yerkes, R. M. 1932. p. 396, p. 396

John Broadus Watson
Watson, J. B. 1913. p. 158

Max Wertheimer
Wertheimer, M. 1938. p. 2

Arnold Lucius Gesell
Gesell, A. 1925. p. 15, p. 26

Adelbert Ames
Ames, A., C. A. Proctor, and B. Ames. 1923. p. 3

Elton George Mayo
Brown, J. A. C. 1954. p. 78

Clark Leonard Hull
Hull, C. L. 1952b. p. 154
Hull, C. L. 1952a. pp. 355–356

Hermann Rorschach
Diamond, S. 1974. p. 629

Kurt Koffka
Koffka, K. 1935. p. 680
Diamond, S. 1974. p. 488
Koffka, K. 1935. p. 22

Edward Chace Tolman
Tolman, E. C. 1949. p. 21, p. 414, p. 343

Leta Stetter Hollingworth
Shields, S. A. 1991. p. 247
Hollingworth, L. S. 1923. p. 196
Shields, S. A. 1991. p. 252

Frederic Charles Bartlett
Bartlett, F. 1932. p. 213
Bartlett, F. 1958. pp. 13–14

Edwin Garrigues Boring
Boring, E. G. 1950. pix, p. xiii

Wolfgang Köhler
Köhler, W. 1942. p. 40
Köhler, W. 1927. p. 241

Louis Leon Thurstone
Thurstone, L. L. 1959. p. 19, pp. 182–183

Ruth Fulton Benedict
Benedict, R. 1935. p. 1, p. 183
Benedict, R. 1942. p. vii

Ronald Aylmer Fisher
Fisher, R. A. 1946. p. 211
Gridgeman, N. T. 1972. pp. 10–11

Karl Spencer Lashley
Lashley, K. S. 1960. p. 500
Lashley, K. S. 1929. p. 68

Kurt Lewin
Lewin, K. 1936. p. 12, p. 9

Wilder Graves Penfield
Penfield, W., and T. Rasmussen. 1950. p. 224

Jean Piaget
Piaget, J. 1929. p. 60
Piaget, J. 1952. p. 245

Lev Semionovich Vygotsky
Vygotsky, L. S. 1978. p. 24
Vygotsky, L. S. 1962. p. 153

Gordon Willard Allport
Allport, G. W. 1937. p. 260, p. 207, p. 369, p. 246

Alexander Romanovich Luria
Luria, A. R. 1974. p. 277
Luria, A. R. 1973. p. 290

Carl Ransom Rogers
Rogers, C. R. 1961. p. 5
Rogers, C. R. 1963. p. 426
Rogers, C. R. 1961. p. 189

Egon Brunswik
Brunswik, E. 1956. p. 4, p. 48
Brunswik, E. 1966. pp. 510–511

Burrhus Frederic Skinner
Skinner, B. F. 1969. p. 75
Skinner, B. F. 1950. p. 194

James Jerome Gibson
Gibson, J. J. 1979. p. 303
Gibson, J. J. 1950. p. 1
Gibson, J. J. 1959. p. 459

Donald Olding Hebb
Hebb, D. O. 1949. p. 62
Hebb, D. O. 1959. p. 629

Stanley Smith Stevens
Stevens, S. S. 1961. p. 80
Stevens, S. S. 1975. p. 16

Abraham Harold Maslow
Maslow, A. H. 1968. p. iii, p. 24
Maslow, A. H. 1954. pp. 89–90

Roger Walcott Sperry
Sperry, R. 1983. p. 55
Sperry, R. W. 1972. p. 365
Sperry, R. 1983. p. 124

Kenneth John William Craik
Craik, K. J. W. 1943. pp. 120–121
Craik, K. J. W. 1966. pp. 23–24

Ivo Kohler
Kohler, I. 1964. p. 39, p. 17

Fergus William Campbell
Campbell, F. W., and L. Maffei. 1976. p. 30
Braddick, O. J., F. W. Campbell, and J. Atkinson. 1978. p. 4

Donald Eric Broadbent
Broadbent, D. E. 1958. p. 297
Broadbent, D. E. 1973. p. 206

Allen Newell
Newell, A., J. C. Shaw, and H. A. Simon. 1958. pp. 165–166
Newell, A. 1990. p. 39

David Courtenay Marr
Marr, D. 1982. pp. 24–25

Bibliography

Alexander, F. G., and S. T. Selesnick. 1967. *The History of Psychiatry: An Evaluation of Psychiatric Thought and Practice from Prehistoric Times to the Present.* London: Allen & Unwin.

Allport, G. W. 1937. Personality. *A Psychological Interpretation.* New York: Holt.

Allport, G. W. 1954. *The Nature of Prejudice.* Cambridge, Mass.: Addison-Wesley.

Allport, G. W. 1961. *Pattern and Growth in Personality.* New York: Holt, Rinehart & Winston.

Allport, G. W. 1967. Gordon W. Allport. In *A History of Psychology in Autobiography,* Vol. 5, E. G. Boring and G. Lindzey, eds. New York: Appleton-Century-Crofts, pp. 3–25.

Ames, A. 1925. Depth in pictorial art. *Art Bulletin 8*:5–24.

Ames, A. 1951. Visual perception and the rotating trapezoidal window. *Psychological Monographs 65.* Whole No. 324.

Ames, A., C. A. Proctor, and B. Ames. 1923. Vision and the technique of art. *Proceedings of the American Academy of Arts and Sciences 58*:3–47.

Arieti, S., ed. 1974. *American Handbook of Psychiatry.* Vol. 1. *The Foundations of Psychiatry.* New York: Basic Books.

Aubert, H. 1865. *Physiologie der Netzhaut.* Breslau: Morgenstern.

Bacon, F. 1605. *The Twoo Bookes of Francis Bacon. On the Proficience and Aduancement of Learning, Diuine and Humane.* London: Henrie Tomes.

Bacon, F. 1620. *Novum Organum sive Indicia Vera de Interpretatione Naturae.* Londini: Billius.

Bacon, F. 1855. *The Novum Organon, or a True Guide to the Interpretation of Nature.* G.W. Kitchin, trans. Oxford: Oxford University Press.

Bacon, F. 1857. *The Works of Francis Bacon,* Vol. 3. J. Spedding, R. L. Ellis, and D. D. Heath. eds. London: Longman, Simpkin, Hamilton, Wittaker, Bain, Hodgson, Wasbourne, Bohn, Richardson, Houlston, Bickers and Bush, Willis and Sotheran, Cornish, Booth, and Snow.

Bain, A. 1855. *The Senses and the Intellect.* London: Parker.

Bain, A. 1859. *The Emotions and the Will.* London: Parker.

Bain, A. 1873. *Mind and Body. The Theories of their Relation.* London: Henry King.

Bain, A. 1904. *Autobiography.* London: Longmans, Green.

Baldwin, A. L. 1967. *Theories of Child Development.* New York: Wiley.

Bartlett, F. C. 1927. *Psychology and the Soldier.* Cambridge, England: Cambridge University Press.

Bartlett, F. 1932. *Remembering: A Study in Experimental and Social Psychology.* Cambridge, England: Cambridge University Press.

Bartlett, F. C. 1946. Kenneth J. W. Craik, 1914–1945. *British Journal of Psychology 36*:109–116.

Bartlett, F. 1958. *Thinking. An Experimental and Social Study.* London: Allen & Unwin.

Beach, F. A., D. O. Hebb, C. T. Morgan, and H. W. Nissen, eds. 1960. *The Neuropsychology of Lashley.* New York: McGraw-Hill.

Becker, R. J. 1959. Outstanding contributors to psychology. *American Psychologist 14*:297–298.

Bell, C. 1811. *Idea of a New Anatomy of the Brain; Submitted for the Observations of his Friends.* London (published privately). Reprinted: Gordon-Taylor, G., and E. W. Walls. 1958. *Sir Charles Bell. His Life and Times.* Edinburgh: Livingstone.

Bell, C. 1844. *The Anatomy and Philosophy of Expression as Connected with the Fine Arts,* ed. 3. London: John Murray.

Bell, G. J. 1870. *Letters of Sir Charles Bell, Selected from His Correspondence with His Brother George Joseph Bell.* London: John Murray.

Bell, J., and C. Bell. 1803. *Anatomy of the Human Body,* Vol. 3. London: Longmans, Rees, Cadell and Davies.

Beloff, J. 1993. *Parapsychology. A Concise History.* London: Athlone Press.

Benedict, R. 1935. *Patterns of Culture.* London: Routledge & Kegan Paul.

Benedict, R. 1942. *Race and Racism.* London: Routledge & Kegan Paul.

Benedict, R. 1946. *The Chrysanthemum and the Sword. Patterns of Japanese Culture.* Boston: Houghton Mifflin.

Bennett, J. H., ed. 1974. *Collected Papers of R. A. Fisher,* Vol. 5. 1948–62. Adelaide, Australia: University of Adelaide Press.
Berkeley, G. 1709. *An Essay Towards a New Theory of Vision.* Dublin: Pepyat.
Bernard, C. 1866. *Leçons sur les propriétés des tissus vivants.* Paris: Baillière.
Binet, A. 1896. *Alterations of Personality.* H. G. Baldwin, trans. London: Chapman & Hall.
Binet, A. 1899. *The Psychology of Reasoning. Based on Experimental Researches in Hypnotism.* A. G. Whyte, trans. Chicago: Open Court Publishing.
Binet, A. 1900. *La suggestibilité.* Paris: Schleicher.
Binet, A., and C. Féré. 1885. L'hypnotisme chez les hystériques: Le transfert. *Revue Philosophique 19*:1–25.
Binet, A., and T. Simon. 1905. Methodes nouvelle pour le diagnostic du niveau intellectual des anormaux. *L'Anée Psychologique 11*:191–244.
Binet, A., and T. Simon. 1908. La développment de l'intelligence chez les infants. *L'Anée Psychologique 14*:1–94.
Binet, A., and T. Simon. 1916. *The Development of Intelligence in Children.* E. S. Kite, trans. Baltimore: Williams & Wilkins.
Binet, A., and T. Simon. 1916. *The Intelligence of the Feeble-minded.* E. S. Kite, trans. Baltimore: Williams & Wilkins.
Blakemore, C. 1977. *Mechanics of the Mind.* Cambridge, England: Cambridge University Press.
Blakemore, C. 1988. *The Mind Machine.* London: BBC Books.
Blum, M. L., and J. C. Naylor. 1968. *Industrial Psychology. Its Theoretical and Social Foundations.* New York: Harper & Row.
Bolles, R. C. 1993. *The Story of Psychology. A Thematic History.* Belmont, Calif.: Wadsworth.
Boring, E. G. 1933. *The Physical Dimensions of Consciousness.* New York: Century.
Boring, E. G. 1942. *Sensation and Perception in the History of Experimental Psychology.* New York: Appleton-Century.
Boring, E. G. 1950. *A History of Experimental Psychology,* ed. 2. New York: Appleton-Century.
Boring, E. G. 1952. Edwin Garrigues Boring. In *A History of Psychology in Autobiography,* Vol. 4. E. G. Boring, H. Werner, H. S. Langfeld, and R. M. Yerkes, eds. New York: Russell & Russell. pp. 27–52.
Boring, E. G. 1961. *Psychologist at Large. An Autobiography and Selected Essays.* New York: Basic Books.
Boring, E. G. 1963. *History, Psychology, and Science: Selected Papers.* New York: Wiley.
Boring, E. G., and G. Lindzey, eds. 1967. *A History of Psychology in Autobiography,* Vol. 5. New York: Appleton-Century-Crofts.
Boring, E. G., H. Werner, H. S. Langfeld, and R. M. Yerkes, eds. 1952. *A History of Psychology in Autobiography,* Vol. 4. New York: Russell & Russell.
Bowman, W. 1891. Obituary of F.C. Donders. *Proceedings of the Royal Society of London 49*:vii–xxiii.
Braddick, O. J., F. W. Campbell, and J. Atkinson. 1978. Channels in vision. In *Handbook of Sensory Physiology,* Vol. 8. *Perception,* R. Held, H. W. Leibowitz, and H.-L. Teuber, eds. Berlin: Springer, pp. 3–38.
Bradshaw, J. L. 1989. *Hemispheric Specialization and Psychological Function.* Chichester: Wiley.
Brain, Lord. 1961. *Speech Disorders. Aphasia, Apraxia and Agnosia.* London: Butterworths.
Brentano, F. 1874. *Psychologie vom empirischen Standpunkt.* Leipzig: Duncker & Humblot.
Brentano, F. 1892. Über ein optisches Paradoxen. *Zeitschrift für Psychologie 3*:349–358.
Brentano, F. 1973. *Psychology from an Empirical Standpoint.* A. C. Rancurello, D. B. Terrell, and L. L. McAlister, trans. O. Kraus and L. L. McAlister., eds. London: Routledge & Kegan Paul.
Brett, G. S. 1912. *A History of Psychology,* Vol. 1. *Ancient and Patristic.* London: George Allen.
Brett, G. S. 1921. *A History of Psychology,* Vol. 2. *Mediaeval & Modern Period.* London: Allen & Unwin.
Brett, G. S. 1921. *A History of Psychology,* Vol. 3. *Modern Psychology.* London: Allen & Unwin.
Breuer, J., and S. Freud. 1895. *Studien über Hysterie.* Vienna: Deuticke.
Brewster, D. 1819. *A Treatise on the Kaleidoscope.* Edinburgh: Constable.
Brewster, D. 1844. Observations on colour-blindness, or insensibility to the impressions of certain colours. *London, Edinburgh and Dublin Philosophical Magazine and Journal of Science. 25*:134–141.
Brewster, D. 1855. *Memoirs of the Life, Writings, and Discoveries of Sir Isaac Newton.* Edinburgh: Constable.
Brewster, D. 1856. *The Stereoscope. Its History, Theory, and Construction.* London: John Murray.
Broadbent, D. E. 1958. *Perception and Communication.* Oxford: Pergamon Press.
Broadbent, D. E. 1961. *Behaviour.* London: Eyre & Spottiswoode.
Broadbent, D. E. 1971. *Decision and Stress.* London: Academic Press.
Broadbent, D. E. 1973. *In Defence of Empirical Psychology.* London: Methuen.

Broca, P. 1888. *Mémoires sur le cerveau de l'homme et des primates.* Paris: Reinwald.
Brown, J. A. C. 1954. *The Social Psychology of Industry. Human Relations in the Factory.* Harmondsworth, England: Penguin Books.
Bruce, D. 1991. Integrations of Lashley. In *Portraits of Pioneers in Psychology.* G. A. Kimble, M. Wertheimer, and C. L. White, eds. Hillsdale, N.J.: Erlbaum. pp. 307–323.
Bruce, D. 1994. Lashley and the problem of serial order. *American Psychologist 49*:93–103.
Brunswik, E. 1956. *Perception and the Representative Design of Psychological Experiments.* Berkeley: University of California Press.
Brunswik, E. 1966. Historical and thematic relations of psychology to other sciences. In *The Psychology of Egon Brunswik.* K. R. Hammond, ed. New York: Holt, Rinehart & Winston. pp. 495–513.
Cahan, D. ed. 1994. *Hermann von Helmholtz and the Foundations of Nineteenth-Century Science.* Berkeley: University of California Press.
Calkins, M. W. 1896. Association: An essay analytic and experimental. *Psychological Review. Monograph Supplement 1.* No.2.
Calkins, M. W. 1930. Mary Whiton Calkins. In *A History of Psychology in Autobiography,* Vol. 1. C. Murchison, ed. Worcester, Mass.: Clark University Press, pp. 31–62.
Campbell, F. W., and L. Maffei. 1976. Contrast and spatial frequency. In *Recent Progress in Perception.* R. Held and W. Richards, eds. San Francisco: Freeman, pp. 30–36.
Campbell, F. W., and J. G. Robson. 1968. Application of Fourier analysis to the visibility of gratings. *Journal of Physiology 197*:551–566.
Campbell, L., and W. Garnett. 1882. *The Life of James Clerk Maxwell.* London: Macmillan.
Cannon, W. B. 1932. *The Wisdom of the Body.* New York: Norton.
Charcot, J. M. 1892. *Oeuvres complètes de J. M. Charcot. Leçons sur les maladies du système nerveux.* Paris: Baittaille.
Charcot, J. M., and P. Richer. 1887. *Les démoniaques dans l'art.* Paris: Delahaye et Lecrosnier.
Clarke, E., and K. Dewhurst. 1972. *An Illustrated History of Brain Function.* Berkeley: University of California Press.
Cobb, W. A., ed. 1971. *Handbook of Electroencephalography and Clinical Neurophysiology,* Vol. 1. Amsterdam: Elsevier.
Cohen, J. 1969. *Personality Assessment.* Chicago: Rand McNally.
Cole, M., and I. Maltzman, eds. 1969. *A Handbook of Contemporary Soviet Psychology.* New York: Basic Books.
Comte, A. 1865. *A General View of Positivism.* J. H. Bridges, trans. London: Trübner.
Comte, A. 1896. *The Positive Philosophy of Auguste Comte,* Vol. 1. H. Martineau, trans. London: George Bell.
Comte, A. 1968. *Oeuvres d'Auguste Comte,* Vol. 1. Paris: Anthropos.
Comte, A. 1968. *Oeuvres d'Auguste Comte,* Vol. 11. Paris: Anthropos.
Cowles, M. 1989. *Statistics in Psychology: An Historical Perspective.* Hillsdale, N.J.: Erlbaum.
Craik, K. J. W. 1943. *The Nature of Explanation.* Cambridge, England: Cambridge University Press.
Craik, K. J. W. 1966. *The Nature of Psychology. A Selection of Papers, Essays and Other Writings by the Late Kenneth J. W. Craik.* S. L. Sherwood. ed. Cambridge, England: Cambridge University Press.
Danziger, K. 1990. *Constructing the Subject: Historical Origins of Psychological Research.* Cambridge, England: Cambridge University Press.
Darnton, R. 1968. *Mesmerism and the End of the Enlightenment in France.* Cambridge, Mass.: Harvard University Press.
Darwin, C. 1871. *The Descent of Man, and Selection in Relation to Sex.* London: John Murray.
Darwin, C. 1872. *The Expression of the Emotions in Man and Animals.* London: John Murray.
Darwin, C. 1877. A biographical sketch of an infant. *Mind 2*:285–294.
Darwin, C. 1900. *The Origin of Species by Means of Natural Selection or the Preservation of Favoured Races in the Struggle for Life,* ed 6. London: John Murray.
Davis, S. F., R. L. Thomas, and M. S. Weaver. 1982. Psychology's contemporary and all-time notables: Student, faculty, and chairperson viewpoints. *Bulletin of the Psychonomic Society 20*:3–6.
Day, R. H. and H., Knuth. 1981. The contributions of F C Müller-Lyer. *Perception 10*:126–146.
Delboeuf, J. R. L. 1889. *Le magnétisme animal: A propos d'une visite a l'école de Nancy.* Paris: Alcan.
Delboeuf, J. R. L. 1892. Sur une nouvelle illusion d'optique. *Bulletin de l'Académie Royale de Belgique 24*:545–558.
des Cartes, Renatus. 1662. *De homine figuris et latinitate.* F. Schuyl, trans. Lugduni Batavorum: Leffen & Moyardum.

Descartes, R. 1664/1909. *Traité de l'homme.* In *Oeuvres de Descartes.* Vol. 11, C. Adam and P. Tannery, eds. Paris: Cerf.
Diamond, S., ed. 1974. *The Roots of Psychology. A Sourcebook in the History of Ideas.* New York: Basic Books.
Donders, F. C. 1869. Over de snelheid van psychische processen. *Nederlandsch Archief voor Genees- en Natuurkunde* 4:117–145.
Donders, F. C. 1969. On the speed of mental processes. *Acta Psychologica 30*: 412–431.
Donders, F. C. 1972. *On the Anomalies of Accommodation and Refraction of the Eye.* W. D. Moore, trans. Boston: Milford House.
Drabble, M., ed., 1985. *The Oxford Companion to English Literature.* Oxford: Oxford University Press.
Duke-Elder, S. 1968. *System of Ophthalmology,* Vol. 4. *The Physiology of the Eye and of Vision.* London: Henry Kimpton.
Duke-Elder, S., and K. C. Wybar. 1961. *System of Ophthalmology,* Vol. 2. *The Anatomy of the Visual System.* London: Henry Kimpton.
Dulany, D. E., R. L. DeValois, D. C. Beardslee, and M. R. Winterbottom, eds. 1963. *Contributions to Modern Psychology. Selected Readings in General Psychology,* ed 2. New York: Oxford University Press.
Ebbinghaus, H. 1885. *Über das Gedächtnis. Untersuchungen zur experimentellen Psychologie.* Leipzig: Duncker & Humblot.
Ebbinghaus, H. 1897. *Grundzüge der Psychologie.* Leipzig: Veit.
Ebbinghaus, H. 1964. *Memory. A Contribution to Experimental Psychology.* H. A. Ruger and C. E. Bussenius, trans. New York: Dover.
Ellenberger, H. F. 1970. *The Discovery of the Unconscious. The History and Evolution of Dynamic Psychiatry.* London: Allen Lane.
Ellenberger, H. F. 1974. Psychiatry from ancient to modern times. In *American Handbook of Psychiatry,* Vol. 1. *The Foundations of Psychiatry.* S. Arieti, ed. New York: Basic Books.
Ellis, W. D. 1938. *A Source Book of Gestalt Psychology.* London: Routledge & Kegan Paul.
Esper, E. A. 1964. *A History of Psychology.* Philadelphia: Saunders.
Everson, S. ed. 1991. *Companions to Ancient Thought: 2. Psychology.* Cambridge, England: Cambridge University Press.
Fancher, R. E. 1990. *Pioneers of Psychology,* ed 2. New York: Norton.
Fechner, G. T. 1860. *Elemente der Psychophysik.* Leipzig: Breitkopf & Härtel.
Fechner, G. T. 1966. *Elements of Psychophysics,* Vol. 1. H. E. Adler, trans. D. H. Howes and E. G. Boring, eds. New York: Holt, Rinehart & Winston.
Ferrier, D. 1876. *The Functions of the Brain.* London: Smith, Elder.
Ferrier, D. 1878. *The Localisation of Cerebral Disease.* London: Smith, Elder.
Fisher, R. A. 1946. *Statistical Methods for Research Workers,* ed. 10. Edinburgh: Oliver & Boyd.
Fisher, R. A. 1956. *Statistical Methods and Scientific Inference.* Edinburgh: Oliver & Boyd.
Flanagan, O. 1991. *The Science of the Mind,* ed. 2. Cambridge, Mass: MIT Press.
Flourens, P. 1824. *Recherches expérimentales sur les propriétés et les fonctions du système nerveux dans les animaux vertébrés.* Paris.
Flourens, P. 1858. *De la vie et de l'intelligence.* Paris.
Flourens, P. 1863. *De la phrénologie et des études vraise sur le cerveau.* Paris: Garnier.
Flourens, P. 1864. *De la raison du génie et de la folie.* Paris: Garnier.
Flugel, J. C. 1933. *A Hundred Years of Psychology.* London: Duckworth.
Forrest, D. W. 1974. *Francis Galton. The Life and Work of a Victorian Genius.* London: Paul Elek.
Fraser, A. C. 1871. *Life and Letters of George Berkeley, D.D. Formerly Bishop of Cloyne; and an Account of his Philosophy.* Oxford: Clarendon Press.
Freud, S. 1933. *Neue Folge der Vorlesungen zur Einführung in die Psychoanalyse.* Vienna: Internationaler Psychoanalytischer Verlag.
Freud, S. 1953. *The Standard Edition of the Complete Psychological Works of Sigmund Freud,* Vol. 5. (1900–1901). *The Interpretation of Dreams* (second part) and *On Dreams.* J. Strachey, trans. London: Hogarth Press.
Freud, S. 1955. *The Standard Edition of the Complete Psychological Works of Sigmund Freud,* Vol. 18. J. Strachey, trans. London: Hogarth Press.
Fritsch, G., and E. Hitzig. 1870. Über die elektrische Erregbarkeit des Grosshirns. *Archiv für Anatomie, Physiologie, und wissenschaftliche Medicin* 1:300–332.
Fulton, J. F. 1966. *Selected Readings in the History of Physiology,* ed. 2. Springfield, Ill.: Thomas.

Gall, F. J. 1835. *On the Functions of the Brain and Each of Its Parts, with Observations on the Possibility of Determining the Instincts, Propensities and Talents, and the Moral and Intellectual Dispositions of Men and Animals by the Configuration of the Brain and Head.* W. Lewis, trans. Boston.
Galton, F. 1869. *Hereditary Genius.* London: Macmillan.
Galton, F. 1889. *Natural Inheritance.* London: Macmillan.
Galton, F. 1908. *Memories of My Life.* London: Macmillan.
Gardner, H. 1987. *The Mind's New Science. A History of the Cognitive Revolution.* New York: Basic Books.
Garrett, H. E. 1930. *Great Experiments in Psychology.* New York: Appleton-Century.
Garrison, F. H. 1913. *An Introduction to the History of Medicine.* Philadelphia: Saunders.
Gesell, A. 1925. *The Mental Growth of the Pre-school Child. A Psychological Outline of Normal Development from Birth to the Sixth Year, Including a System of Developmental Diagnosis.* New York: Macmillan.
Gesell, A. 1934. *An Atlas of Infant Behavior. A Systematic Delineation of the Forms and Early Growth of Human Behavior Patterns,* Vol. 1. New Haven, Conn: Yale University Press.
Gesell, A. 1934. *An Atlas of Infant Behavior. A Systematic Delineation of the Forms and Early Growth of Human Behavior Patterns,* Vol. 2. New Haven, Conn: Yale University Press.
Gesell, A. 1940. *The First Five Years of Life. A Guide to the Study of the Preschool Child.* London: Methuen.
Gesell, A. 1952. Arnold Gesell. In *A History of Psychology in Autobiography,* Vol. 4. E. G. Boring, H. Werner, H. S. Langfeld, and R. M. Yerkes. eds. New York: Russell & Russell. pp. 123–142.
Gibson, J. J. 1950. *The Perception of the Visual World.* Boston: Houghton Mifflin.
Gibson, J. J. 1959. Perception as a function of stimulation. In *Psychology: A Study of a Science,* Vol. 1. *Sensory, Perceptual, and Physiological Formulations,* S. Koch, ed. New York: McGraw-Hill, pp. 456–501.
Gibson, J. J. 1966. *The Senses Considered as Perceptual Systems.* London: Allen & Unwin.
Gibson, J. J. 1967. James J. Gibson. In *A History of Psychology in Autobiography,* Vol. 5, E. G. Boring and G. Lindzey, eds. New York: Appleton-Century-Crofts. pp. 125–143.
Gibson, J. J. 1979. *The Ecological Approach to Visual Perception.* Boston: Houghton Mifflin.
Gillespie, C. C., ed. 1970–1978. *Dictionary of Scientific Biography.* 15 volumes. New York: Scribner's.
Gloor, P. 1969. *Hans Berger—On the Encephalogram of Man.* Amsterdam: Elsevier.
Goethe, J. W. 1810. *Zur Farbenlehre.* Stuttgart: Cotta.
Goethe, J. W. 1840. *Theory of Colours.* C. L. Eastlake, trans. London: John Murray.
Gordon-Taylor, G., and E. W. Walls. 1958. *Sir Charles Bell. His Life and Times.* Edinburgh: Livingstone.
Goshen, C. E., ed. 1967. *Documentary History of Psychiatry. A Source Book on Historical Principles.* London: Vision Press.
Gregory, R. L. 1981. *Mind in Science. A History of Explanations in Psychology and Physics.* London: Weidenfeld & Nicolson.
Gregory, R. L. 1981. Editorial: the Nobel Prizes. *Perception 10*:243–244.
Gregory, R. L. 1986. *Odd Perceptions.* London: Methuen.
Gregory, R. L., ed. 1987. *The Oxford Companion to the Mind.* Oxford: Oxford University Press.
Gridgeman, N. T. 1972. Ronald Aylmer Fisher. In *Dictionary of Scientific Biography,* Vol. 5, C. C. Gillespie, ed. New York: Scribner. pp. 7–11.
Grmek, M. D. 1970. Claude Bernard. In *Dictionary of Scientific Biography,* Vol. 2, C. C. Gillespie, ed. New York: Scribner's, pp. 24–34.
Grüsser, O.-J. 1984. J. E. Purkyne's contributions to the physiology of the visual, the vestibular and the oculomotor systems. *Human Neurobiology 3*:129–144.
Grüsser, O.-J. and T. Landis. 1991. *Vision and Visual Dysfunction,* Vol. 12. *Visual Agnosias and Other Disturbances of Visual Perception and Cognition.* London: Macmillan.
Guthrie, D. 1945. *A History of Medicine.* London: Thomas Nelson.
Hall, G. S. 1904. *Adolescence. Its Psychology and its Relation to Physiology, Anthropology, Sociology, Sex, Crime, Religion and Education,* Vol. 1. New York: Appleton.
Hall, G. S. 1922. *Senescence. The Last Half of Life.* New York: Appleton.
Hall, T. S. 1972. *Treatise of Man. René Descartes.* Cambridge, Mass.: Harvard University Press.
Hammond, K. R., ed. 1966. *The Psychology of Egon Brunswik.* New York: Holt, Rinehart & Winston.
Hartenstein, G., ed. 1853. *Immanuel Kant's Kritik der reinen Vernunft.* Leipzig: Leopold Voss.
Haymaker, W., and F. Schiller, eds. 1970. *The Founders of Neurology,* ed 2. Springfield, Ill.: Thomas.
Hearnshaw L. 1987. *The Shaping of Modern Psychology.* London: Routledge.
Hearnshaw, L. S. 1964. *A Short History of British Psychology.* 1840–1940. London: Methuen.
Hearst, E. ed. 1979. *The First Century of Experimental Psychology.* Hillsdale, N.J.: Erlbaum.

Hebb, D. O. 1949. *The Organization of Behavior*. New York: Wiley.
Hebb, D. O. 1959. A neuropsychological theory. In *Psychology: A Study of a Science,* Vol. 1. *Sensory, Perceptual, and Physiological Formulations.* S. Koch, ed. New York: McGraw-Hill. pp. 622–643.
Hebb, D. O. 1980. *Essays on Mind.* Hillsdale, N.J.: Erlbaum.
Hebb, D. O. 1980. D. O. Hebb. In *A History of Psychology in Autobiography,* Vol. 7. G. Lindzey, ed. San Francisco: Freeman. pp. 272–303.
Helmholtz, H. 1873. *Popular Lectures on Scientific Subjects.* first series. E. Atkinson, trans. London: Longmans, Green.
Helmholtz, H. 1881. *Popular Lectures on Scientific Subjects.* second series. E. Atkinson, trans. London: Longmans, Green.
Helmholtz, H. von. 1896. *Handbuch der physiologischen Optik,* ed. 2. revised. Hamburg: Voss.
Helmholtz, H. von. 1924. *Helmholtz's Treatise on Physiological Optics,* Vol. 1. J. P. C. Southall, trans. Washington D.C.: Optical Society of America.
Helmholtz, H. von. 1924. *Helmholtz's Treatise on Physiological Optics,* Vol. 2. J. P. C. Southall, trans. Washington D.C.: Optical Society of America.
Helmholtz, H. von. 1925. *Helmholtz's Treatise on Physiological Optics,* Vol. 3. J. P. C. Southall, trans. Washington D.C.: Optical Society of America.
Henle, M. ed. 1961. *Documents of Gestalt Psychology.* Berkeley: University of California Press.
Hergenhahn, B. R. 1992. *An Introduction to the History of Psychology,* ed.2. Belmont, Calif.: Wadsworth.
Hering, E. 1942. *Spatial Sense and Movements of the Eyes.* Baltimore: American Academy of Sciences.
Herrnstein, R. J., and E. G. Boring. 1965. *A Source Book in the History of Psychology.* Cambridge, Mass.: Harvard University Press.
Hiebert, E. N. 1973. Ernst Mach. In *Dictionary of Scientific Biography,* Vol. 8, C. C. Gillespie, ed. New York: Scribner's. pp. 595–607.
Hilgard, E. R. 1987. *Psychology in America. A Historical Survey.* San Diego: Harcourt Brace Jovanovich.
Hilgard, E. R. 1993. Which psychologists prominent in the second half of this century made lasting contributions to psychological theory? *Psychological Science* 4:70–80.
Hilgard, E. R., and J. R. Hilgard. 1975. *Hypnosis in the Relief of Pain.* Los Altos, Calif.: Kaufmann.
Hirschmüller, A. 1989. *The Life and Work of Josef Breuer: Physiology and Psychoanalysis.* New York: New York University Library.
Hobbes, T. 1651. *Leviathan: or, the Matter, Form, and Power of Commonwealth, Eccliastical and Civil.* London: Andrew Crooke.
Hollingworth, L. S. 1920. *The Psychology of Subnormal Children.* New York: Macmillan.
Hollingworth, L. S. 1923. *Special Talents and Defects. Their Significance for Education.* New York: Macmillan.
Hollingworth, L. S. 1926. *Gifted Children.* New York: Macmillan.
Hollingworth, L. S. 1928. *The Psychology of Adolescence.* New York: Appleton.
Hoorn, W. van. 1972. *As Images Unwind. Ancient and Modern Theories of Visual Perception.* Amsterdam: University Press.
Hull, C. L. 1943. *Principles of Behavior. An Introduction to Behavior Theory.* New York: Appleton-Century.
Hull, C. L. 1952a. *A Behavior System. An Introduction to Behavior Theory Concerning the Individual Organism.* New Haven, Conn.: Yale University Press.
Hull, C. L. 1952b. Clark L. Hull. In *A History of Psychology in Autobiography,* Vol. 4, E. G. Boring, H. Werner, H. S. Langfeld, and R. M. Yerkes, eds. New York: Russell & Russell. pp. 143–162.
Hume, D. 1740. A *Treatise of Human Nature.* London: Borbet.
Hume, D. 1748. *An Enquiry Concerning Human Understanding.* London.
Hume, D. 1772. *Essays and Treatises on Several Subjects,* Vol. 2. *Containing An Enquiry Concerning Human Understanding; A Dissertation on the Passions; An Enquiry Concerning the Principles of Morals; and The Natural History of Religion. A New Edition.* London: T. Cadell.
Humphrey, N. 1992. *A History of the Mind.* London: Chatto & Windus.
Hunter, R., and I. MacAlpine. 1963. *Three Hundred Years of Psychiatry. 1535–1860. A History Presented in Selected English Texts.* London: Oxford University Press.
Irvine, W. 1955. *Apes, Angels, and Victorians. A Joint Biography of Darwin and Huxley.* London: Weidenfeld and Nicolson.
James, H., ed. 1920. *The Letters of William James,* Vol. 2. London: Longmans, Green and Co.
James, W. 1890. *Principles of Psychology.* New York: Holt.
Janet, P. 1889. *L'automatisme psychologique. Essai de psychologie expérimentale sur les formes inférieures de l'activité humaine.* Paris: Baillière.

Janet, P. 1925. *Psychological Healing.* E. and C. Paul, trans. London: Allen & Unwin.
Jung, C. G. 1923. *Psychological Types or the Psychology of Individuation.* H. G. Baynes, trans. New York: Harcourt, Brace.
Jung, C. G. 1953. *Psychology and Alchemy.* R. F. C. Hull, trans. London: Routledge & Kegan Paul.
Jung, C. G. 1977. *The Collected Works of C. G. Jung,* Vol. 18. *The Symbolic Life. Miscellaneous Writings.* R.F.C. Hull, trans. London: Routledge & Kegan Paul.
Kant, I. 1964. *Critique of Pure Reason,* J. M. D. Meiklejohn, trans. New York: Dutton.
Kantor, J. R. 1969. *The Scientific Evolution of Psychology,* Vol. 2. Chicago: Principia.
Kemp, M. 1990. *The Science of Art. Optical Themes in Western Art from Brunelleschi to Seurat.* New Haven, Conn.: Yale University Press.
Kemp, S. 1990. *Medieval Psychology.* Westport, Conn.: Greenwood.
Kepler, J. 1604. *Ad Vitellionem Paralipomena.* Frankfurt: Marinium & Aubrii.
Kimble, G. A. and K. Schlesinger, eds. 1985. *Topics in the History of Psychology,* Vol. 1. Hillsdale, N.J.: Erlbaum.
Kimble, G. A., M. Wertheimer, and C. L. White, eds. 1991. *Portraits of Pioneers in Psychology.* Hillsdale, N.J.: Erlbaum.
Klopfer, B., and D. McG. Kelley. 1942. *The Rorschach Technique. A Manual for a Projective Method of Personality Diagnosis.* New York: World Book Company.
Koenigsberger, L. 1902. *Hermann von Helmholtz,* Vol. 1. Braunschweig: Vieweg.
Koenigsberger, L. 1906. *Hermann von Helmholtz* F. A. Welby, trans. Oxford: Clarendon.
Koffka, K. 1922. Perception: An introduction to Gestalt-theorie. *Psychological Bulletin 19*:531–585.
Koffka, K. 1924. *The Growth of Mind. An Introduction to Child-Psychology.* New York: Harcourt, Brace.
Koffka, K. 1935. *Principles of Gestalt Psychology.* New York: Harcourt, Brace.
Kohler, I. 1964. *The Formation and Transformation of the Perceptual World.* H. Fiss, trans. New York: International Universities Press.
Kohler, I. 1972. Experiments with goggles. In *Perception: Mechanisms and Models,* R. Held and W. Richards, eds. San Francisco: Freeman, pp. 299–309.
Köhler, W. 1920. *Die physischen Gestalten in Ruhe und im stationären Zustand.* Braunschweig: Vieweg.
Köhler, W. 1927. *The Mentality of Apes,* ed. 2, revised. E. Winter, trans. London: Kegan Paul, Trench, Trubner.
Köhler, W. 1930. *Gestalt Psychology.* London: Bell.
Köhler, W. 1942. *Dynamics in Psychology.* London: Faber and Faber.
König, E. 1901. *W. Wundt. Seine Philosophie und Psychologie.* Stuttgart: Fromanns.
Korn, J. H., R. Davis, and S. F. Davis. 1991. Historians' and chairpersons' judgments of eminence among psychologists. *American Psychologist 46*:789–792.
Koster, W. G. ed. 1969. *Attention and Performance II.* Amsterdam: North-Holland.
Kozulin, A. 1990. *Vygotsky's Psychology. A Biography of Ideas.* London: Harvester Wheatsheaf.
Kraepelin, E. 1899. *Psychiatrie. Ein Lehrbuch für Studierende und Aertze.* Vol. 2. *Klinische Psychiatrie.* Leipzig: Barth.
Kraepelin, E. 1906. *Lectures on Clinical Psychiatry,* ed. 2. T. Johnstone, trans. - ed. London: Baillière, Tindall & Cox.
Kunke, J. E. 1892. *Gustav Theodor Fechner (Dr. Mises). Ein deutsches Gelehrtenleben.* Leipzig: Breitkopf & Härtel.
Lashley, K. S. 1929. *Brain Mechanisms and Intelligence.* Chicago: University of Chicago Press.
Lashley, K. S. 1930 The mechanism of vision. I. A method of rapid analysis of pattern-vision in the rat. *Journal of Genetic Psychology 37*:453–460.
Lashley, K. S. 1960. In search of the engram. In *The Neuropsychology of Lashley.* F. A. Beach, D. O. Hebb, C. T. Morgan, and H. W. Nissen, eds. New York: McGraw-Hill, pp. 478–505.
Lashley, K. S. 1960. The problem of serial order in behavior. In *Cerebral Mechanisms in Behavior.* L. A. Jeffress, ed. New York: Wiley. pp. 112–136.
Lewin, K. 1935. *A Dynamic Theory of Personality. Selected Papers.* New York: McGraw-Hill.
Lewin, K. 1936. *Principles of Topological Psychology.* F. and G. M. Heider, trans. New York: McGraw-Hill.
Lewin, K. 1952. *Field Theory in Social Science. Selected Theoretical Papers.* London: Tavistock.
Lindberg, D. C. 1976. *Theories of Vision from Al-Kindi to Kepler.* Chicago: University of Chicago Press.
Lindberg, D. C., ed. 1978. *Science in the Middle Ages.* Chicago: University of Chicago Press.
Lindzey, G. ed. 1974. *A History of Psychology in Autobiography,* Vol. 6. Englewood Cliffs, N.J.: Prentice-Hall.

Lindzey, G. ed. 1980. *A History of Psychology in Autobiography,* Vol. 7. San Francisco: Freeman.
Locke, J. 1690. *An Essay Concerning Humane Understanding.* London: Thomas Baffet.
Locke, J. 1695. *An Essay Concerning Humane Understanding,* ed. 2. London: Thomas Baffet.
Locke, J. 1823. *The Works of John Locke,* Vol. 1. London: Tegg, Sharpe, Offor, Robinson, Evans, Griffin, Cumming.
Lück, H. E., and R. Miller, eds. 1993. *Illustrierte Geschichte der Psychologie.* Munich: Quintessenz.
Luria, A. R. 1968. *The Mind of a Mnemonist.* New York: Avon.
Luria, A. R. 1969. The neuropsychological study of brain lesions and restoration of damaged brain functions. In *A Handbook of Contemporary Soviet Psychology.* M. Cole and I. Maltzman, eds. New York: Basic Books. pp. 277–301.
Luria, A. R. 1970. *Traumatic Aphasia. Its Syndromes, Psychology and Treatment.* The Hague: Mouton.
Luria, A. R. 1972. The functional organization of the brain. In *Physiological Psychology.* R. F. Thompson, ed. San Francisco: Freeman. pp. 406–413.
Luria, A. R. 1973. *The Working Brain. An Introduction to Neuropsychology.* B. Haigh, trans. Harmondsworth, England: Penguin.
Luria, A. R. 1974. A. R. Luria. In *A History of Psychology in Autobiography,* Vol. 6, G. Lindzey, ed. Englewood Cliffs, N.J.: Prentice-Hall, pp. 253–292.
McDougall, W. 1908. *An Introduction to Social Psychology.* London: Methuen.
McDougall, W. 1920. *The Group Mind. A Sketch of the Principles of Collective Psychology with some Attempt to Apply them to the Interpretation of National Life and Character.* Cambridge, England: Cambridge University Press.
McDougall, W. 1923. *Outline of Psychology.* New York: Scribner's.
McDougall, W. 1930. The hormic psychology. In *Psychologies of 1930.* C. Murchison, ed. Worcester, Mass.: Clark University Press, pp. 3–36.
McHenry, L. C. 1969. *Garrison's History of Neurology. Revised and Enlarged with a Bibliography of Classical, Original and Standard Works in Neurology.* Springfield, Ill.: Thomas.
Mach, E. 1875. *Grundlinien der Lehre von der Bewegungsempfindungen.* Leipzig: Engelmann.
Mach, E. 1886. *Beiträge zur Analyse der Empfindungen.* Jena: Fischer.
Mach, E. 1897. *Contributions to the Analysis of Sensations.* C. M. Williams, trans. Chicago: Open Court.
Macmillan, M. B. 1986. A wonderful journey through skull and brains: The travels of Mr. Gage's tamping iron. *Brain and Cognition* 5:67–107.
Macmillan, M. B. 1991. *Freud Evaluated. The Completed Arc.* Amsterdam: North-Holland.
Macmillan, M. B. 1992. Inhibition and the control of behavior. *Brain and Cognition 19*:72–104.
Magendie, F. 1822. Expérience sur les fonctions des racines des nerfs rachidiens. *Journal de Physiologie Expérimentale et Pathologique* 2: 276–279.
Marr, D. 1982. *Vision. A Computational Investigation into the Human Representation and Processing of Visual Information.* New York: Freeman.
Marx, M. H., and W. A. Hillix. 1963. *Systems and Theories in Psychology.* New York: McGraw-Hill.
Maslow, A. H. 1954. *Motivation and Personality.* New York: Harper & Brothers.
Maslow, A. H. 1968. *Toward a Psychology of Being,* ed. 2. New York: Van Nostrand.
Maxwell, J. C. 1890. *The Scientific Papers of James Clerk Maxwell,* Vol. 1, W. D. Niven, ed. Paris: Hermann.
Mayo, E. 1933. *The Human Problems of an Industrial Civilization.* New York: Macmillan.
Mayo, E. 1945. *The Social Problems of an Industrial Civilization.* New York: Macmillan.
Mead, M. 1959. *An Anthropologist at Work. Writings of Ruth Benedict.* London: Secker & Warburg.
Meischner, M., and E, Eschler. 1979. *Wilhelm Wundt.* Cologne: Pahl-Rugenstein.
Mesmer, A. 1948. *Dissertation on the Discovery of Animal Magnetism.* G. Frankau, trans. London: MacDonald.
Miller, J. 1978. *The Body in Question.* London: Cape.
Molesworth, W. 1839. *The English Works of Thomas Hobbes,* Vol. 1. London: Bohn.
Molesworth, W. 1839. *The English Works of Thomas Hobbes,* Vol. 3. London: Bohn.
Morgan, C. L. 1894. *An Introduction to Comparative Psychology.* London: Walter Scott.
Morgan, C. L. 1900. *Animal Behaviour.* London: Arnold.
Morgan, C. L. 1932. C. Lloyd Morgan. In *A History of Psychology in Autobiography,* Vol. 2. C. Murchison, ed. Worcester, Mass.: Clark University Press. pp. 237–264.
Müller, J. 1826. *Zur vergleichenden Physiologie des Gesichtssinnes des Menschens und der Thiere, nebst einen Versuch über die Bewegungen der Augen undüber den menschlichen Blick.* Leipzig: Cnobloch.
Müller, J. 1833. *Handbuch der Physiologie des Menschens,* Vol. 1. Coblenz: Hölscher.

Müller, J. 1840. *Handbuch der Physiologie des Menschens,* Vol. 2. Coblenz: Hölscher.
Müller-Lyer, F. C. 1889. Optische Urteilstäuschungen. *Archiv für Anatomie und Physiologie. Physiologische Abteilung* 2:263–270.
Müller-Lyer, F. C. 1896. Zur Lehre von den optischen Täuschungen. Über Kontrast und Konfluxion. *Zeitschrift für Psychologie.* 9:1–16.
Müller-Lyer, F. C. 1931. *The Family.* F. W. S. Browne, trans. London: Allen & Unwin.
Münsterberg, H. 1889. *Beiträge zur experimentellen Psychologie.* Freiburg: Mohr.
Münsterberg, H. 1897. Die verschobene Schachbrettfigur. *Zeitschrift für Psychologie* 15:184–188.
Münsterberg, H. 1899. *Psychology and Life.* London: Constable.
Münsterberg, H., ed. 1906. *Harvard Psychological Studies,* Vol. 2. Boston: Houghton Mifflin.
Münsterberg, H., ed. 1909. *Subconscious Phenomena.* London: Rebman.
Münsterberg, H. 1909. *On the Witness Stand.* New York: Clark Boardman.
Münsterberg, H. 1913. *Psychology and Industrial Efficiency.* New York: Houghton Mifflin.
Murchison, C., ed. 1926. *Psychologies of 1925.* Worcester, Mass.: Clark University Press.
Murchison, C., ed. 1930. *A History of Psychology in Autobiography,* Vol. 1. Worcester, Mass.: Clark University Press.
Murchison, C., ed. 1930. *Psychologies of 1930.* Worcester, Mass.: Clark University Press.
Murchison, C., ed. 1932. *A History of Psychology in Autobiography,* Vol. 2. Worcester, Mass.: Clark University Press.
Murphy, G. 1928. *An Historical Introduction to Modern Psychology.* New York: Harcourt Brace.
Murray, D. J. 1983. *A History of Western Psychology.* Englewood Cliffs, N.J.: Prentice-Hall.
Newell, A. 1990. *Unified Theories of Cognition.* Cambridge, Mass.: Harvard University Press.
Newell, A., J. C. Shaw, and H. A. Simon. 1958. Elements of a theory of human problem solving. *Psychological Review* 65:151–166.
Newell, A., and H. A. Simon. 1972. *Human Problem Solving.* Englewood Cliffs, N.J.: Prentice-Hall.
Newton, I. 1704. *Opticks: or, a Treatise of the Reflections, Refractions, Inflections and Colours of Light.* London: Innys.
Nicholson, J., and H. Beloff, eds. 1984. *Psychology Survey 5.* Leicester, England: British Psychological Society.
Nuttin, J. 1961. *Psychology in Belgium.* Louvain: Studia Psychologica.
O'Connell, A. N., and N. F. Russo. 1990. *Women in Psychology. A Bio-Bibliographic Source Book.* New York: Greenwood Press.
Pavlov, I. P. 1927. *Conditioned Reflexes. An Investigation of the Physiological Activity of the Cerebral Cortex.* G. V. Anrep, trans. - ed. Oxford: Oxford University Press.
Pavlov, I. P. 1928. *Lectures on Conditioned Reflexes. Twenty-five Years of Objective Study of the Higher Nervous Activity (Behaviour) of Animals.* W. H. Gantt, trans. London: Martin Lawrence.
Pavlov, I. P. 1955. *Selected Works.* K. S. Koshtoyants, ed. Moscow: Foreign Languages Publishing House.
Peacock, G. 1855. *Life of Thomas Young.* London: John Murray.
Pearson, E. S. 1938. Karl Pearson. *An Appreciation of Some Aspects of His Life and Work.* Cambridge, England: Cambridge University Press.
Pearson, E. S., ed. 1978. *The History of Statistics in the 17th & 18th Centuries against the Changing Background of Intellectual, Scientific and Religious Thought.* London: Charles Griffin.
Pearson, K. 1880. *The New Werther.* London: Kegan.
Pearson, K. 1890. *The Grammar of Science.* London: Adam & Charles Black.
Pearson, K. 1900. *The Grammar of Science,* ed. 2. London: Adam & Charles Black.
Pearson, K. 1914–1930. *The Life, Letters and Labours of Francis Galton,* 3 volumes Cambridge, England: Cambridge University Press.
Penfield, W. 1947. Ferrier Lecture. Some observations on the cerebral cortex of man. *Proceedings of the Royal Society of London. Series B* 134:329–347.
Penfield, W. 1958. *The Excitable Cortex in Conscious Man.* Liverpool: Liverpool University Press.
Penfield, W., and T. Rasmussen. 1950. *The Cerebral Cortex of Man. A Clinical Study of Localization of Function.* New York: Macmillan.
Peterman, B. 1932, *The Gestalt Theory and the Problem of Configuration.* M. Fortes, trans. London: Kegan Paul, Trench, Trubner.
Piaget, J. 1929. *The Child's Conception of the World.* J. and A. Tomlinson, trans. London: Routledge & Kegan Paul.

Piaget, J. 1952. Jean Piaget. In *A History of Psychology in Autobiography,* Vol. 4, E. G. Boring, H. Werner, H. S. Langfeld, and R. M. Yerkes, eds. New York: Russell & Russell, pp. 237–256.
Piaget, J., and B. Inhelder. 1948. *La représentation de l'espace chez l'enfant.* Paris: Presses Universitaires de France.
Pinel, P. 1806. *Treatise on Mental Alienation.* D. D. Davis, trans. London.
Pinel, P. 1818. *Nosographie philosophique, ou la méthode de l'analyse appliqué a la médecine,* ed. 6. Paris: Brosson.
Plateau, J. 1850. Vierte Notiz über neue, sonderbare Anwendungen des Verweilens der Eindrücke auf die Netzhaut. *Annalen der Physik und Chemie 80*:287–292.
Plateau, J. 1878. Bibliographie analytique des principaux phénomènes subjectifs de la vision. Troisème section. Images qui succèdent a la contemplation d'object d'un éclat ou même d'objects blanc bien éclairés. *Memoires de l'Académie Royale de Belgique 14*:1–26.
Polyak, S. 1957. *The Vertebrate Visual System.* Chicago: University of Chicago Press.
Postman, L. ed. 1963. *Psychology in the Making. Histories of Selected Research Problems.* New York: Knopf.
Purkinje, J. 1823. *Beobachtungen und Versuche zur Physiologie der Sinne. Beiträge zur Kenntniss des Sehens in subjectiver Hinsicht,* Vol. 1. Prague: Calve.
Purkinje, J. 1825. *Beobachtungen und Versuche zur Physiologie der Sinne. Neue Beiträge zur Kenntniss des Sehens in subjectiver Hinsicht,* Vol. 2. Berlin: Reimer.
Quetelet, A. 1842. *Treatise on Man and the Development of his Faculties.* Edinburgh: W. & R. Chambers.
Rand, B. 1912. *The Classical Psychologists.* Boston: Houghton Mifflin.
Ratliff, F. 1965. *Mach Bands: Quantitative Studies on Neural Networks in the Retina.* San Francisco: Holden-Day.
Reid, T. 1821. *An Inquiry into the Human Mind, On the Principles of Common Sense.* London: Bumpus, Sharpe, Samms, Warren, & Reilly.
Reid, T. 1846. *The Works of Thomas Reid, D. D.* W. Hamilton, ed. Edinburgh: MacLachlan, Stewart.
Riehl, A. 1897. *Friedrich Nietzsche. Der Künstler und der Denker.* Stuttgart: Frommanns.
Robinson, D. N. 1978. *The Mind Unfolded. Essays on Psychology's Historic Texts.* Washington, D.C.: University Publications of America.
Robinson, D. N. 1982. *Toward a Science of Human Nature. Essays on the Psychologies of Mill, Hegel, Wundt, and James.* New York: Columbia University Press.
Robinson, J. O. 1972. *The Psychology of Visual Illusion.* London: Hutchinson.
Roche, K. F., 1974. *Rousseau. Stoic and Romantic.* London: Methuen.
Rogers, C. R. 1951. *Client-Centered Therapy: Its Current Practice, Implications, and Theory.* Boston: Houghton Mifflin.
Rogers, C. R. 1961. *On Becoming a Person. A Therapist's View of Psychotherapy.* London: Constable.
Rogers, C. R. 1963. "Client-centered" psychotherapy. In *Contributions to Modern Psychology. Selected Readings in General Psychology,* ed. 2. D. E. Dulany, R. L. DeValois, D. C. Beardslee, and M. R. Winterbottom, eds. New York: Oxford University Press, pp. 425–434.
Rogers, C. R. 1967. Carl R. Rogers. In *A History of Psychology in Autobiography,* Vol. 5 . E. G. Boring, and G. Lindzey, eds. New York: Appleton-Century-Crofts, pp. 343–384.
Rorschach, H. 1921. *Psychodiagnostik.* Bern: Huber.
Rose, F. C., and W. F. Bynum. 1982. *Historical Aspects of the Neurosciences. A Festschrift for Macdonald Critchley.* New York: Raven Press.
Rosenzweig, M. R. 1963. The mechanisms of hunger and thirst. In *Psychology in the Making. Histories of Selected Research Problems.* Postman, L., ed. New York: Knopf, pp. 73–143.
Ross, H. E., and D. J. Murray. 1978. *E. H. Weber: The Sense of Touch.* London: Academic Press.
Rousseau, J.-J. 1911. *Émile.* B. Foxley, trans. London: Dent.
Runes, D. G. 1959. *Pictorial History of Philosophy.* New York: Philosophical Library.
Russell, B. 1948. *History of Western Philosophy and Its Connection with Political and Social Circumstances from the Earliest Times to the Present Day.* London: Allen & Unwin.
Russell, B. 1959. *Wisdom of the West.* New York: Doubleday.
Sahakian, W. S. ed. 1968. *History of Psychology. A Source Book in Systematic Psychology.* Itasca, Illinois: Peacock.
Sanford, E. C. 1924. Granville Stanley Hall 1846–1924. *American Journal of Psychology 35*:313–321.
Sarris, V. 1989. ed. Max Wertheimer memorial issue. *Psychological Research. 51*:43–85.
Scheerer, E. 1987. The unknown Fechner. *Psychological Research 49*:197–202.
Schopenhauer, A. 1883. *The World as Will and Idea,* 3 volumes. R. B. Haldane and J. Kemp, trans. London: Routledge & Kegan Paul.

Schopenhauer, A. 1896. *The Art of Controversy and Other Posthumous Papers.* T. B. Saunders, trans. London: Swan Sonnenschein.
Schultz, D. P., and S. E. Schultz. 1987. *A History of Modern Psychology,* ed. 4. San Diego: Harcourt Brace Jovanovich.
Semeonoff, B. and E. Trist. 1958. *Diagnostic Performance Tests. A Manual for Use with Adults.* London: Tavistock Publications.
Sheer, D. E. ed. 1961. *Electrical Stimulation of the Brain. An Interdisciplinary Survey of Neurobehavioral Integrative Systems.* Austin, Tex.: University of Texas Press.
Sherrington, C. S. 1947. *The Integrative Action of the Nervous System.* Cambridge, England: Cambridge University Press.
Shields, S. A. 1991. Leta Stetter Hollingworth: "Literature of opinion" and the study of individual differences. In *Portraits of Pioneers in Psychology.* G. A. Kimble, M. Wertheimer, and C. L. White, eds. Hillsdale, N.J.: Erlbaum, pp. 243–255.
Skinner, B. F. 1938. *The Behavior of Organisms: An Experimental Analysis.* New York: Appleton-Century.
Skinner, B. F. 1950. Are theories of learning necessary? *Psychological Review 57*:193–216.
Skinner, B. F. 1957. *Verbal Behavior.* Englewood Cliffs, N.J.: Prentice-Hall.
Skinner, B. F. 1967. B. F. Skinner. In *A History of Psychology in Autobiography,* Vol. 5, E. G. Boring and G. Lindzey, ed. New York: Appleton-Century-Crofts. pp. 387–413
Skinner, B. F. 1969. *Contingencies of Reinforcement. A Theoretical Analysis.* New York: Appleton-Century-Crofts.
Skinner, B. F. 1971. *Beyond Freedom and Dignity.* New York: Knopf.
Sokal, M. M., and P. A. Rafail. 1982. *A Guide to Manuscript Collections in the History of Psychology and Related Areas.* Millwood, New York: Kraus.
Spearman, C. E. 1923. *The Nature of "Intelligence" and the Principles of Cognition.* London: Macmillan.
Spearman, C. E. 1927. *The Abilities of Man. Their Nature and Measurement.* London: Macmillan.
Sperry, R. 1983. *Science and Moral Priority. Merging Mind, Brain, and Human Values.* Oxford: Blackwell.
Sperry, R. W. 1962. Some general aspects of interhemispheric integration. In *Interhemispheric Relations and Cerebral Dominance,* V. B. Mountcastle, ed. Baltimore: Johns Hopkins Press. pp. 43–49.
Sperry, R. W. 1972. The eye and the brain. In *Perception: Mechanisms and Models.* R. Held and W. Richards, eds. San Francisco: Freeman. pp. 362–366.
Sperry, R. W. 1974. Lateral specialization in the surgically separated hemisphere. In *The Neurosciences: Third Study Program.* F. O. Schmitt and F. G. Worden, eds. Cambridge, Mass.: MIT Press. pp. 5–19.
Sperry, R. W. 1982. Forebrain commissurotomy and conscious awareness. In *Neuropsychology after Lashley. Fifty Years Since the Publication of Brain Mechanisms and Intelligence.* J. Orbach, ed. Hillsdale, N.J.: Erlbaum, pp. 497–522.
Spillane, J. D. 1981. *The Doctrine of the Nerves.* Oxford: Oxford University Press.
Spillmann, L., and B. Wooten., eds. 1984. *Sensory Experience, Adaptation, and Perception. Festschrift in Honor of Professor Ivo Kohler.* Hillsdale, N.J.: Erlbaum.
Stevens, S. S. 1961. To honor Fechner and repeal his law. *Science 133*: 80–86.
Stevens, S. S. 1974. S. S. Stevens. In *A History of Psychology in Autobiography,* Vol. 6, G. Lindzey, ed. Englewood Cliffs, N.J.: Prentice-Hall. pp. 395–420.
Stevens, S. S. 1975. *Psychophysics.* New York: Wiley.
Taylor, W. C. 1867. *The National Portrait Gallery of Illustrations and Eminent Persons,* Vol. 2. London: Jackson.
Thorndike, E. L. 1898. Animal intelligence. An experimental study of the associate processes in animals. *Psychological Review. Monograph Supplement 2.* No.4 (Whole No. 8).
Thorndike, E. L. 1903. *Educational Psychology.* New York: Science Press.
Thorndike, E. L. 1905. *The Elements of Psychology.* New York: Seiler.
Thorndike, E. L. 1949. *Selected Writings from a Connectionist's Psychology.* New York: Appleton-Century-Crofts.
Thorndike, E. L., and Lorge, I. 1944. *The Teacher's Word Book of 30,000 Words.* New York: Columbia Teachers College.
Thorndike, E. L., and R. S. Woodworth. 1901. The influence of improvement in one mental function upon the efficiency of other functions. *Psychological Review 8*:247–256.
Thurstone, L. L. 1944. *A Factorial Study of Perception.* Chicago: University of Chicago Press.
Thurstone, L. L. 1952. L. L. Thurstone. In *A History of Psychology in Autobiography,* Vol. 4, E. G. Boring, H. Werner, H. S. Langfeld, and R. M. Yerkes, eds. New York: Russell & Russell. pp. 295–321.

Thurstone, L. L. 1959. *The Measurement of Values.* Chicago: University of Chicago Press.
Titchener, E. B. 1898. The postulates of a structural psychology. *Philosophical Review* 7:449–465.
Titchener, E. B. 1901. *Experimental Psychology. A Manual of Laboratory Practice,* Vol. 1. *Qualitative Experiments. Part 1. Student's Manual.* New York: Macmillan.
Titchener, E. B. 1910. *A Textbook of Psychology.* New York: Macmillan.
Tolman, E. C. 1949. *Purposive Behavior in Animals and Men.* Berkeley: University of California Press.
Tolman, E. C. 1952. Edward Chace Tolman. In *A History of Psychology in Autobiography,* Vol. 4. E. G. Boring, H. Werner, H. S. Langfeld, and R. M. Yerkes, eds. New York: Russell & Russell, pp. 323–339.
Trahair, R. S. 1984. *The Humanist Temper: The Life and Work of Elton Mayo.* New Brunswick, N.J.: Transaction Books.
Urmson, J. O., ed. 1960. *The Concise Encyclopaedia of Western Philosophy and Philosophers.* London: Hutchinson.
Urwick, L., and E. F. L. Brech. 1948. *The Making of Scientific Management,* Vol. 3. *The Hawthorne Investigations.* London: Management Publications Trust.
Vieth, G. U. A. 1818. Über die Richtung der Augen. *Annalen der Physik und Chemie 58*:233–255.
Viney, W. 1993. *A History of Psychology: Ideas and Context.* Boston: Allyn & Bacon.
Volkelt, J. 1900. *Arthur Schopenhauer. Seine Persönlichkeit, seine Lehre, sein Glaube.* Stuttgart: Frommanns.
Vygotsky, L. S. 1962. *Thought and Language.* E. Hanfmann and G. Vakar, ed. - trans. Cambridge, Mass.: MIT Press.
Vygotsky, L. S. 1978. *Mind in Society. The Development of Higher Psychological Processes.* Cole, M., V. John-Steiner, S. Scribner, and E. Souberman, eds. Cambridge, Mass.: Harvard University Press.
Wade, N. J., ed. 1983. *Brewster and Wheatstone on Vision.* London: Academic Press.
Wade, N.J. 1987. On the late invention of the stereoscope. *Perception 16*:785–818.
Wade, N. 1990. *Visual Allusions: Pictures of Perception.* London: Erlbaum.
Wade, N. 1992. Faces of psychology. *Perception, 21* (Suppl. 1):1–107
Warren, R. M., and R. P. Warren. 1968. *Helmholtz on Perception: Its Physiology and Development.* New York: Wiley.
Washburn, M. F. 1908. *The Animal Mind. A Text-book of Comparative Psychology.* New York: Macmillan.
Washburn, M. F. 1916. *Movement and Mental Imagery.* Boston: Houghton Mifflin.
Washburn, M. F. 1917. *The Animal Mind. A Text-book of Comparative Psychology,* ed. 2. New York: Macmillan.
Washburn, M. F. 1930. A system of motor psychology. In *Psychologies of 1930.* C. Murchison, ed. Worcester, Mass.: Clark University Press. pp. 81–94.
Washburn, M. F. 1932. Margaret Floy Washburn. In *A History of Psychology in Autobiography,* Vol. 2. C. Murchison, ed. Worcester, Mass.: Clark University Press. pp. 333–358.
Watson, J. B. 1913. Psychology as the behaviorist views it. *Psychological Review 20*:158–177.
Watson, J. B. 1919. *Psychology from the Standpoint of the Behaviorist.* Philadelphia: Lippincott.
Watson, J. B. 1930. *Behaviorism.* revised ed. New York: Norton.
Watson, J. B., and W. McDougall. 1929. *The Battle of Behaviorism.* New York: Norton.
Watson, R. I. 1968. *The Great Psychologists. From Aristotle to Freud,* ed. 2. Philadelphia: Lippincott.
Watson, R. I. 1979. *Basic Writings in the History of Psychology.* New York: Oxford University Press.
Wertheimer, M. 1912. Experimentelle Studien über das Sehen von Bewegung. *Zeitschrift für Psychologie 60*:321–378.
Wertheimer, M. 1922. Untersuchungen zur Lehre von der Gestalt. I. Prinzipielle Bemerkungen. *Psychologische Forschung* 1:47–58.
Wertheimer, M. 1923. Untersuchungen zur Lehre von der Gestalt. II. *Psychologische Forschung* 4:301–350.
Wertheimer, M. 1938. Gestalt theory. In *A Source Book of Gestalt Psychology.* W. D. Ellis, ed. New York: Humanities Press, pp. 1–11.
Wertheimer, M. 1945. *Productive Thinking.* New York: Harper.
Wertheimer, M., D. B. King, M. A. Peckler, S. Raney, and R. W. Schaef. 1992. Carl Jung and Max Wertheimer on a priority issue. *Journal of the History of the Behavioral Sciences 28*:45–56.
Westfall, R. S. 1980. *Never at Rest. A Biography of Isaac Newton.* Cambridge, England: Cambridge University Press.
Wheatstone, C. 1838. Contributions to the physiology of vision—Part the first. On some remarkable, and hitherto unobserved, phenomena of binocular vision. *Philosophical Transactions of the Royal Society 128*:371–394.

Wheatstone, C. 1852. Contributions to the physiology of vision—Part the second. On some remarkable, and hitherto unobserved, phenomena of binocular vision. *Philosophical Transactions of the Royal Society 142*:1–17.
Wheatstone, C. 1879. *The Scientific Papers of Sir Charles Wheatstone, D.C.L., F.R.S.* London: Physical Society of London.
Whipple, G. M. 1910. *Manual of Mental and Physical Tests. A Book of Directions Compiled with Special Reference to the Experimental Study of School Children in the Laboratory or Classroom.* Baltimore: Warwick & York.
Whyte, L. L. 1962. *The Unconscious before Freud.* London: Tavistock.
Wilshire, B. 1968. *William James and Phenomenology: a Study of "The Principles of Psychology."* Bloomington: Indiana University Press.
Wolf, T. H. 1973. *Alfred Binet.* Chicago: University of Chicago Press.
Wolman, B. B. 1968. *Historical Roots of Contemporary Psychology.* New York: Harper & Row.
Woodworth, R. S. 1901. On the voluntary control of the force of movement. *Psychological Review 8*:350–359.
Woodworth, R.S. 1918. *Dynamic Psychology.* New York: Columbia University Press.
Woodworth, R.S. 1931. *Contemporary Schools of Psychology.* New York: Ronald Press.
Woodworth, R. S. 1932. Robert S. Woodworth. In *A History of Psychology in Autobiography,* Vol. 2. C. Murchison, ed. Worcester, Mass.: Clark University Press, pp. 359–380.
Woodworth, R.S. 1938. *Experimental Psychology.* New York: Holt.
Woodworth, R.S. 1939. *Psychological Issues. Selected Papers of Robert S. Woodworth.* New York: Columbia University Press.
Worden, F. G., J. P. Swazey, and G. Adelman, eds. 1975. *The Neurosciences: Paths of Discovery.* Cambridge, Mass.: MIT Press.
Wright, W. A., ed. 1900. *Bacon. The Advancement of Learning,* ed. 5. Oxford: Clarendon Press.
Wundt, W. 1874. *Grundzüge der physiologischen Psychologie.* Leipzig: Engelmann.
Wundt, W. 1898. Die geometrisch-optischen Täuschungen. *Abhandlungen der mathematisch-physischen Classe der Königlichen Sächsischen Gesellschaft der Wissenschaften 42*:55–178.
Wundt, W. 1912. *Völkerpsychologie.* Leipzig: Engelmann.
Wundt, W. 1916. *Elements of Folk Psychology. Outlines of a Psychological History of the Development of Mankind.* E. L. Schraub, trans. New York: Macmillan.
Yerkes, R. M. 1906. The mutual relations of stimuli in the frog *Rana clamata* Daudin. In *Harvard Psychological Studies,* Vol. 2. H. Münsterberg, ed. Boston: Houghton Mifflin. pp. 545–574.
Yerkes, R. M. 1923. Testing the human mind. *Atlantic Monthly 121*:358–370.
Yerkes, R. M. 1932. Robert Mearns Yerkes. In *A History of Psychology in Autobiography,* Vol. 2. C. Murchison, ed. Worcester, Mass.: Clark University Press, pp. 381–407.
Yerkes, R. M., J. W. Bridges, and R. S. Hardwick. 1915. *A Point Scale for Measuring Mental Ability.* Baltimore: Warwick & York.
Yerkes, R. M., and J. D. Dodson. 1908. The relation of strength of stimulus to rapidity of habit-formation. *Journal of Comparative and Neurological Psychology 18*:459–482.
Yerkes, R. M. , and J. B. Watson. 1911. Method of studying vision in animals. *Behavior Monographs 1.* No. 2.
Yerkes, R. M., and A. W. Yerkes. 1929. *The Great Apes. A Study of Anthropoid Life.* New Haven, Conn.: Yale University Press.
Yoakum, C. S., and R. M. Yerkes. 1920. *Mental Tests in the American Army.* London: Sidgwick & Jackson.
Young, R. M. 1970. *Mind, Brain and Adaptation in the Nineteeth Century. Cerebral Localization and its Biological Context from Gall to Ferrier.* Oxford: Clarendon Press.
Young, T. 1801. On the mechanism of the eye. *Philosophical Transactions of the Royal Society 91*:23–88.
Young, T. 1802. On the theory of lights and colours. *Philosophical Transactions of the Royal Society 92*:12–48.
Young, T. 1807. *A Course of Lectures on Natural Philosophy and the Mechanical Arts.* London: Johnson.
Zangwill, O. L. 1970. Sir Frederic Bartlett (1886–1969). *Quarterly Journal of Experimental Psychology 22*:77–81.
Zangwill, O. L. 1972. Remembering revisited. *Quarterly Journal of Experimental Psychology 24*:123–138.
Zilboorg, G., and G. W. Henry. 1941. A *History of Medical Psychology.* New York: Norton.
Zusne, L. 1975. *Names in the History of Psychology. A Biographical Sourcebook.* New York: Wiley.

List of Psychologists

The page numbers in boldface indicate the text describing their contributions to psychology. The italicized numbers refer to the pages on which the sources of the quotations are given.

Subject Index

The italicized names refer to journals, which are typically cited for the date of their foundation.